DEDICATION

I would like to dedicate this book to my parents, Alma and A.D. Shirley. My parents are models of fiscal responsibility, frugality, and life enrichment through a strong faith in God. They are model parents who instilled self-confidence in all three of us at early ages and helped us realize the joys of doing our best at everything we attempted. They taught us by example many lessons of life regarding time management, organization, and responsibility. I discovered through their examples the importance of time with family and friends that I am still striving to duplicate.

Live Long & Profit

Wealthbuilding Strategies for Every Stage of Your Life

Kay R. Shirley, Ph.D., CFP

Dearborn
Financial Publishing, Inc.®

This publication is designed to provide accurate and authoritative information in regard to the subject matter covered. It is sold with the understanding that the publisher is not engaged in rendering legal, accounting, or other professional service. If legal advice or other expert assistance is required, the services of a competent professional person should be sought.

Executive Editor: Cynthia A. Zigmund
Managing Editor: Jack Kiburz
Interior Design: Lucy Jenkins
Cover Design: S. Laird Jenkins Corporation
Typesetting: Elizabeth Pitts

Printed in the United States of America

97 98 99 10 9 8 7 6 5 4 3 2 1

Library of Congress Cataloging-in-Publication Data

Shirley, Kay R.
    Live long and profit : wealthbuilding strategies for every stage
of your life / Kay R. Shirley.
        p.   cm.
    Includes index.
    ISBN 0-7931-2662-2
    1. Finance, Personal. 2. Investments   I. Title.
HG179.S468   1997
332.024'01—dc21   97-17561
                                                          CIP

CONTENTS

FOREWORD

One morning recently I woke up and I was 60 years old. I looked in the mirror just to confirm that reality and sure enough I was staring into a face that bore the inevitable flaws and furrows of one who had run the good race, fought the good fight, and occasionally wondered, "What's it all about?" Yet, without the ungraceful reminder by that mischievous piece of glass I would have attached no particular significance to my birthday. I felt energetic. My mind was already perking the possibilities of the day and I was about to dress for my 6 A.M. workout.

Perhaps a better indicator of my true age would have been to arise and look at an account of the net worth statement that my financial adviser, Kay Shirley, had prepared for me a few weeks earlier. At the age of 60 I had some real options. I could continue to work as editor-in-chief of *Atlanta* magazine, consider some new and exciting job offers, take time to do that "serious writing" editors are always threatening the world with, or just sit on the front porch of our cabin and pick fuzz out of my belly button until the urge to go places and do things rousted me from contemplative serenity. All of which is to say, that with the exception of health, you are as old as your bank account says you are. You see, at age 60 I realized that the attention I had or had not paid to my financial lifestyle over the decades was analogous to the long-term effects of what I had or had not attended to in the way of nutrition and lifestyle.

In my earlier years, there would have been no reason to suspect that I would arrive at age 60 in robust financial health. I was born as the shadow of the Great Depression began to recede, but I was marked by my parent's generation, a generation that was always glancing back over their shoulders lest another monetary disaster overtake them. For many years it would have been very difficult for anyone to convince me that for the average person life did not consist of working as long as you could, then hoping the company pension and Social Security would at least lend some dignity to the years that were left. For years, this cynicism led me to do little in the way of educating myself in even the basics of financial wellness.

Financial cynicism remains a prevalent mind-set for many people, although for baby boomers the manifestations of that cynicism have mutated into an anxiety that differs from that of my generation. Nevertheless, from an era in which government and corporate institutions were viewed as the front-line defense against retirement disasters, we have come to a time in which it may well be every family for itself. One thing remains constant, however: We all need to become less naïve when it comes to our finances.

By the time I was introduced to Dr. Shirley I was already past 50. Out of naïveté, cynicism, and absolute bone-chilling fear, I had already squandered several opportunities that would have advanced my current options by several years. For example, by 1972 I had drifted through a series of low-paying jobs before opening a public relations firm in Atlanta. Five years later, we were not only established as a thriving business, but we had received and accepted a buyout offer from J. Walter Thompson, Inc., at the time the largest advertising company in the world. By today's standards, the payout would seem insignificant, but in its time and especially to someone who had lived paycheck to paycheck, it was heady financial territory. In many ways, however, I was like the dog that chases and finally catches the car and wonders, "What do I do now?"

It's amazing how many people know how to make money through personal service or product development, then don't know what to do after that. I was in that category. I called a stockbroker located in the same building as my office and turned my money over to him without having done any research on my own. It was not a horrible mistake, for he turned out to be honorable. He just didn't turn out to be particularly astute.

Years later, I was lucky enough to cash in some company stock that had soared in value. Learning little, I turned the money over to the investment wing of my bank, just in time for the great market crash of 1987. Since I had never stayed with one company long enough to acquire any retirement benefits, visions of homelessness for my wife and me danced in my head. As soon as the market regained its value, I withdrew from the mutual fund and socked my money into certificates of deposit.

About 1990, it occurred to me that I knew practically nothing about investments and I was ashamed that I had created this scenario of financial confusion. The stock market had regained its vigor and there I was, missing about three years of prime earning potential. That same year I was introduced to Kay Shirley. She began to teach and I began to learn. What I learned is that the earlier you cast off the robes of cynicism and begin to trust that the brain that made money for you in the first place will serve you well in future investments, the sooner you will harvest more options for your life that you ever dreamed possible.

Much of what Kay has taught me can be found in the pages of this book. I try not to allow myself to think of the all the options I might have had if, in 1976, when I sold Walburn & Associates, I had simply had access to a book as easy to understand and as fundamentally wise as this one.

Two major points in this book are illustrated by the personal ruminations of the preceding paragraphs. The first is that investing is not a cold and scientific venture. Financial decisions, she says, are driven "not by investment returns, not by analytical spreadsheets, not by the numbers, but by family pressures and emotional concerns." She points out that a couple will often say to their financial adviser, "We know we're here to talk about money, but . . ." And the "buts" range from changing or not changing jobs, moving an aging parent into a nursing home or their home, planning a family with or without a working mother, planning for the children to receive proceeds from the estate upon one's death, keeping the office in the home or not, or even concerns about dealing with a high-pressure, highly social, high-cost-of-living lifestyle that precludes relaxing and enjoying friends and each other.

The second point is that our money needs change by the decade. That's what makes this book a financial friend for a person of any age group. Starting at age four and continuing by decade to 70 and beyond, Dr. Shirley analyzes the needs of each particular group and gives concise, practical advice in a book that actually is more of a portable classroom. I stand as living proof that it is never too late to learn. And more important, it is never too *early* to learn.

Lee Walburn
Editor in Chief, *Atlanta Magazine*

PREFACE

Do you remember what was going on 25 years ago? In 1972, Nixon was President; *The Godfather* won the Academy Award for best movie; "All in the Family" was the most popular TV show; Roberta Flack had a hit called "The First Time Ever I Saw Your Face"; and Helen Reddy was singing "I Am Woman"!

That was only 25 years ago? Time flies, they say. And the closer you get to retirement, the faster it flies.

This can be good news if you have planned and are prepared. Because the economy is always changing, I can only suggest what you'll be up against a quarter century from now. And I'm not preaching gloom and doom either. There is a lot you can do to ensure a happy and prosperous retirement. You may need some help from a broker or financial planner, but you will have to do most of it yourself. After all, it *is* your money. And it *is* your future.

What sort of financial future are you facing? Nothing is certain. Nothing except change.

Change will affect us all. You have a choice: Do nothing, and change will almost surely affect you badly; plan carefully, and the effects can be to your advantage.

The economy and the markets will stay on the roller coaster they've ridden the last 25 years. But if you plan your financial future carefully, you can enjoy the ride.

I want to help you: to show you how to take advantage when appropriate and how to keep others or outside circumstances from taking advantage of you.

Let's think about money.

YOUR ATTITUDES, HABITS, AND PLANS

What Is Your Real Attitude about Money?

To find out, answer these simple questions:

- **Do you think money is the root of all evil?** By the way, the Bible doesn't say that: It says the *love of money* is the problem.
- **Do you like money? Do you like it enough to work to keep it?** You already work to earn it, but that is not enough.
- **Do you have a budget?** Or is your "budget" mainly a matter of saying "I think I can afford it?" If that's the way it is, then you may think you're like the little engine that could. Remember? The one who kept saying "I think I can, I think I can, I think I can." Well, that's fine for a child's story. But in the real world, saying "I think I can" about a budget won't make you like the little engine that could. It will give you a little bank account that can't.
- **How much money do you have left at the end of the month?** Or do you wind up, more often than not, with more month at the end of your money?
- **How soon do you plan to retire?** And how well do you want to live?

If you are around 40, retirement is only 25 years away. Sounds like a long time, doesn't it? But the time will fly by. Nobody *can* do it for you. Nobody *will* do it for you. And the financial playing field is not level. When the Declaration of Independence talks about all of us being created equal, that is a philosophical concept. And it's very true another way: You don't know and nobody can tell anyone what the world or the world's economy will do.

So think about the first question again: what is your real attitude about money? And what are you going to do about it? Whatever else may happen, we all head toward what's coming at the same sure pace. No matter what the speed at which the economy's operating, the future comes at us one day at a time. And every day you don't do something to make sure your financial future is firm, you lose more than 24 hours.

How Are You Supposed to Know What to Do?

What if the economy continues to be inflationary, and you had been planning to convert to bonds with fixed income for retirement? Inflation makes stocks good things to have and at the same time can ruin a bond portfolio. So how much should you have of each, if any?

In the final analysis, there's not a lot you can do about inflation—it appears to be here to stay. But that doesn't mean you should do nothing. What you can and must do is have a plan for every stage of your life.

Let me ask you this: Have you taken a vacation lately or are you about to? Remember how you planned for it? You probably looked for the best, least expensive way to get where you wanted to go. You figured out how to get the most advantage for the least cost. And you may have gotten help and advice from a professional.

That was just for two weeks of your life.

But when it comes to financial planning, we are talking about the rest of your life. Have you spent as much time planning that as you spent planning your last vacation?

FINANCIAL PLANNING FOR THE AGES

Do you know where you want to be, as far as financial security is concerned? How much do you need in your nest egg to support your cost of living for the rest of your long, long life? Is your act together so you can live a healthy life, wisely with plenty of money if you should live to be 100?

What should you be doing in your 20s, 30s, 40s, 50s, 60s, 70s, 80s and beyond to make sure you profit? What should you be doing during those decades to make sure your life is long and has the quality you deserve as you age?

Live Long and Profit will take you through life's major financial milestones. You will be challenged to master the financial aspects of your life decade by decade.

It is necessary to use sound financial judgment throughout your life. Many considerations come into play:

- Your judgment may be unduly influenced by a distorted psychological view of money.
- Your judgment and choices almost certainly will be influenced by your relationships.
- As the years go by, your needs and priorities will change, and you will find it necessary to revisit and revise your financial plan again and again. This is a lifelong endeavor.

This book is based on the fact that most of us will live longer than our parents and grandparents; many of us to age 100. It is based on my knowledge that most investors these days are relatively conservative and not willing to see their money go down a dramatic amount in any year. The decrease in return that is tolerable differs from person to person but, generally, most people expect about 10 percent to 14 percent returns annually and can tolerate the associated decreases. Finally, because of our long life expectancies, it will be necessary to continue investing for growth, even into retirement.

The chapters of this book build logical steps to support the above assumptions for each stage of life.

I want to make sure you have every advantage working for you as you seek to build wealth through every stage of your life. Please turn to the first chapter of this book. That's the first step you need to take to *Live Long and Profit*.

Within these pages are the keys to success. Read, heed, and enjoy.

ACKNOWLEDGMENTS

Many people have contributed to this book. First, I would like to thank my husband, Billy Lovett, for showing me patience, love, and encouragement. Throughout this long project, he has been kind and supportive, always offering an uplifting word at just the right time. Freelance writer Beth Bassett has contributed immeasurably to the organization of the material and the creative expression of many ideas. Jim Pritchett gave me the newest technology to prepare this manuscript efficiently. Don Smith, executive producer for CNN's "Talk Back Live," pushed me to go the extra step to perfect this manuscript for publication. He is a tough taskmaster. Jody Owenby, my longtime assistant, very capably, willingly, and gladly helped me through the myriad details and was always there when I needed him. I am most appreciative and indebted to each of them.

Over 17 years, many clients have shared their most private particular situations in confidence with me. This has given me unique insight into the challenges facing each of us as we progress through each stage of our lives. I want to thank each and every one of them for the trust and confidence they have placed in me. Working intensely with them over the years has allowed me to begin understanding the vast complexity of financial decisions.

All the identities and names of the people used to illustrate the points of this book—with the exception of my parents and aunts and uncles—have been changed to protect their confidentiality. I have even changed the occupations of the people discussed so as to further protect each real person's privacy. Any similarity to actual people, alive or dead, is purely coincidental.

I also want to thank all my staff for their help along the way and their willingness to carry the load at the office while I devoted time to preparing this book.

PART ONE

A View from the Financial Counselor's Couch

When I became a financial planner, I found that I was dealing with the nuances of human personalities and relationships as much as I was with the abstract, mathematically exacting aspects of money. I found I really was a financial psychiatrist.

CHAPTER 1

MIND, MONEY, AND ACTION
How Compulsive Behavior Can Ruin You

When I was forced into planning my own financial future due to significant losses incurred in my portfolio by a stockbroker (who turned out to be incompetent), I was fully aware of what I did not know about investments. So I reluctantly set out to learn all I could to analytically create a plan for financial independence. My background as a mathematical analyst and math teacher lent itself to focusing on the numbers, and I soon grew to love that aspect of what I found myself doing. I was actually learning about investments—and was becoming somewhat of an expert.

When I began sharing my newfound analytical knowledge with others who had been burned by bad brokers, however, I began to understand that most money decisions are first emotional, then analytical! I had to learn to deal with the emotional aspects of financial decision-making as well. I had to become a money psychiatrist.

My clients' money decisions, small as well as large, were driven not only by investment returns, but also by emotional pressures. Those pressures resulted from the circumstances of their lives—their families, or the lack thereof. And those had to be dealt with right along with the dollar-and-cent details.

The most ruinous emotion-based attitudes toward money are the irrational compulsion to save or the irrational compulsion to spend. People who compulsively save money, never enjoying today the things it can buy, do so in order to satisfy some longing to feel forever, once-and-for-all secure. Those who compulsively spend money do so because they have a deep need to find happiness, to be liked, or to fit into a society from which they somehow felt alienated. Obviously, neither compulsion makes for sound money management. Often, these compulsions are not so obvious to the person caught in the trap and therefore must be dealt with before financial solidarity can be achieved.

But aside from compulsions, money decisions are guided by our stages of life. That is, for each decade of life, decisions made focus on the following:

- 20s—What to buy, where to work, where to live, whom to befriend and/or marry, and how to begin investing
- 30s—How to live better for less (or the same) whether single or married, how to pay for children and their activities, how to teach children the basics of money management, and how to invest for college funding and retirement
- 40s—How to maintain sanity in the face of work pressures, costly lifestyles, marriage complexities, aging parent concerns, education of children, and how to invest for retirement
- 50s—How to save for retirement while focusing on the demands of a successful career or, conversely, how to maintain your lifestyle while coping with the loss of a job due to corporate downsizing; preparing wills that take multiple marriages into consideration; intensifying the care of aging parents; and deciding where to invest
- 60s—How to stay healthy, how to manage those precious retirement dollars, and how to prevent long-term care costs in the future from potentially eroding your estate

- 70s—If not cared for in the 60s, attention is devoted to estate planning, long-term care funding, and portfolio rebalancing to ensure growth as well as income
- 80s—Enjoying the rewards of many years of good decisions about money management, gifting to loved ones, and nurturing friendships

Because the effects of the financial choices we make are cumulative, the choices at each juncture affect our options at the next. If our decisions are sound along the way, we can usually avoid the financial crises created by excessive debt, funding lifestyles we cannot afford to the detriment of our relationships, and feeling the helplessness of being unable to properly educate our children, help our parents, or prepare for our own retirement.

What follows is a look at typical financial challenges that arise during each decade, and some examples of people responding well or not so well to them.

I hope that the right decisions will inspire you and the wrong decisions will alert you to potential problems so you can avoid them.

THE IRRATIONAL COMPULSION TO SAVE

"Wealth unused might as well not exist."
—Aesop's Fables

Most of us have seen cartoons about Donald Duck's uncle, Scrooge McDuck. Uncle Scrooge is forever fending off Huey, Dewey, and Louie, and, of course, Donald himself, when they interrupt Scrooge's favorite pastime: communing with his money. There he sits with his wild shock of white hair, throwing gold coins into the air, counting them, stacking and restacking them. Is Uncle Scrooge a compulsive saver? He may be, because compulsive saving involves an ongoing preoccupation with hoarding money.

But while Scrooge McDuck may give us a chuckle, the compulsion to hoard money is not so funny in the real world. It may be, in reality, an out-of-control, compulsive way of handling insecurities, anxiety, fear of the future, and sometimes guilt. The compulsive saver may use money to provide a security blanket for the calm that is missing otherwise.

Jim: An Unfounded Compulsion to Save

Often the compulsion to hoard is rooted in early deprivations people have undergone or in fears of potential deprivations. Take Jim, a top executive with a major company, who came to me for financial planning. In discussing Jim's situation, I found that although he had an annual income of $300,000, his family lived very modestly and had $200,000 in a money market account earning less than inflation after taxes!

Jim explained to me that there was a reason for his frugality— a reason for putting his money in this absolutely safe place.

His grandfather, he said, had lost everything in the Depression, and Jim's father had never recovered financially from the older man's failure. Jim, who had grown up with stories of the Depression, was determined that nothing remotely resembling his grandfather's failure would ever happen to him. He was willing to give up economic return on a substantial sum of money for emotional peace of mind.

Jim's financial situation. Jim and his family live in a home with no mortgage and drive cars with no debt. They own a beach condo with no mortgage. He has more than $500,000 in his company 401(k) (invested 50 percent in guaranteed interest, and the other 50 percent invested in his company stock). At 60 he will receive a pension of $75,000 per year.

He is a vice president with a large Fortune 500 company. His job is secure. His wife earns about $40,000 a year from a very secure job. Their children are educated, on their own, and have no debt.

Together, Jim and his wife earn about $340,000 per year. At the time Jim and his wife came to see me, they had been earning this high income for five years. During those years, they had paid off their home, beach house, and cars; had traveled; and had accumulated the money they now had in the money market account. Their net worth and tax plan looked like this:

Jim's Net Worth

Assets

Money market	$200,000	
401(k)s	500,000	
Total Invested Assets		$ 700,000
Home	$400,000	
Cars	100,000	
Beach home	250,000	
Total Use Assets		$ 750,000
Total Assets		**$1,450,000**
Liabilities	0	0
Net Worth		**$1,450,000**

Jim's Tax Plan

	His	*Hers*
Income	$300,000	$40,000
FICA	(8,240)	(3,060
401(k) (15%)	(9,500)	(6,000
Adjusted gross income	$282,260	$30,940

Deductions

Exemptions	$ 5,100
State income tax withheld	16,000
Real estate taxes	7,000
Car license and fees	1,000
Charitable contributions	20,000
Total deductions	$ 49,100
Taxable Income	**$264,100**
Federal income taxes	$ 79,145
State income taxes	$ 15,476
Total income	$340,000
401(k)s	(15,500)
FICA	(11,300)
Federal income tax	(79,145)
State income tax	(15,476)
Income to Spend	**$218,579**
Cost of living	(120,000)
Excess Income to Spend or Invest	**$ 98,579**

Analysis. You're probably thinking, "I wish I had his problem!" That is just the extreme we are pointing out here. Here is a couple living modestly in relation to their income. Their jobs are secure, their retirement income is secure, Jim's family's farming past is safely behind them, yet Jim's subconscious can't let him do something productive with his money. The psychological has superimposed itself over his analytical sense, rendering his financial decision-making inadequate.

Jim is suffering from an irrational fear of a family financial crisis that is highly unlikely to recur in the future. Sure, it is okay—even smart—to have some money in a money market. But $200,000 when there is virtually is no debt or threat of job loss? Jim's retirement, his marriage, and his children are secure. Jim can finally relax. He won't be repeating the problems of the past. And he can invest a good portion of that $200,000 to be a better steward of the money. Further, to the extent he can, Jim wants to leave some money to his children, so they won't have to ever worry about what his parents and grandparents did. Properly investing the cash will allow him to leave potentially even more for his children.

Result. With Jim, we discussed potential returns for that large sum of cash sitting in his 401(k) as well as for the $200,000 in the money market. Jim, 48, wants to work until he is 60. He has 12 more years for the money to grow. He is earning 6 percent a year on the $250,000 in the 401(k) and 3 percent a year on the $200,000 in his money market account.

Since Jim is very nervous about taking risks, we suggested he begin by seeking to earn a higher rate of return on part of his money inside the 401(k) as well as in the money market.

We showed him the potential he was missing this way:

Amount Invested	No. of Years	Result at Per-Year Returns		
		3%	6%	10%
$100,000	12	$142,576	$201,219	$313,842
$200,000	12	$285,152	$402,439	$627,685

Notice the almost threefold increase when the return is increased from 3 percent to 10 percent! Of course, if he chose to invest more, his rewards in 12 years would be much greater.

After studying this example, Jim decided to initially place $100,000 of his 401(k) money into the unmanaged equity index fund offered by his company plan. This fund would be purchasing an equal number of shares of each of the Fortune 500 companies and holding them over time. According to Ibbottson and Associates reporting service, the unmanaged S&P 500 index has produced a 10 percent per year return since 1926. It represents stock of the largest 500 companies in our country. In order for Jim to lose all his money, each of those companies would have to go out of business—on the same day! Jim had taken his first step out of his past.

As for his money market account, Jim decided to place $100,000 in a team-managed mutual fund comprised of the same Fortune 500 companies as those in the equity index fund. However, because it would be managed, a team of managers would be deciding on a daily basis if it would be appropriate to sell a stock while high and wait until it dropped to repurchase it—thus "managing" the portfolio. This team-managed mutual fund has produced average annual returns of about 13 percent a year since 1934.

After two years of watching his initial $100,000 in the 401(k) and his $100,000 of money market cash fluctuate on a quarterly basis, Jim was surprised and pleased to see he had earned much better than the 3 percent and 6 percent returns the balance of his money was earning. More important, he had not panicked when his value had been down—as indeed, it had been from time to time. So he felt he was now ready to take steps to invest more of the idle cash. With retirement still ten years away, he would reap significant rewards by making this decision.

Bob, the Savings Addict

Bob, a computer systems designer, was so caught up in saving it almost had become an addiction. He got pleasure only from seeing his investment accounts grow. He didn't care that the dishwasher and sofa needed to be replaced. He wasn't interested in taking vacations, because if he didn't take them, his company would pay him cash instead. He could invest the cash, and his investment accounts would grow faster.

As a result of Bob's fixation on saving for the future, his family was suffering today and, in recent months, had developed indications of potentially falling apart. Bob, who had a personal income of $64,000 a year, had doggedly saved 25 percent of his earnings for the past ten years. Furthermore, he had demanded that his wife and two children account in a daily ledger for every dime they spent. He routinely denied his family modern conveniences, comfortable furnishings, and periodic vacations that their friends on much smaller budgets routinely enjoyed. As a last resort, Bob's wife and children rebelled and insisted he see a financial planner.

Together, we evaluated Bob's financial needs, current and future, and determined that, although he was only 42, he was already almost financially independent. He was shocked to realize that he had almost completely met his retirement needs for age 60. He had invested conservatively in stock mutual funds and his annual average returns were in the 12 percent range. His bigger shock came when his family revealed how unhappy they were under his financial dictatorship. He had been truly oblivious to the day-to-day needs of his wife and children, so much so that he turned red with embarrassment in my presence while the whole family explained how they felt.

We then reconfirmed when he wanted to quit work. We set a realistic saving goal so that his family could enjoy some of the fruits of his labor right away. Their first decision was to purchase a dishwasher and new furnishings for the family room right away. Then together, he and his wife decided to continue saving 25 percent of his earnings, with half earmarked for retirement (a long-term goal); and the other half for vacations and a down payment on a second home (an intermediate goal).

Bob now had a partner in his plan. Because he was willing to compromise on the amount he was saving for retirement, and to begin to save for more immediate goals, his wife felt a part of the plan and was happy to participate.

Analysis. An in-depth discussion led us to learn that Bob's father had jumped from job to job and thus was never vested in a retirement plan. Bob was highly anxious about making sure he tightly secured his own retirement—even to the sacrifice of to-day—almost completely.

In all fairness, had we met earlier in the program, I'm not at all sure Bob could have changed his goal—regardless of the pressure his wife exerted. His retirement anxiety was so deeply rooted, he literally couldn't focus attention anywhere else until that retirement was wrapped up and tied with a bow!

Now, with his retirement secure, Bob was able to let go of some money to enjoy today. Needless to say, Bob's whole family is more relaxed now that Bob's anxiety is satisfied.

Bob was fortunate. His wife didn't leave him during all those painful penny-pinching years. This couple survived the compulsive behaviors and even profited by them. But there truly is a balance to achieve when juggling long-term with short-term and mid-term goals.

Wealth Unused

There is an Aesop's fable about a man who hid his gold at the foot of a tree in his garden. Every week he happily dug it up and gloated over it. One day, however, he found an empty hole. A robber who had seen the man digging up the money had come and taken it away. Discovering his loss, the man tore his hair and wailed so loudly that his neighbors came to see what was the matter. When he told them, they asked, "Did you ever take any of the money out?" "Nay," he told them, "I only came to look at it." "Then come again and look at the hole," they said. "It will do you just as much good." The moral to the story is this: "Wealth unused might as well not exist."

Seven Habits of Compulsive Savers

Compulsive savers may:

1. Use money as a security blanket for a calm that is otherwise missing.
2. Use money to cover an unfounded fear.
3. Constantly worry about their financial condition.
4. Place large sums of money in low-yielding savings accounts.
5. Hoard money in cookie jars, coat pockets, drawers, or safe-deposit boxes.
6. Refuse to owe money for any reason.
7. Sincerely believe that investments with even a little risk will cause them undue stress.

THE IRRATIONAL COMPULSION TO SPEND

At the opposite end of the spectrum from compulsive saving is compulsive spending, but the two ways of dealing with money have much in common: Both compulsive spending and compulsive saving involve an irrational approach to money management driven by pressures and emotional concerns often only indirectly related to money.

Are you a compulsive spender if you went out yesterday and shopped until you dropped? Not necessarily. Compulsive spending involves a long-term, ongoing abuse of money, checks, credit cards, and in some cases loans, which negatively impacts not only your financial situation, but also your work and relationships.

Compulsive spenders buy things they don't need, live beyond their means, and believe that on some bright day in the future they will magically pay off their debts with no trouble at all (although the way this will be accomplished has not yet been worked out). Yet they constantly fret about their money situation and feel guilty and depressed about it. To keep worry at bay, moreover, they go out and spend more money. Probably, they reason, an elaborate meal at an expensive restaurant, a love-boat cruise, or a new car will make it all okay.

Shirley, the Big Spender

Let's look at the example of Shirley, a woman who was managing her finances fairly well on the $30,000-a-year salary she was earning from her job at the post office until she woke up one morning a wealthy woman due to a large inheritance. The money, about $1 million, came to her at the death of her father (who probably was a compulsive saver). Her mother had previously passed away.

According to the provisions of Shirley's mother's will, she was to receive $500,000 right away, and the remaining $500,000 designated for her benefit in her father's will was to be held in trust until she was 58 years old. Shirley should not spend any of the principal from the trust established by her father's will, only the income it earned. She was also named the trustee of her own trust. In Shirley's case, this was akin to putting the fox in charge of the henhouse.

Shirley came to me for help

- in figuring out what to spend for a new car;
- in deciding what amount to spend remodeling her home; and
- at the same time determining how to invest her money so she could quit her job.

We worked out a plan whereby she could buy a new car and improve her home for about $50,000 total and quit her job within two years and never have to work again. Presently, however, it became evident that Shirley could not stick to the plan, and after a year she abandoned it altogether. She could not resist the temptation to spend large sums of money.

Instead of improving her home, she bought a new home for $225,000; five cars for $150,000; a $100,000 beach cottage; a $100,000 boat; and $25,000 worth of miscellaneous "stuff" totalling $600,000.

Here's how her million dollars looked after her spending spree:

$1,000,000 Inheritance – 600,000 Spent = $400,000 Left

From time to time during the spending spree, she would call me and say: "I know you're not going to like this, but I've bought . . ."

What happened to Shirley?   Since she was named both trustee and beneficiary of her father's estate, she was in total control. So first she spent all the principal from her mother's trust. Then, against her father's wishes, Shirley spent $100,000 of her remaining principal, and if the $400,000 she had left yielded an average of 6 to 7 percent interest (a conservative yield one can realistically expect to spend from a lump sum such as this), she would have an income of $24,000 to $28,000 a year, barely enough to maintain all the "things" she had bought. She undermined her own success.

Shirley could not quit her job. And her father, poor man, is probably spinning in his grave!

Analysis.   Shirley's spending was driven by emotional considerations. Even she knew this. At 48 she had been divorced for many years. She told me that she was lonely and wanted desperately to "be like everybody else and fit in—to have a traditional relationship like her married friends." By buying things, she was trying to buy love. But we all know that love cannot be bought and so did she. She said that she just "couldn't help it."

Her emotions sabotaged the financial freedom she had said she so badly wanted, and in the meantime, she denied herself the self-confidence and satisfaction that comes with financial independence. It is that self-confidence, ironically, that probably could have led her to a successful relationship. She had truly sabotaged her own success on every front—and no one had been able to stop her.

Result.   After two years of unbridled spending, Shirley started seeing a counselor. Three years later, Shirley did find a mate—about five years after her father died. She continued to work and so did her husband. She sold three of the cars and gave one to her son who had just graduated from high school. She did leave her remaining principal of $400,000 invested.

Over the five years she realized a 12 percent-a-year return. Five years after her father's death, she has rebuilt the estate to $700,000. Her new cost of living is $60,000 a year to support her boat, beach house, cars, and new house.

She is now 53 and plans to retire at age 58. Her husband will have no retirement income, although he earns about $35,000 a year as a self-employed plumber. Since he is three years her senior, she plans to use her investment income to support both of them in retirement. Even if her investment return drops to 10 percent per year between now and five years from now, she will have $1,127,357 to invest for income and growth. Five years hence, she will need about $70,000 to support their cost of living. This includes projected inflation of about 3 percent a year. At that time, her investment capital of $1 million will produce between $66,000 and $77,000 per year in income.

While she had to work ten years longer than she had hoped initially, Shirley will be fine.

Jane, Robert, and Their Credit Cards

In less extreme cases of compulsive spending than Shirley's, people slip into the trap of building up credit-card debt. Some use the plastic to reward themselves with toys and pleasures of various kinds—fancier televisions, expensive clothing and jewelry, or eating out too often. But those seemingly innocuous and justified credit-card purchases quickly add up, and the interest on the debt begins to eat away at both the amount of money people have to spend and their peace of mind.

Clients Jane and Robert serve as an example of the insidious nature of credit-card debt. By the time they came to see me, this couple had realized that their debt payments had become an obstacle to saving for their son's college education as well as their own retirement.

We worked out a debt-consolidation plan that cut their monthly payments in half. This was accomplished through the use of a home equity loan. The remaining half was to be saved for their son's college fund and their retirement. Under the plan, they also resolved to cut down on their spending in ways both small and large. As for the small ways—they often indulged themselves with expensive appetizers before their evening meal and with expensive cuts of meat or seafood for the entree. They decided they would eat raw veggies and dip before dinner instead of shrimp cocktails and try some casseroles for the main dish. Expensive vacations also had to go.

Analysis.   This couple had allowed credit-card balances to creep up in small ways—there had been no big expenditures. They indulged their expensive tastes frequently. They ate out often, and took frequent short, but expensive weekend trips. Taking care of the credit-card balance was the first step. But lifestyle changes were needed to keep the balances from recurring. They had to stop and think before pulling out the cards.

Rule of Thumb

Keep your credit cards in your sock drawer so you won't be tempted.

The result: putting on the brakes.   People who suspect they may have a tendency toward compulsive credit-card spending should consolidate their credit-card debt as Jane and Robert did and pay it off as soon as possible. For most, this decision will require major changes and a major joint commitment. The only thing worse than having large credit-card balances is consolidating the large credit-card balances and then building up yet another credit-card balance. Destroy all but one card and pay the total monthly.

The reality.   Many items purchased by compulsive spenders are things they don't even need, and some purchases are things they don't even want. They may have clothes in the closet they have never worn or items on the shelves they have never taken out of the packages. Compulsive spending must be controlled either at the point of purchase or before entering the store. In other words, by not going to the store at all. For those who enter the store and find themselves in front of the cashier, the point-of-purchase question is this: Am I sure I need this item?

RULE OF THUMB

When in doubt, don't.

What an interesting rule. It's one my father taught me about any decision in life, and it works here. Think about the dress or shirt you bought and have worn only once. Had you checked your purchase against "when in doubt" would you own it now? Think about other things in your life—perhaps something you said, or a relationship you may have entered even though you had questions about it. Think about an investment you made despite questions lurking in your mind. Would you have been better off if you had followed our rule?

For compulsive spenders, like compulsive savers, one way to achieve moderation is through counseling to address any underlying issues such as loneliness, stress, or fear and the emotions that often accompany them, such as anger, depression, and insecurity. Whatever the problem, you must take action. Remember, even no decision is a decision. Decide to act, then act.

Four Habits of Compulsive Spenders

Compulsive spenders may do the following:

1. Display irrational or compulsive spending patterns.
2. Have unrealistic expectations about their ability to pay off debt.
3. Constantly worry about finances to the point that their uneasiness affects their work and relationships.
4. Use money as a way to handle tension, anxiety, boredom, anger, joy, rejection, or loneliness.

SOME HELP FOR COMPULSIVE SAVERS AND SPENDERS

The solution to compulsive saving or spending lies in taking control of the compulsiveness, step-by-step:

1. **Do a reality adjustment about your liquidity needs.** Evaluate the worst-case financial scenario you could encounter and specify the money you would need if such a scenario became reality. Keep only that amount in a liquid low-yielding instrument.

2. **List and prioritize your financial goals.** Determine the goals that you wish to accomplish in one year; on a three-to-five-year horizon and goals for the more-than-five-year time frame. Then allocate your investable resources accordingly, being careful to give equal attention to each goal.

3. **Get sound financial counseling.** If you have trouble compartmentalizing your goals and thus, your money allocations, go see a good financial planner who can help you reach objectivity. That planner can also help you identify investments that will allow you to reach your goal.

4. **Address the personal issues that really concern you, such as fear, anger, depression, and insecurity.** Recognize the economic loss that you are trading for psychological gain, which may be false gain.

5. **Finally, take action.** Once you've specified your goals and quantified the allocation of your resources, you're ready to act. Don't wait until tomorrow. Act today.

CHAPTER 2

THE BASICS OF INVESTING

Before we get into the specifics for our life decades, let's briefly discuss some investment basics we will need as we move forward through life. Let's focus on choosing a financial planner, evaluating our risk tolerance, avoiding scam artists, selecting a suitable mutual fund, and allocating assets as you invest for retirement.

CHOOSING SOMEONE TO HELP YOU

Successful, busy people recognize the importance of finding a professional to help them manage various aspects of their lives. Unless you can devote almost full-time to it, you will be smart to find a good professional adviser to help you with your investments.

In their book, *Ask the Conservative Investor* (Scott, Foresman), Bruce P. Bagge and Christopher Channer suggest you seek a financial adviser much as you would look for a doctor or lawyer.

nd for referrals, especially from people who have in-
:essfully," they say. Then interview several.

Of all the financial advisers available to the average person, the Certified Financial Planner is perhaps the best. They are required to be recertified annually by completing a required number of continuing education courses, as well as a specific course on the ethics of financial planning. Financial planners understand the pros and cons of most investment opportunities as well as the behavior of money in most every circumstance. Overall, they are honest and your well-being is their overriding concern.

However, just about anyone who is smart enough and willing to go through the educational experiences required can become a Certified Financial Planner. Therefore, it is not unusual to find that your financial planner originally began his or her career in a different profession. That first profession will greatly color the opinions the adviser holds toward certain areas of financial planning.

For instance, if the person was first an insurance agent, he or she may give more attention to insurance with less to tax planning or investments. If the person was an accountant, the first priority might naturally be to taxes. If a stockbroker, to stocks. If a lawyer, to estate planning. The very best financial planner is one whose background was unrelated to any of the specific areas addressed by financial planning. That way you are more likely to find his or her advice will be balanced across all areas—not biased to one.

Qualities of a Good Financial Planner

Here are some specifics to look for in your financial planner. Find someone who is:

- **Smart, competent, and well-educated.** Look for a person who has invested the time and effort to become licensed as a securities representative, Registered Investment Adviser, Certified Financial Planner, CPA, or attorney. Whatever the license they hold, the person deserves your attention if he or she is a recognized professional in the business and has meaningful credentials.

- **Experienced.** While everyone has to start somewhere, you'll be entrusting decisions about your life's savings to this person. A great majority of financial planners have been in the business less than four years. Look for someone with at least five years' experience.
- **A good listener.** Find someone who is really willing to listen to your concerns and ideas. Look for a person who is simply knowledgeable in a number of fields and not pushing a product.
- **Not pushy.** Don't be rushed or intimidated into decisions. Be especially wary of anyone you don't know who wants you to send them money after a sales pitch over the phone.
- **A good example of practicing what they preach.** Why not ask to see the investment portfolio of the financial planner you are planning to choose? If the planner has done a good job for themselves, he or she will be proud of it and willing to show you. If the planner makes excuses about failure, remember, it is not true that the people who have made all the mistakes know how to avoid them. The fact is, they are probably psychologically prone to making mistakes and emotionally hooked on creating problems to solve. As a friend has said, "It's easier to jump on a moving train than it is to start one." Make sure you are jumping on a train that is moving in a positive direction.
- **Trustworthy.** Listen to your feelings. Make sure the person you choose cares about you and the quality of work he or she does. Financial planning is a people business and your decision should be a people decision. Inspirational speaker Zig Ziglar has said: "People do not care how much you know until they first know how much you care." The best financial planners practice this in their relationships with the people they serve.

How Financial Planners Are Paid

Financial planners are paid by fees, commissions, or both. The fees range from a one-time flat fee for a plan to annual fees charged as a percentage of the amount of money you invest with them. Commissions are charged as a percentage of the total amount you spend to buy an investment, or as a percentage of the total when you sell out of the investment, or both. Mutual fund commissions are structured as fees when you invest, a fee when you get out of the investment, *or* a fee (called a 12b-1 fee) charged against your total account value every year.

Do not expect to pay a fee when you meet the planner on the first visit. In fact, if the planner charges you a fee on the first visit, rule that person out. The first meeting should be one of getting acquainted and determining if the two of you can work together. Expect to provide complete information for the planner to review at the first meeting. In return at the end of the meeting, a fee schedule or method of compensation should be discussed or given to you along with a complete description of the plan that will be produced for you.

Here's a list of resources to help you locate a financial planner.

Where to Find a Financial Planner

The Institute of Certified Financial Planners, based in Denver, is the professional organization that represents more than 1,000 Certified Financial Planners from coast to coast. To contact them, call 800-282-7526.

Members of the **International Association for Financial Planning** have an academic degree in planning and meet certain other qualifications. To contact them, call 800-945-4237.

The International Association for Financial Planning (IAFP) is the membership organization for financial planners. According to their 1996 internal survey, there are 15,744 members. The average member is 48 years old and has been a member for five years. Only 4,000 have been members for more than eight years. Twenty percent are women. Almost 40 percent are CFPs, 20 percent are Chartered Life Underwriters (CLUs), and 6 percent are CPAs. About 32 percent are paid through a combination of fees and commissions, about 20 percent are salaried, 13 percent are commission-based only, and only 7.2 percent are fee-only.

Members of **The National Association of Personal Financial Advisors** include financial advisers who charge a fee for their advice and collect no commissions from sales of investments. To contact them, call 800-366-2732.

AVOIDING SCAM ARTISTS

In your early years you may think you can speculate, and if it's not too big a risk, maybe you'll recover. It's much better, however, to avoid the unnecessary risk and protect your invested capital at all costs.

Just remember what you've always heard: If it sounds too good to be true, it probably is.

As you enter your retirement years, be especially wary. It is well documented that the 60s and up are the years during which a person has the most money accumulated. You must be on guard to make sure you don't let any unscrupulous people get their hands on your gold.

Don't get sucked into someone's crooked scheme. Here is some advice that may seem obvious when you read it, but is not at all obvious if you get caught up in the scam.

- Never give out your Social Security number, credit-card number or other personal information such as your birth-date to a person you don't know.
- Always ask for proof of identity. Write down the name and check out the person. Call the National Association of Securities Dealers, Inc., 301-590-6500, or the Securities and Exchange Commission, 202-942-7040, and your state securities regulator.Never send money for any investment to a person you don't know. Just hang up the phone if a stranger calls asking you to invest. Don't even discuss it.
- Ask for a written explanation of the investment the person is selling—whether you know the person or not.
- Never allow an adviser to use his or her address on your account. Mutual funds only send checks to the address of record. Make sure your address is the address of record. It is fine for the adviser to receive a copy, but not to be the primary address on the account.

EVALUATING RISK TOLERANCE

Determining the amount of downward fluctuation you can tolerate, as in the amount that will allow you to still sleep at night, is necessary for you to select the right mutual fund for yourself no matter what your age.

To define a rate of return you would consider good, but one with whose fluctuations downward you would also be able to sleep, ask yourself the questions in Figure 2.1.

Based on your selected rate of return target and your willingness to leave the money alone until age 65—retirement age—select a mutual fund whose average rate of return since 1973 has met your goal as determined in Figure 2.1.

SELECTING A MUTUAL FUND

Recently a well-read, smart, successful business owner came to see me for financial advice. We discussed his objectives relative to retiring as well as his criteria for selecting the hodge-podge of 32 mutual funds he and his wife were holding. "The first thing I do," he said, "is rule out the fund if it has a load."

This man is uninformed. *All mutual funds have a load.* It is either paid as a commission deducted up front, a surrender penalty deducted when you sell, or a fee that is deducted every year to reimburse the company for its sales and marketing expenses—which they all have, whether load or no-load. And don't be fooled by the ads that sometimes run telling you they are "no-load and no 12b-1 fees."

About a year ago, I saw an ad on CNBC purporting to sell a fund with "absolutely no load, and no 12b-1 fee." Having been in this business for 16 years at the time, I knew they were misleading the public, so I requested the prospectus. True to their ad, they had no load and no 12b-1 fee. But they had a "miscellaneous" category, which covered sales and marketing expenses (in the footnotes) raising their total annual fees to 3.3 percent—the absolute highest in the entire mutual fund industry. The ad ran for about two weeks, and then, I suspect, the NASD required

FIGURE 2.1   Risk Tolerance Self-Analysis

Ask Yourself Two Questions

1. **Which rate of return would you like in an "upward-swinging" market?** An *upward-swinging market* is defined as one where stocks of the Fortune 500 companies (measured by the S&P 500) are positive from one year to the next. (This may include negative swings during the course of the years.) As a frame of reference, be aware that stocks have averaged 10 percent a year since 1926, bonds about 5 percent, and Treasury bills about 3.5 percent; and inflation has averaged about 3 percent per year over that same time period.

   Now from the choices below, circle the rate of return you would like to have.

   5%   7%   10%   12%   15%   20%   25%   greater: __ %

2. Now place a minus sign before the return you selected. **If in a downward-swinging market your investment went down that much, could you sleep?** Would you worry? A downward swinging market is defined as one where the S&P 500 is negative from one year to the next.

Evaluate Your Answers

If you would worry about your investments when they might go down the noted amount, then you should select a return that is lower—one that will allow you to sleep nights if the negative should occur. If you chose 15 percent, ask yourself if your money went down 15 percent, would it worry you?

Once you reach a number that you can tolerate in *down markets,* you have correctly identified the rate of return you can target that is within your risk tolerance.

Write that number here: _____ is my expected rate of return given my risk tolerance.

them to pull it for misleading the public. But our uninformed investor owns that fund and thinks he is paying no load.

According to John Dixon, president of Mutual Service Corporation, the point is not "load or no load." The point is are you going to "do it yourself" or have a professional help you. Successful people pay professionals to help them. How you're paying doesn't matter: salary, hourly fee, percentage fee, or commission. What matters is that you probably need someone to help you and, as with everything else, you have to pay for the help.

Too often, "no loads" become an excuse not to pay for a professional. Rarely can you be successful that way—unless you are yourself an investment professional and have the time, interest, and energy to stay on top of your investments.

If you are the do-it-yourself type, you have probably already found that selecting a mutual fund from the 8,000+ available is no easy job. To help you wade through the data, I offer three criteria for the conservative investor to consider when selecting a mutual fund:

Criteria for Selecting a Mutual Fund

1. Review the fund's track record back to 1973. Evaluating a fund's performance back to 1973 is the only way to assess the fund management's ability to weather very bad markets, which will inevitably recur in the future.
2. Look for performance better than the unmanaged S&P 500 Index, especially during 1973 and 1974; that is, 12 percent per year average annual return.
3. Look for a fund managed by a "systems approach" (that is, multiple managers or an analytical model that must be followed regardless of the person guiding the fund).

According to CDA/Wiesenberger, the leading provider of mutual fund information services to financial professionals for more than 55 years, as of December 31, 1996, there were 8,365 mutual funds available from which to select. The following is a summary of the data according to our criteria for selecting a mutual fund:

Mutual Fund Data from CDA/Wiesenberger
(as of 12/31/96)

Total number of mutual funds:	8,365
Total number of mutual funds that began in 1973 or earlier	306
Total number of mutual funds that began in 1973 or earlier with a multiple manager system	14
Total number of mutual funds that began in 1973 or earlier with a minimum annual rate of return of 12 percent (since that time) and managed by a multiple manager system	11

This decision strategy makes selection of a mutual fund much easier. It is difficult to make a decision from among the more than 8,000 different funds. It is manageable to make a decision from among 11. The 11 funds that meet our criteria are as follows:

1. Amcap Fund
2. American Mutual Fund
3. Dodge & Cox Balanced
4. Dodge & Cox Stock
5. Growth Fund of America
6. Income Fund of America
7. Investment Company of America
8. 20th Century Growth
9. 20th Century Select
10. New Perspective Fund
11. Washington Mutual Investors Fund

As you can see from our CDA/Wiesenberger analysis—long-term results back to the bear markets of 1973 and 1974—the team-managed fund families are American, with 7 of the 11 funds; 20th Century with 2 of the funds; and Dodge & Cox with 2 funds.

Of the 11 funds, 7 are load and 4 are no-load. The investor who restricts himself or herself to no-load funds would arbitrarily eliminate seven of the best funds available.

There are also good funds that meet our criteria but are managed not by multiple managers but by a system, such as a set of technical criteria strictly followed regardless of the person or persons managing the fund. Examples of those funds are the Pioneer Fund, Pioneer II, Aim Weingarten, and Aim Charter. A complete list of funds that are "system driven" is more difficult to identify because the available databases do not provide screening by that variable.

Teams Win

Mary Rowland reports in her article, "Power Play" (*Bloomberg Personal,* November–December 1996) "that team-managed funds perform better than those managed by individual managers, according to an exclusive analysis of data by *Bloomberg Personal.* The returns are consistently higher than the returns of individually managed funds, while their average risk levels and expenses are the same." The team-managed funds for the past 15 years significantly outpaced those of individually managed funds—by 1.18 percentage points per year. That would mean the investor with $10,000 invested in the average team-managed fund at the beginning of that period had $74,150 at the end of the 15 years versus $63,460 for the person who invested the same amount in the average individually managed fund. *Bloomberg Personal,* whose analysis had used the Morningstar database, asked Lisa Grossmann at Morningstar to review their numbers, and she verified them.

Don Phillips of Morningstar said: "Team-managed funds do better. The numbers seem to get bigger over the longer term." "If there is a single word that accounts for the fact that teams do better than individually managed funds, it is discipline," says Robert Puff, chief investment officer at Twentieth Century, which has always used teams.

The Capital Research–managed American Funds have been called by respected financial planner Alexandra Armstrong the *crème de la crème* of funds. The team management system has been firmly entrenched for 30 years. Manager compensation is tied to four-year averages, according to John Lawrence, a company spokesman.

Putnam Investments installed a team management approach in 1985. Carol McMullen of Putman Investments says: "One of the differences between a team-oriented place and a star-system place is that of process—a process on the buy side and one for the sell side."

John Gunn, a member of the management team at Dodge & Cox says, "You get the advantage of people looking at it from a lot of different angles." That creates style consistency, and the 15-year results for Aim Constellation, Putnam Vista, and Dodge & Cox Stock that haven't varied at all.

Facts about Load Funds

Load funds aren't necessarily bad. A load is the mechanism by which the mutual fund company gets reimbursed for distribution and marketing expenses. All front-load (called Class A shares) mutual funds offer a "volume discount feature" often referred to as "break points." The more dollars you have to invest, the lower the percentage charged as a front load. For example, such a chart looks somewhat like this:

Volume Discount Feature

Investment	Front Load
Less than $50,000	5.75%
$50,000 but less than $100,000	4.50
$100,000 but less than $250,000	3.50
$250,000 but less than $500,000	2.50
$500,000 but less than $1,000,000	2.00
$1,000,000 +	0

It would not be smart to invest in a front-load fund one year and cash out of the fund one or two years later. If the investor planned to cash out in a short period of time, it would be wiser to use a no-load fund. If, however, the investor planned to be a long-term investor, it would be smarter to invest in a front-load fund.

By biting the bullet and paying the load up front, the investor's biggest cost would be spread out over all the years he or she would be holding the fund. If the fund's annual operating expenses are low (and they usually are lower with a front-load fund), it would be a better move than a no-load option.

There is another type of load fund. It is called a back-end load or a fund with Class B shares. Instead of paying a fee to buy the mutual fund, the investor pays a fee to get out of the mutual fund if he or she chooses to get out within seven years. After seven years, there is no fee to get out. Following is an example of the declining schedule of typical surrender penalties:

Number of Years in Fund	1	2	3	4	5	6	7
% Deducted	5	4	4	3	2	1	0

Class B shares usually have higher annual fees than Class A shares, but those fees are reduced after the seven-year surrender penalty period has expired.

Facts about No-Load Funds

If you didn't know better, you might be led to believe there are no costs associated with no-load funds. This is a common misconception about no-load funds.

Here are the facts: Both a load and a 12b-1 fee are defined as ways for the mutual fund company to obtain a reimbursement of marketing or distribution expenses.

All other expenses fall under the category of operating expenses. Operating expenses cover all overhead expenses such as office and furniture rental, telephone, mail, administrative, legal, accounting, travel, and so on. Operating expenses also include payment of compensation to the person or persons managing the portfolio of stocks or bonds into which you are invested. Operating expenses are deducted from your account as a percentage of your total account balance on a daily basis. The deductions for such are never shown on your statement. The numbers shown on your statement already have all fees deducted.

There is absolutely, unequivocally, no mutual fur
ence that has zero operating expenses.

RULE OF THUMB

There's no such thing as a free lunch . . . especially in the investment world.

No-load (called Class C shares) funds deduct no fee upon investing and no fee upon liquidating. Instead, they deduct about 1 percent every year you own the fund. This fee, called a 12b-1 fee, is added to the annual operating expenses discussed previously. It is assessed on the total account balance each year.

Front-load and back-load funds also charge a 12b-1 fee annually. The difference in the 12b-1 fee is related to how quickly the fund management company gets its marketing and distribution costs reimbursed. If, for example the fund charges a front load, the 12b-1 fee will be the lowest because the front load gave the company some money for sales and marketing expense reimbursements. If they charge a back load that expires in seven years, the 12b-1 fee will be a bit higher but will be reduced after the seven-year penalty period is up.

If, however, no load is charged, the 12b-1 fee is the highest—and it never goes down. Therefore, if you are in a no-load fund for ten years, your "load" could be as high as 10 percent. To see how this works, consider the examples shown in Figure 2.2.

The following is a simple, step-by-step way to decide which expense structure is best for your objectives:

1. Decide how long you will hold the fund. If you are going to hold it for three years or less, choose Class C shares.
2. If you are going to hold the fund for more than seven years and you don't have $50,000 to invest, choose Class B shares.
3. If you are going to hold the fund for longer than four years and you can get at least a $50,000 break point, choose Class A shares.

FIGURE 2.2   An Analytical Comparison of Load Versus No-Load

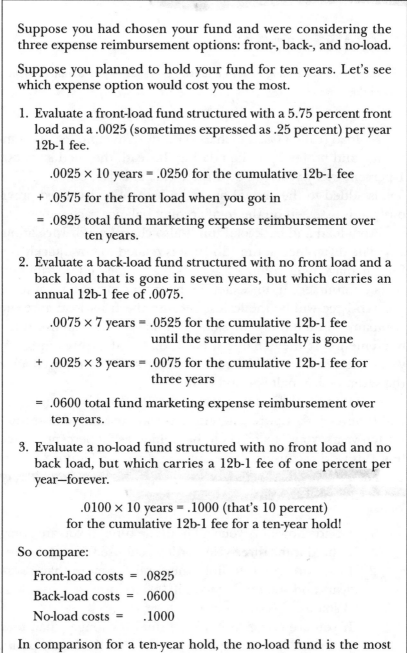

Suppose you had chosen your fund and were considering the three expense reimbursement options: front-, back-, and no-load.

Suppose you planned to hold your fund for ten years. Let's see which expense option would cost you the most.

1. Evaluate a front-load fund structured with a 5.75 percent front load and a .0025 (sometimes expressed as .25 percent) per year 12b-1 fee.

    .0025 × 10 years = .0250 for the cumulative 12b-1 fee

    + .0575 for the front load when you got in

    = .0825 total fund marketing expense reimbursement over ten years.

2. Evaluate a back-load fund structured with no front load and a back load that is gone in seven years, but which carries an annual 12b-1 fee of .0075.

    .0075 × 7 years = .0525 for the cumulative 12b-1 fee until the surrender penalty is gone

    + .0025 × 3 years = .0075 for the cumulative 12b-1 fee for three years

    = .0600 total fund marketing expense reimbursement over ten years.

3. Evaluate a no-load fund structured with no front load and no back load, but which carries a 12b-1 fee of one percent per year—forever.

    .0100 × 10 years = .1000 (that's 10 percent) for the cumulative 12b-1 fee for a ten-year hold!

So compare:

    Front-load costs = .0825
    Back-load costs = .0600
    No-load costs =   .1000

In comparison for a ten-year hold, the no-load fund is the most expensive option.

In the February 1997 issue of his *Financial Focus* news. Jack Everett, CFP, writes, "Often individuals select a fund be cause it has low costs. Don't let that aspect of greed cause you to overlook the fact that the important factor is how much you can gain from an investment, not how little others are making from managing your assets. I want my managers to make a lot of profit. The only way they can do this is to perform well. If they perform well, then I will also make money. If they don't perform well, I will move my money elsewhere."

Deciding Between Load or No-Load Funds

If the funds under consideration have the same performance over the same time frame, the expenses are irrelevant. Make sure you are reviewing numbers that are net of all fees and expenses. Here are the three most important criteria to consider if the performance numbers are the same:

1. **What system of management created the performance?** A system of management is one whose day-to-day management decisions are driven by either a team of people or by a set of strict criteria that are implemented irrespective of the person who may be managing the fund at the time. While a system of management won't guarantee good results, its past results will at least provide more evidence of the hope of future performance in any type of market than that of a completely different person making decisions in a totally individualistic way.

2. **What is the chance it can be replicated in the future?** The danger of selecting a mutual fund managed by one manager is not only the fact that rarely does one person possess enough information to make the best decision. But the biggest problem is that the turnover of managers is extremely high.

   Industry-wide, the average age of fund managers is 29 years. The average length of time a fund manager stays with one fund is 4.33 years. Furthermore, the conservative investor will want his or her fund management system to have lived through and survived a bad market.

If fund managers have only been there four to five years, they will not have had the chance to have lived through even one bad year, given today's market.

3. **If the fund is not managed by a team, is there a system of management?** If your fund is not managed by multiple managers or a team, make sure an analytical system or decision-making model is in place that must be adopted by anyone who manages the fund. Make sure the model has been in place since 1973 and that it has produced results that outperform the unmanaged S&P 500, especially in bad markets.

EMOTIONS:
THEY CAN SABOTAGE OR SAVE YOUR INVESTMENTS

While investment goals and strategies change through the decades, we must live with our emotions day in and day out through the course of our lives. And we must constantly reconcile the conflicting messages our emotions sometimes send our brain when it comes to investment decisions. Our emotions can lead us to make either disastrous or brilliant decisions.

Two personality types characterize the opposite ends of a spectrum with regard to investment action: "Nervous Nellie" or "Instant Guru Gary." Do either of these sound like you? Perhaps you're in the middle, like "Careful Carla."

Nervous Nellie: A Case of Analysis Paralysis

Nervous Nellie knows she should be investing. So with highlighter in hand she sits down to read the recent magazines that contain charts ranking mutual funds according to various criteria: *Money, U.S. News and World Report, Barron's, Business Week, Forbes, Mutual Fund Selector,* etc. Nellie highlights the best-performing funds on each set of charts. Then she makes a list of the funds she highlighted. Next, she looks for funds that appear consistently on each chart—there are none. She discovers that each rating service has used different criteria on which to compare the funds, so there is no consistency.

Nellie decides that perhaps the one-, three-, and five-year averages reported in this year's magazines might not contain enough information. Not discouraged, Nellie goes to the library to see if last year's issue containing the fund rankings would show any consistencies. They don't. So nervous about investing in the wrong fund, Nellie decides to wait for next year's issues to come out. Perhaps then she would find some funds.

Nervous Nellie has analysis paralysis, which will keep her from making any decision. Eventually she probably will get fed up and make a decision by throwing a dart.

This person is typical of some people who at 53 wake up and admit they have been negligent in managing their money. And at 53 it is time to begin a serious program of investing to make up for lost time. The danger is that, even after months of research, the person will end up making a decision based on the wrong criteria.

Instant Guru Gary:
A Little Bit of Knowledge Is a Dangerous Thing

You've met Instant Guru Gary over the water cooler at work or over finger foods at a cocktail party. He's the one who's quick to tell you what you're doing wrong. He throws around names of funds he's using. He's on the Internet and subscribes to six newsletters. He manages his portfolio himself.

Here's how he does it: Every week, Gary reads his newsletters and magazines. He is particularly attracted to a fund written up in a magazine. He places some money in that fund. That fund does fine for the next several months, then it begins to level off. What happened? Instant Guru Gary overlooked one little piece of information: By the time the article about the fund was published, it had already made its move. Remember, many articles in monthly magazines were written at least 30 days before you read them. As a general rule, by the time you read it, it's too late!

With the rest of his money, Gary moves often from fund to fund. Then his job takes him out of town and he misses a week. It happens to be a week during which the market drops and one fund manager quits. His fund goes down. By the time Gary checks back in, he can't believe what's happened to his money.

Why didn't someone tell him the fund manager left? Now it's too late. So he takes his loss and jumps back in. The cycle repeats.

The research says. Dalbar Financial Services, a Boston-based research firm, conducted a study to evaluate the investment results of investors who moved their money around among funds often with the results of those who didn't. According to their study, reported in the February 18, 1994 issue of *Investor's Business Daily*, investors who traded their investments more frequently received lower overall returns than those who held their investments longer, regardless of whether the funds were purchased load or no-load. The study included the returns of stock and bond mutual fund investors for a period of roughly ten years (January 1, 1984 through September 30, 1993).

Careful Carla: Making a Sound Decision

Never having been taught in college when she got her degree in math (or marketing, English, psychology, education, etc.) about investments, Carla doesn't know where to invest. She doesn't even know how various asset classes perform. But she is determined to learn.

Here's how she goes about it.

1. Research. The reference librarian directs her to the Ibbotson Associates *Stocks, Bonds, Bills and Inflation 1996 Yearbook* to learn the average rates of return for the various asset classes. From that source, Carla learns the average annual compounded rates of return with all dividends and capital gains reinvested since 1926:

Consumer Price		Government	
Index	3.1%	Bonds	5.1%
Treasury Bills	3.7	Corporate	
Common Stocks	10.3	Bonds	5.7

2. The process of elimination. Armed with these numbers as indications of what might be reasonable to expect, Carla determines that she doesn't want Treasury bills. She is shocked to learn that government and corporate bonds sometimes have negative years. She had always thought bonds were safe.

She notices that the two worst consecutive years for sto ket performance were 1930–31—the Great Depression. The next two worst consecutive years were 1973–74. During those two years, we experienced the oil embargo and the resignation of a U.S. Vice President and President. She notices that since 1974, our market as measured by the unmanaged S&P 500 has not even experienced a 10 percent correction, even in the crash of 1987. She determines that she wants to invest in the stock market.

She is sure individual stocks are not for her. The risk of selecting a few stocks is too great for her. And she doesn't have enough money to be as diversified as she'd like. She decides she wants growth stock mutual funds. She determines she is willing to take the risk of fluctuations in order to receive at least the 10 percent-a-year average return turned in by the S&P 500. In her research, she learns that a 12 percent-a-year return net of fees is possible if a mutual fund management system is employed. She is convinced she can expect that return with modest volatility. She also knows there are more than 8,000 from which to choose—she just doesn't know which one.

3. Researching specific funds. Carla is looking for a track record that dates back to 1973 so she can see if the fund family is still in business after those devastating years of 1973 and 1974. From Morningstar, she learns that no funds are star rated on performance dating back longer than ten years. She turns to CDA/ Wiesenberger's *Investment Company Yearbook*.

4. Setting standards. Carla's criteria are as follows: the fund must have a track record back to 1973 and must have produced at least 12 percent a year on average since then. In addition, the track record must have been created either by a team of portfolio counselors or through a disciplined decision-making model regardless of the person at the helm.

Looking only at year-by-year returns is not enough. Carla determines that for her peace of mind she wants to select funds that are managed in a way that will not require her attention on a daily, weekly, monthly, or even yearly basis. She will choose funds with track records that are above average, that are only modestly volatile, and that are managed by a systems approach time-tested to survive the bad times, especially. She isn't as concerned about doing better than the averages in the good times—just wants to do better in the worst times.

Overcoming bad times. Here's why. If $10,000 invested goes down 50 percent, resulting in a $5,000 loss, then the $5,000 value must go up 100 percent just to allow the $10,000 investor to break even. Here's another example: If $10,000 invested goes down 20 percent, resulting in a $2,000 loss, then the $8,000 value must go up 25 percent just to allow the $10,000 investor to break even.

Now, let's compare market fluctuations with bank rates for the various market types. In the chart that follows, one market cycle includes one bull (or up) and one bear (or down) market; thus we show three market cycles. To calculate our returns, we assume an initial $10,000 in each asset class (i.e. the bank, stock market, and managed mutual funds). We then applied the specific percentages of growth or loss to the investment:

	$10,000 went up	30% to 13,000
Then	13,000 went down	15% to 11,050
Then	11,050 went up	40% to 15,470
Then	15,470 went down	20% to 12,376
Then	12,376 went up	50% to 18,564
Then	18,564 went down	25% to 13,923

13,923 − 10,000 = 3.923 profit or about 5.7% annual compound rate of return

Each asset class rate of return was calculated in the same way.

Market Fluctuations Compared with Bank Rates

Three Market Cycles	Bank Account	Stock Market*	Managed Funds
1a. Bull market	6%	30%	25%
1b. Bear market	6%	(15%)	(5%)
2a. Bull market	6%	40%	35%
2b. Bear market	6%	(20%)	(5%)
3a. Bull market	6%	50%	45%
3b. Bear market	6%	(25%)	(5%)
Value of $10,000	$14,200	$13,900	$21,100
Compound Annual Return	6.00%	5.7%	13.25%

*Performance of S&P 500

Reprinted with permission of Keystone Capital Management, Inc., Gulfport, Mississippi.

Carla's theory: In a good market, anyone can do a good job. As her father had said, "Even a blind squirrel can find acorns in a field of oak trees!"

A consistent investment program provides better long-term success than does volatile performance with high returns in some years and losses in others, because the loss years can lead to the devastation of uncompounding.

The previous chart graphically illustrates the importance of avoiding losses. With bull market gains of 30 percent, 40 percent, and 50 percent followed by bear market losses of only half as much, the investor ends up with a return lower than bank rates!

The well-managed fund alternative can turn this roller coaster into a stairway by participating in the uptrends and missing some of the downtrends. To be effective it doesn't have to be perfect and catch the exact top and bottom. The information in the previous chart was calculated assuming that each turning point in the market cycle was missed by 5 percent. Obviously, the key to success in the markets is protection of assets from the downside.

5. Calculating expenses.   Carla wants to make sure the expenses of the mutual fund she selects are reasonable. She knows mutual funds are divided into two camps: load and no-load. No-load funds are sold direct to the public. They are marketed through ads in magazines, commercials on TV, and mail-outs. Their costs of marketing are covered by levying an annual 12b-1 fee. Load funds cover marketing costs by charging a fee upon investing or a fee to get out. In addition, both load and no-load funds levy an annual fee that covers such costs as shareholder service, portfolio counselor compensation, and legal, accounting, and general administrative expenses.

Annual operating expenses and loads are important, but they are not as important as some advertisements might lead you to believe. This is because the expenses are already factored in when you look at the results of these funds. They have affected the track record before we even see the track record. There is no need to factor them again.

The decision about buying a load or no-load fund should be based first on the results, second on the load structure.

A no-load fund would be a better choice for the investor who plans to invest for a short period—say less than four years, or for those who want to move their funds around frequently. As for a load fund, as long as annual fees are under the industry average (see following chart), a front-load fund is a good choice for the investor who plans to stay invested for more than four years, with every intention of riding out the ups and downs.

Annual Expense Ratios

Category	Industry Average*
Growth	1.41%
Growth and Income	1.35
International/Global	1.83
Equity–Income	1.33[†]
Balanced	1.35
Taxable bond	1.14
Tax-exempt bond	1.02
Money market	0.58[‡]

*All data from CDA/Wiesenberger unless otherwise noted.
[†]From Morningstar.
[‡]From IBC/Donoghue's *Money Fund Report*®.

6. Making the decision.   Carla's goal is to invest for retirement, which she expects at age 65, 30 years from now. She set her rate of return goal at 12 percent and decided a front-load fund was best for her. Her research directed her to a choice among American, Pioneer, or Aim Funds. She chose American since the fund family offered 28 funds from which she could seek diversification.

WHAT ABOUT INDEX FUNDS?

An index fund is a mutual fund consisting of an equal number of shares of the companies that make up the "index." For example, the S&P 500 index is made up of an equal number of shares of stocks from each of the Fortune 500 companies. If you like the idea of owning the largest 500 companies in our country, consider investing in an index fund.

These funds are simple to operate: no decision-ma
quired; no research is required; no adjustments are
market or economic fluctuations. These funds are always fully in
vested. Because no management is required, the fees are very
low.

With the unprecedented growth of the stock market over the
past 20 years, index funds have done well.

In a downtrending market, however, index funds may not
perform as well. Since they do not have the benefit of management, they are unable to reposition investments as a defensive
measure against potential market downturns. In other words, if
a company's stock goes up in a year, there is no one to decide to
sell while high and wait until it drops lower to buy it back, thus
increasing the number of shares.

Let's contrast the unmanaged approach with the managed
approach: Consider the example of an unmanaged fund of 100
shares valued at $40 per share. If they go up to $50 per share and
then back down to $40, where they started, the unmanaged port-
folio would have gone from $4,000 up to $5,000 and back down
to $4,000.

If managed, the management system would be likely to trigger
a sale at $50 per share, creating $5,000 in cash. When the stock
drops to $40 per share, the managers can buy it back, creating a
block of 125 shares. Then when the price goes back to $50 per
share, the 125 shares will create value of $6,250, not $5,000 as
with the unmanaged index portfolio. However, the more the fund
managers buy and sell stocks with gains within a fund during one
year, the greater the tax owed on the capital gains generated.

In short, an advantage to owning an index fund is that the
companies are just bought and held. There is no trading. They
are only sold from the portfolio if they are dropped from the
index. Therefore such funds tend not to create large tax bills. By
contrast, mutual funds that are actively managed can create capital gains on which the shareholders must pay taxes.

ASSET ALLOCATION FOR RETIREMENT PLANNING

It is now a broadly accepted concept that diversification among asset classes is a smart thing to do when managing your assets for retirement. There are many ideas of how to diversify your assets as they grow for retirement. Some think you should have assets (such as stocks and bonds) that can be sold at a moment's notice; others think you should have assets (such as real estate and gold) that are illiquid, that is, cannot be sold at a moment's notice. There are people who like to manage rental property. Still others think you should have some of all. The "some of all" is a good theory until you reach your 50s and beyond. At that point, you should probably begin moving almost 100 percent into liquid assets, since they will probably be called on to provide income within 10 to 15 years.

Illiquid Assets

I have found that *gold* is a good investment only if you don't plan to use the money in your lifetime. Therefore, buy it for the next generation. Rarely does gold appreciate fast enough nor is it possible to sell it for enough during your lifetime to make it a good retirement planning investment.

RULE OF THUMB

Invest in gold only if you don't plan to use the money in your lifetime. An investment in gold is an investment for future generations.

Real estate has been in and out of favor during the past 30 years. When real estate was in favor during the late 1970s and early 1980s, people made money. When the tax law changed taking away many of the tax benefits of owning real estate, people lost money. Many think the late 1990s are a good time to again own real estate.

To own real estate, you must choose between two forms of ownership and management: direct and indirect. If you directly own real estate, you will have to manage the property an ble for all the responsibilities of ownership. This is not possible for many people who have full-time jobs, since real estate ownership takes a lot of time.

The second method of management is indirect. In order to participate in real estate indirectly, you must buy a limited partnership or a real estate investment trust, such as the one offered by Inland Real Estate Corp. There are now even a few mutual funds of real estate investment trusts (Franklin Real Estate Shares, Pioneer Real Estate Fund, and Dodge and Cox Real Estate Shares are a few). In each of these forms of ownership, you have no management responsibility and no financial exposure for the liabilities associated with owning property.

You can achieve both diversification and liquidity by selecting a real estate investment trust (REIT). Be sure you carefully check out the management of the properties. Make certain the company is a real estate company first and an investment company second.

If, however, during your earning years when your taxes are the highest, you can find real estate that offers you tax credits or write-offs, it is often worth taking the chance. If you don't need the write-offs but still want to diversify with a small amount of real estate, look for good real estate investment trusts. Especially seek those managed by a company that has been doing it for at least 20 years. This will assure you that they survived the bad years of the late 1980s. Real estate is considered a growth investment, so if you'd like, use it as a part of that portion of your asset allocation.

Liquid Assets

The liquid portion of your portfolio should consist of cash and stock and bond mutual funds. I favor mutual funds because, according to a 1984 to 1994 study conducted by Sanford Bernstein and Co., a renowned research firm dedicated to market research for the securities industry, 90 percent of the trades on the New York Stock Exchange in 1984 were done by small investors. But by 1994, 90 percent of the trades were being done by large mutual fund and large pension fund managers. No longer can the small investor with 100 to 1,000 shares compete. Large fund managers are trading in blocks of 100,000 shares. That is a formidable competitor for the small investor.

Your diversification among mutual funds should be among growth-oriented and balanced domestic and global stock funds. The balanced portion of the portfolio should contain bond funds or should be a mutual fund where your fund manager can choose to place bonds in your portfolio when and if he or she thinks appropriate. Use the balanced portion of your portfolio to provide stability and lower volatility. Often, younger people or those with more tolerance for volatility use stock funds that pay dividends (called equity income) for the balanced portion of the portfolio. *Balanced* is a word often used to describe growth *and* income.

Whatever your risk tolerance, be sure to include global funds. In 1984, 67 percent of the world's wealth was based in the U.S. stock markets. In 1994, a short ten years later, 60 percent of the world's wealth was based outside the United States. This does not mean you will be investing in a mom-and-pop foreign business in a country whose economy is unstable. Instead, you will want to be investing in countries whose economic and political base is strong and in large, well-run companies.

Are you aware that you cannot now buy a television or VCR that is manufactured by a U.S.–owned company? Did you know that Nestlé is a Swiss company? That Bayer is a German company? That Motel 6 is a French company? That Bridgestone Tire is a Japanese company? A very high percentage of the revenues of these companies comes from the U.S. marketplace.

On the other hand, some companies based in the United States derive a great percentage of their revenue from abroad. Did you know, for example, that the Coca-Cola Co. gleans 80 percent of its revenue from the international marketplace? Yes, you can benefit from the international marketplace by investing in a mutual fund that owns companies like Coca-Cola, and whose revenue base is diversified worldwide. But you must look hard and do a considerable amount of research to find out which companies those are. It is usually easier to designate a portion of your

assets for global funds and then let your experienced m
fund manager select the particular companies.

As you seek to find mutual funds with an international focus,
look for management experience that goes back many years—at
least 20 years. Don't put your money with a fund whose manager
has only been managing stocks abroad for ten years or less.
There are too many complexities with foreign markets for anyone to become an expert in less than ten years.

As you read through the following chapters, you will find suggestions for allocating your assets as you progress through the
decades. You can be a millionaire at retirement with considerable
ease if you follow the steps outlined in Part Two of this book.
Many people, perhaps even someone as unsuspecting as your
own next-door neighbor, have proven it can be done. You can do
it too. Read on to find out how.

PART TWO

FINANCIAL PASSAGES
HOW OUR MONEY NEEDS CHANGE BY DECADES

*Because the effects of the financial choices
we make are cumulative, the choices at each
juncture affect our options at the next one.*

*As the years go by, your needs and priorities will
change, and you will find it necessary to revisit
and revise your financial plan again and again.*

This is a lifelong endeavor.

THE SHIFTING MOSAIC OF LIFE

As day follows night and is as little under our control, so do our lives move through the decades. On this journey, the pieces of our life mosaics shift and shift again as the years go by. We are the children of our parents. We are the parents of our children. Often we then become the support system of our parents, and finally, our children often become our support system. Accompanying each shift of the mosaic, we face complex psychological, relationship, career, and financial challenges.

Life's Major Financial Milestones

Chances are you're going to live to be 100. If not, you'll more than likely outlive your ancestors. By decade, here are the major tasks you'll need to master as you build, preserve, and finally spend your wealth.

Ages 4 to 10.   Learn and practice the rudimentary aspects of handling money: spending, saving, giving.

Ages 10 to 20.   Learn and begin to practice good habits of spending, saving, giving, using credit, and borrowing.

Ages 20 to 30.   Establish and practice adult habits of spending, saving, and giving. You may purchase a first home and furniture, save at least 4 percent of your income for retirement, and invest for growth—pretax if your company provides a plan.

When children are a part of the picture, you will need to buy life insurance, set up college funding accounts, and establish a will; you may begin to teach your own children the basics of money management.

Ages 30 to 40.   You may buy a larger home, an upgraded car, and better furniture; continue feeding college funding accounts; increase retirement savings to 10 percent; and invest for growth—pretax if your company provides a plan. Make sure you are properly insured, and establish a will. When children are in your life, buy insurance.

Ages 40 to 50.   Continue to save for retirement—by this age, at least 12 and up to 30 percent of your income should be saved for this purpose. Invest for growth—pretax if your company provides a plan. You may be able to send your children to college by using the funds you've created. You may find it necessary to revise your will or begin to care for older parents.

Ages 50 to 60.   Continue to save for retirement—by this age, at least 15 and up to 50 percent of your income should be saved for this purpose. Invest for growth—pretax if your company provides a plan. You may find yourself caring for older parents.

Begin to make serious plans for retirement. Revise your will if necessary.

Age 60 and beyond.   Invest for preservation of principal, income, and growth. Enjoy your money, your family, your friends, and your life. Remember that exercise and good nutrition is essential to your well-being! You may decide to work part-time, and to pursue continuing learning opportunities.

At Each Juncture

Because the effects of the financial choices we make are cumulative, the choices at each juncture affect our options at the next one. If our decisions are sound all along the way, we usually can avoid the financial crises of:

- Excessive debt
- Funding lifestyles we can afford only to the detriment of our relationships
- Being unable to properly educate our children
- Helping our parents when they need us
- Preparing for our own retirement with insufficient funds

Let's take a closer look at some of the typical financial challenges that arise during given decades and consider some examples of people who have adequately or inadequately responded to these challenges.

Perhaps the right decisions that were made will inspire you and the wrong decisions will alert you to potential problems so you can avoid making them.

CHAPTER 3

THE TRANSITIONAL 20S: FROM LEARNING TO EARNING

"Daughter I am in my mother's house,
But mistress in my own."

"Our Lady of the Snows"
Author unknown

MAJOR FINANCIAL TASK

Establishing Good Spending and Saving Habits

In her 1976 bestselling book *Passages,* Gail Sheehy calls this decade the "trying 20s." The decade confronts us, she writes, "with the question of how to take hold in the adult world. Our focus shifts from the interior turmoils of late adolescence—'Who am I?' 'What is truth?'—and we become almost totally preoccupied with working out the externals."

MANAGING THE EXTERNALS INVOLVES MONEY AND ITS USE

While Sheehy sees late adolescence as the time for working out the question of "Who am I?," many have not completed that phase by their 20s. This may come as a surprise to those, who, while in college, were led to believe they would be totally prepared for the world beyond after graduation. As these young people enter the work world, they are many times disillusioned to find that much of what they learned in college is irrelevant when performing their jobs. It is only later that most also learn how unprepared they are to manage their newly acquired salaries.

So, as we move from dependence on our parents for support to independence, we begin to sort through the data that will be relevant for managing our initial expectations about our careers and financial potential.

Typically, the financial challenges predominate our thinking when we are in our 20s. Remember, while in college learning, most of us approached adulthood principally as money *spenders*, depending on our parents to do the heavy money earning. Then, somewhere in our early 20s, the picture changes completely. Suddenly we are expected to earn our own money and to spend no more than we earn. We are expected to establish an affordable lifestyle for ourselves. We wake up one day and realize we can't start in the same type of lodging or drive the same type of car our parents enjoy today.

We must make decisions, based on affordability, about the furniture we choose, the car we drive, the way we dress, and the leisure activities we pursue. We find there are choices to be made. Do we choose moderation and make choices that fall within our income or do we run up the credit cards? Do we blow our money on expensive nonessential purchases, hoping that our parents won't let us starve, or do we make mature decisions that require patience and delayed gratification?

We are faced with problems at the two most important junctures: financial and emotional. Let's deal with the financial issue that is probably farthest from your mind right now—retirement.

LIFE-STAGE RETIREMENT PLANNER FOR THE 20S

True, retirement may be the farthest thing from your mind now. But if you would like to build wealth and be financially independent by age 65, starting now will enable you to do it with the least pain and succeed more effectively.

We're going to assume that you need most of your starting salary to buy your new wardrobe, new furniture, upgrade from

your clunker to a newer car, and get settled into an ap:
But we are going to show you how just a little money inve
retirement beginning with your first paycheck will help you in
the long run. Set your goal at 4 percent of your pay. The easiest
way, of course, is for your employer to deduct it from your paycheck and invest it for you tax-deferred. When you select the investment option for your money, go for growth. Don't worry
about volatility, and don't move your money around unless there
is a manager change in the mutual fund you select. At the very
least, put your money into an indexed fund option.

Invest according to this formula:

$$100 - \text{Your age} = \text{Percentage of assets invested for growth in mutual funds with no more than 10 percent in real estate}$$

$$\text{Your age} = \text{Percentage of assets invested in growth and income mutual funds}$$

Split your mutual fund investments equally between domestic and global mutual funds. If you can tolerate great risk in your
investments, you could move to 100 percent growth with no
growth and income.

Mutual Fund Investments for the 20s

Objective:	Maximize Growth
Time Horizon:	30 to 40 Years
Risk:	Highly Volatile
Investment Vehicle:	Mutual Funds

Investment Type	% Invested
Growth	80% to 100%
U.S. stocks	50%
Global stocks	50%
Growth and Income	20% to 0%
U.S. stocks	10%
Global stocks	10%

FIGURE 3.1   Asset Allocation for the 20s

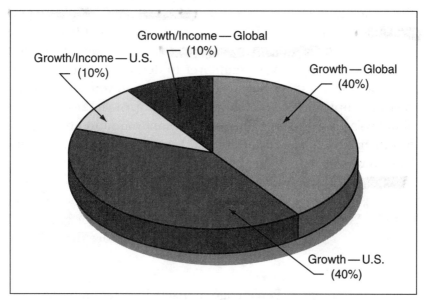

> *Growth–U.S.* = Small and medium-sized companies; REITs; expect fluctuation; minimum holding period: four years.
>
> *Growth/Income–U.S.* = Fortune 500 companies; dividend-paying stocks and bonds; expect modest fluctuation; minimum holding period: three years.
>
> *Growth–Global* = U.S. and non-U.S. small and medium-sized companies; best positioned through mutual funds; expect modest fluctuation; minimum holding period: five years.
>
> *Growth/Income–Global* = U.S. and non-U.S. Fortune 500–sized companies; dividend-paying stocks and bonds; best positioned through mutual funds; expect modest fluctuation; minimum holding period: four years.

When using the diagrams in Figure 3.1 for your own situation, keep in mind your own risk tolerance (the more growth you have the greater risk you will be taking) for all of your invested assets, and your income. Do not include your "use assets" such as your emergency cash, home, car, furniture, boat, or anything else you own that you will not sell to create retirement capital.

The Model Investor Begins at 22

The model 22-year-old begins with a first job straight out of college. We assume a starting salary of between $18,000 and $24,000 a year. With pay increases, this income increases to $30,000 by age 30. This model assumes $1,000 of income per year for each year thereafter. From age 22 to age 29, this person invests only 4 percent per year into a 401(k) plan. He or she selects a growth option that is diversified internationally as well as domestically, realizing returns of 10 percent a year. Note: This projected return is probably low for an aggressive portfolio, but if you can do better, great. The purpose of this example is to show how well you will do if you only receive the average performance of the unmanaged index between now and the time you retire.

Let's move our model investor through the decades and show you how easy it is to accumulate wealth—if you start early! So, our investor began working at age 22 and had no investment dollars accumulated. At the end of the investor's 29th year, he or she will have accumulated $12,582. So from the beginning of the 22nd year to the end of the 29th year, the retirement nest egg will look like this:

22nd Year	29th Year
$0	$12,582

Although $12,582 doesn't sound like much money now, we will show you how it grows as you continue to invest through the years. To recap, while retirement may be the last thing you are thinking about, put your plan into place first and then move on to the time and thought-consuming areas of your life as a maturing twenty-something young person.

Problems That Plague

Money problems. While money is not the be-all or end-all, it clearly is necessary for successful life management. Having money means you now have choices about the lifestyle you want to create. A 20-year-old must make primary decisions about housing, clothing, and transportation. Along with those decisions comes a choice about how to fund each area. If one chooses to "have it all now," credit cards will have to be used. If one chooses to delay having some things now or having less expensive items now, the decisions can be funded with cash. In this section we will look at one young woman who did it with credit and a couple who did it with cash. Cash is clearly better.

Emotional problems.   Emotional problems also plague 20-year-olds. These problems occur in two areas: life lessons and socialization. By life lessons, I refer to the ability to distinguish between information learned in college that is helpful in performing a job or in making day-to-day decisions and discarding or placing "on hold" information learned that is not helpful for now. For example, while you may have been taught in college things you may feel are irrelevant to your job today, such as how to derive a theorem in your geometry course, the analytical skills that helped you get through geometry may prove helpful to you in the future. Don't become bitter. There may be a time you will need those skills in the future.

At the same time, you may need some skills that you weren't taught in college. Such skills include how to appropriately spend and invest your money, how to function in an office setting, and how to relate to peers and to those for whom you work. Again, don't let this discourage you. You will learn as you go. Be open to these lessons of life.

Much of college is focused on skill development in quantitative or objective areas. But when you get out of school, you quickly learn success is largely dependent on your social skills—the skill with which you handle relationships. In fact, in my experience as a consultant to large aerospace companies, the top executives for whom I worked said their criteria for choosing a person for a promotion to top management was largely dependent on that candidate's interpersonal skills. Let's face it: We live in a day where the labor pool is highly educated. There are many competent people from which choices can be made to fill jobs. So, given three people of basically equal competence, the position will go to the most likable person, whose interpersonal skills are genuine and graceful. College does not teach these skills, and probably rarely even mentions the importance of such. So how would a recent graduate know? It's learned through experience.

Good interpersonal skills also are essential for successful after-college friendships and courtships. Choose your relationships carefully. These friends and their behaviors will have a great impact on the way you will shape your life. Twenty-year-olds have to consciously decide about the qualities they value in their

friends; they then have to decide where to look for
ships they wish to cultivate. For example, are they go
by becoming active in a church, on a tennis team, or \
local bar? In this decade, decisions will have to be m   ͡ut
whether the people met will develop into serious relationships or
remain superficial acquaintances.

Taking the Right First Step—Start Investing for Growth

This book is not only about becoming financially independent; it also is about how to build wealth. The most wealth can be
built if you start early. But your spending and saving habits will
have to reflect your interest in wealth-building from the very beginning if you expect to achieve your goal. You can be a millionaire several times over if you start investing regularly and wisely
in your 20s. And most people will need at least a million dollars
by the time they're 65 to support the lifestyle they create today.

Say you like the thought of being a double-millionaire. If you
keep your tax-deferred savings plan in place at 4 percent for now
and also find $2,000 a year, you'll be there by age 65. Take a look
at the following examples:

Investing $2,000 per year. Consider investing only $2,000 a
year from the time you are 20 until you are 65 and compare the
money you will have with what a typical 30-, 40-, or 50-year-old
would have at 65.

Invest $2,000 a Year Until Age 65

Start at	Earn 10% a Year	Earn 12% a Year
Age 20	$1,437,810	$2,716,500
Age 30	$ 542,049	$ 863,327
Age 40	$ 196,694	$ 266,667
Age 50	$ 63,545	$ 74,560

The case of Norma and Al. If this example doesn't motivate
you to start investing in your 20s, consider the case of Norma and
Al. For this example, we are assuming Norma invests from ages
25 through 35 and then stops. Maybe at 35 Norma is paying for
college or investing in her own business and cannot continue

even though it would be preferable for her to do so. Al, on the other hand, at 25 is spending his money on eating out, dates, cars, and clothes. He says he can't afford to invest now. But he plans to play catch-up by investing twice as much as Norma at 45 and for twice as long. Let's see who winds up having the most at age 65.

How Investing Early Pays Off

	Norma	Al
Saves:	$100 a month	$200 a month
Ages:	25 to 35 and stops	45 to 65
Annual investment return:	10%	10%
Approximate Value at Age 65:	$360,000	$153,139
Value at 12% per Year:	$696,000	$199,830

Notice that Norma saved half as much for half as long to net twice as much as Al.

There is another lesson from the illustration with Norma and Al. Note the dramatic difference in Norma's account between investment returns of 10 percent and 12 percent. That is not an error. Only a 2 percent-per-year compounded return over long periods of time means a lot of money in the end. It might be easy to think only 2 percent is not worth taking a risk to seek, until you consider the information in the following chart:*‡

What Is 2 Percent Worth?
$200/Month Invested

Annual Rate of Return	30 Years	2% Is Worth:
8%	$ 298,071	$154,027*
10%	$ 452,098	$246,895†
12%	$ 698,993	$399,601‡
14%	$1,098,594	

*The difference between 8% and 10%
†The difference between 10% and 12%
‡The difference between 12% and 14%

Based on this chart, do you think it is worth it to atte get just 2 percent more return on your investments? After are young and can afford to take some risk.

I hope these charts have convinced you of two things:

1. To start investing in your 20s
2. To start reaching for better than 10 percent per year returns.

For the higher rates of return, look to the stock market through mutual funds. (Remember the criteria for selecting a good mutual fund in Chapter 2?) Be forewarned: Mutual funds that average annual returns of 10 percent or more *will* fluctuate. At your age, you can afford to take the risk of fluctuations. This is especially true for your 401(k) or other tax-deferred investments that you cannot touch before age 59½ without a penalty.

You can make it happen. I have just told you that you can start to be financially independent by placing only 4 percent of your salary into the tax-deferred plan of your company during your 20s.

If you want to build wealth, however, your investment strategy should be to invest the maximum allowed by your tax-deferred plan—not the maximum your company will match—the true maximum allowed by the IRS. Invest in stock mutual funds within the plan. If no mutual funds meet our three criteria for a good mutual fund, invest in the indexed stock fund option that most closely mirrors the unmanaged S&P 500. Then close your eyes and only look at your balance once a year. Even if the balance is down, don't panic. You have plenty of time for it to come back.

Obviously, the more money you invest early, the more you will have in the future. If you still have available money to invest, you should begin investing in a mutual fund outside the plan. It's called a nonqualified investment, meaning it is *not qualified* to be tax-deferred.

Do 20-Year-Olds Invest for Retirement?

Twenty-year-olds may have a reputation for being unmotivated slackers, but when it comes to saving, Generation Xers are focused on their retirement, reports a recent article from *Money Daily* (16 Oct. 1996).

Despite early adult concerns such as repaying student loans and buying a home, 75 percent of 18- to 30-year-olds who own mutual funds are investing for retirement, according to a new study by the Investment Company Institute (ICI). The average size of their holdings: $6,000.

The ICI findings confirm results from previous studies showing that people in their 20s are focused on retirement saving, *Money Daily* reports. A Kemper-Roper Retirement Monitor study released in June 1995 found that twentysomethings are just as likely as baby boomers to say that retirement is something they think about a great deal. That study found that 58 percent of people in their 20s said either they or their spouses had put money into a 401(k) plan, compared with just 52 percent of baby boomers. For the full article on the studies, published in the December 1996 "Planning Matters," by International Association for Financial Planning, please call IAFP-Fax-Info at 800-320-9032 and request document #4043.

While it is important to know where your money is going, in your 20s, it is more important to know exactly what amount you are saving or investing. Don't guess: Sit down and calculate how much 4 percent of your gross pay would be. Make sure you are investing at least that.

THE TRANSITION BEGINS: NEEDS FOR SPENDING ARE HEAVY

The Wardrobe

Right away, we start our first job. We need to make some changes in order to fit into this new environment. In all likelihood, our first expenditures are to upgrade our wardrobes; suits, skirts and jackets. Here's where the first temptation must be handled well. Set a budget you can afford and stick to it. Shopping at expensive stores is out unless the sale is 25 percent off or more. It is wise to spend money for good classic designs that won't have to be replaced from year to year. Basic dark-colored suits with several blouses or shirts help build a flexible yet impressive wardrobe.

Clothing is important—it states at a glance who you are. In these early years, appearances are very important. Details are important: shoes neat and polished, clothing pressed and fresh with no spots or loose pieces of thread.

For women, choose darker colors for fall and winter suits and work your brighter colors into blouses and scarves. For the spring and summer months, choose basic white, taupe, khaki, and lighter colored suits. Again, work in your colors with blouses and scarves. Remember to extend your wardrobe by purchasing in color groups that can be mixed and matched. Separates are invaluable as basics in your beginning wardrobe.

Men should always own a navy suit and sport coat. It is not a bad idea to purchase two pairs of trousers for your suits. Trousers always wear out faster than jackets. Stick with basic white, beige, and blue shirts. Resist the urge to buy avant-garde shirt styles and colors. Don't wear a tee shirt with writing on it underneath your business shirt. Don't go too wild with your tie. Consider your business image and make sure you choose on the conservative side—especially if that is the general tone of the career you have selected.

More and more companies are allowing "business casual" some or all of the time. If you want to continue to stand out from your peers, don't take this "casual day" opportunity to swing into the office in your warm-ups or jeans and tee shirt. For men, stick with dressy casual—khakis and open-collar golf shirt—fresh, pressed, and neat. For women, dressier pants and a more relaxed cotton blouse or golf shirt are advised. The idea is to stand out from your peers.

While you may be able to hit some sales at the better stores, shopping at outlet malls is probably a wiser choice. No matter where you shop, however, the smart rule is: Never pay full price—

even at the outlet stores. The mark-up on clothing is usually 300 percent. And pay cash.

The Car

The next expenditure is usually for a car. Beginning career-people make a big mistake if they think they need a new car. A new car is guaranteed to lose 10 percent to 20 percent of its value the moment it is driven off the lot.

Here's a better idea: Buy a one-year-old car from a dealer—if possible, a demonstrator. Research the car to buy. Put to use those research skills you learned in college. Go to the library, book store, or get on the Internet and find out what the consumer research is saying. And remember, you don't have to rush to buy something. Time is the one sure thing you have. So take your time to find a good, reliable car at a good value.

The choice to lease or to buy.   The car dealer will offer you the opportunity to lease or purchase. Basically the difference between a lease and purchase is when you make your down payment. With a purchase, you make a down payment up front. With a lease, you make your down payment at the end of the lease if you choose to buy the car then. So if you don't have money for a down payment or if you don't have a car to trade in to create the down payment, you may have no choice but to lease. If you have the choice, you will want to determine which is the best financial deal for you.

To determine the most economical way to buy the car, multiply all the payments required by the number of months you will have to pay and add the down payment if it is a purchase option. This will give you the total amount you will pay to purchase the car. Then multiply the lease payment by the number of months on the lease, add any required up-front costs and add the residual value (the end-of-lease buyout cost) to determine the total amount you will have to pay if you lease the car. Compare the two figures and you will see which is the most economical deal.

If you are in business for yourself, you receive tax benefits for the percentage of time you use your car in your business. If you purchase the car, you can write off the depreciation and a ן tion of the payment. If you lease the car, you can write off a percentage of the lease payment.

Auto insurance. One of the biggest expenses for 20-year-olds is auto insurance. Rates are highest for unmarried men under 25, because such drivers tend to have more accidents.

You will need to decide about collision, liability, uninsured motorist, and comprehensive coverage. You will have to determine a deductible amount that you will have to cover if you have an accident. Don't scrimp on the liability coverage. This is what pays if you cause the accident and someone sues you. You can reduce your premium by increasing your deductible. You should always have enough in your savings account to cover your deductible. If you don't, lower your deductible.

Consider the potential insurance cost in deciding the car you will purchase. Insurance is costlier on sports cars and expensive foreign cars. You can lower your costs substantially by driving your clunker for a few more years. But by far, the best way to lower your insurance cost is to drive carefully. A clean driving record will get you "preferred" rates. In your state, you may be able to get a discount by taking a driver improvement course. Look into it.

The Apartment

The third big expense is for housing. This is third and not first because in my experience more and more young people are living with their parents until they have employment and their wardrobe and transportation needs are met. Once you have a job, look carefully at your take-home pay. Housing is an expense that recurs every month. Be sure you can easily make that payment.

RULE OF THUMB

Don't spend more than 30 percent of your take-home pay for rent.

For example, if your take-home pay is $1,500 a month, plan to spend no more than $450 per month for rent. A good way to control this expense is to team up with a roommate. It may also allow you to live in a nicer place still within your budget.

Finally, having a place of your own will mean that you need furniture. This is the time of your life to accept hand-me-downs from willing parents, aunts, uncles, or grandparents. This is not the time to buy new furniture on your credit cards. However, the most important piece of furniture is a good mattress and box spring. Functioning well on your job is important. A good night's sleep is essential. So the bed is the main place not to scrimp. This is usually the place parents are willing to help you. Maybe you can even take your bed from your bedroom at home.

DON'T LET YOUR SPENDING WRECK YOUR WEALTH

The steps we are taking to make the transition to the real world of work, from learning to earning, from dependence to independence, are important in building the foundation for our futures. If we are not careful, we can quickly find ourselves in the first big financial crunch of our lives. This usually happens when we buy everything at once—pulling out the credit cards way too often. So be extra-cautious with your spending during your 20s.

To balance the heavy drain on your income for the "things" you need to get started, be sure you are saving at least 4 percent. It's not necessary to save more for your retirement in your 20s.

Let's take a look at how one single woman and several young couples got started.

Single and Twentysomething

Being single in the 20s can be either heaven or hell, depending on the person. The successful single will begin saving at least 4 percent of each paycheck and will ensure that spending is within the amount of take-home pay he or she has left after saving. This person won't be consumed with finding a mate but will first create a life that is vibrant, balanced, and financially stable.

Rachel is an example of what can happen when priorities are out of order. Rachel is 22 and from an affluent family; her parents recently divorced. She used her business degree to obtain a job as a customer service assistant at a well-known upscale bank making $18,000 a year. The salary was modest, but Rachel liked the idea of saying she worked at that bank. This is called "psychic pay." And after all, everyone knows new hires at banks often aren't paid very much.

Fantasies about life.   Almost immediately, money became a problem for Rachel. She and a roommate found an apartment. She had a small car payment on a used car. So far, her finances were under control. But clothing became her downfall. Used to shopping frequently at outlet mall stores with her father footing the bill, she continued to do so, placing her purchases on credit cards. She rationalized the spending: How could she conduct meetings with upscale bank customers if she were dressed in less than the best? She bought at good prices; she just bought too much.

Her second year with the bank, she qualified to participate in the company 401(k) plan, but she said she couldn't afford it.

Realities about life.   Two years out of college, Rachel had run up credit-card bills totalling $6,000. She didn't control her spending. Her girlfriends didn't help. They were living at home and paying no rent, so they had more money to spend, and Rachel often went along. Her older car began to need expensive repairs and she began to get scared as she saw her credit card balances climb.

One day when her father asked her how her money was working out, she told him about her charge-card balances. After she promised she would not let herself get into debt again, her parents and grandparents bailed her out. A father-daughter talk resulted in Rachel seeking another job

In her new job, she made $28,000 a year working for a relatively obscure company. She had to sacrifice her "psychic pay" to obtain "real" money of $10,000 more a year. This company allowed her to participate in their tax-deferred plan after only three months, so Rachel signed up for a 5 percent contribution.

That translated to about $1,400 investment per year, plus the company match of 3 percent of her salary—about $840 a year.

Her parents and grandparents were thrilled for her. Surely $10,000 a year more money would keep her from falling into the credit-card trap again. But it didn't. She quickly ran up another $2,000 credit-card bill. When asked how it happened, she declared: "How can *anyone* live on $28,000 a year?" Besides, one day soon, she said, she planned to find a husband and she wouldn't have to worry about money herself.

Analysis and results.   Rachel, ever the indulged child while growing up, continued to live in her fantasy world after she graduated from college. Instead of realizing that she was at a juncture in her life where she needed to begin practicing more responsible behaviors and live within her means, she continued irresponsible spending habits. She depended on her father and grandparents to pay her bills. She determined, wrongly, that the way out of her financial trap was to find a husband.

From her mother she learned to spend without control. From her father she learned that control wasn't necessary, since he never said "no," thus not teaching her the value of a dollar or responsible management of money.

Rachel is far from being an isolated case of overspending in the 20s decade. According to national estimates from counseling offices, younger consumers account for 5 percent to 20 percent of all problem debtors. This is bad news indeed: Using credit cards to pay for luxuries may seem so easy, as if there is no bottom to this marvelous pool of money. But people entering the world of adult spending run the risk of establishing some bad habits that are hard to break.

At this stage in our lives, we may set into motion a course of financial negligence that can last a very long time. If we become accustomed to spending above our means, we may never be able to live any other way. If we become accustomed to seeing credit-card balances carry over every month and grow larger and larger, this may become the norm for us.

If, on the other hand, we become careful spenders and users of credit, we can set a course for financial stability for the future.

So much of the financial direction of our lives depends on the difficult choices we make in the 20s.

Today Rachel is not married, nor is she out of the financial trap. Time will only tell how her financial life will progress.

Moonlight and Roses: Couples and Their Money

While many postpone marriage until the 30s, many others are marrying in their 20s. While they face all the same financial challenges of singles in the 20s, they usually benefit from combining two incomes, especially if they are financially responsible. However, they face still more choices. Probably the biggest decision is whether to have children right away or to wait until they are more financially stable.

It's an immutable fact that if you are romantically involved, you are financially involved as well. This begins with the early days of courtship, when couples must decide who is going to pay for the meal they eat together or admission to the movie. These early decisions are important, because they can set the tone for a relationship based on financial equity or one in which one partner wields a disproportionate amount of power. If John always pays for restaurant meals, for example, he will usually gain the power to decide whether he and Jane go to the corner Waffle House or the Ritz-Carlton dining room. Ditto for Jane if she always pays. This can lead to discontent. If Jane always pays and chooses, John may resent her financial ability to afford such an expensive place as the Ritz-Carlton, and if John pays, Jane may inwardly rage over his inability to feed her anything but scrambled eggs.

Some couples try to solve the money dilemma by opting to divide every expense down the middle, but, says Janet Franzoni, PhD, a professor of family therapy at Georgia State University, that is not a good answer either. If expenses are always split equally, she says, a charade of exaggerated attempts at fairness may develop, with a concurrent public haggling over pennies.

Even in the dating stage of a relationship, couples must confront money issues, says Franzoni. They need to talk about what each can afford and how they can share expenses without undue fuss. Perhaps, she says, a common fund can be created, with each person contributing a fair proportion. Then, in addition, they can individually decide how to spend on the relationship: Jane can take John to her beloved R-C dining room and John can treat Jane to a trip to the Bahamas to balance out the scrambled eggs.

If Jane and John decide to marry, the question of how to handle their finances grows even more crucial. Consider the statistics from a Roper/Starch Worldwide poll published in *Worth* magazine (June 1994). Twenty-nine percent of respondents said fights over money were the number one source of discord in their marriages, and 56 percent said there comes a time in every marriage when money becomes more important than sex. Yet even though money is so important in a marriage, communication about finances is extremely difficult: 40 percent said they were uncomfortable discussing money even with a spouse.

Single-income couples.   Problems surrounding the balance of power arise in marriages just as they do in courtships. When one person is the wage-earner and the other tends the home fires, there can be feelings of inadequacy on the part of the stay-at-home. "Society equates money with competence," Franzoni says. "The wage earner is seen as powerful, attractive, intelligent, and clever." The stay-at-home partner, conversely, may begin to harbor resentments, "and may even be prone to depression due to the perception that the other is a more important person."

More often than not, the woman is the marriage partner who stays at home with the children, while her husband earns the living. In some cases, such a woman can exhibit financial infantilism as a result, essentially living like a child, assuming no responsibility for family spending.

In an extreme case, Ted sold his business and wanted Becky's cooperation in reducing their cost of living until he could become readjusted in a new career. She refused, saying her job was to mind the house and their young daughter, and his was to provide income enough so that she could spend whatever she wanted, whenever she wanted. To quote her: "His job is to make sure my checks don't bounce."

Such an attitude may be explained in part by what author Colette Dowling calls the "Cinderella Complex" in her book of the same name. Despite the general protestations of women that they want independence, she writes, some retain a deep "wish to be saved, a deep yearning for dependence."

Unfortunately, Dowling is right in many cases. But women who always depend on the benevolence of a "prince" for economic security sometimes have to face reality due to divorce or the death of their spouse. As Don Cabaniss, president of the Center for Psychotherapy in Atlanta and retired director of the Center for Pastoral Education at Georgia Baptist Hospital, says, sometimes the clock strikes 12 and Cinderella is faced with who she really is. She has to go home and take care of herself.

Dual-income couples: the case of Vic and Barb. While couples who live on the income of one of the partners may have to deal with feelings of powerlessness on the part of the nonwage-earner, marriages in which both partners work can face problems too, although of a different kind. Sometimes these dual-income partners assume a costly lifestyle based on two incomes. When they begin to think about having a child, they face the decision of whether one partner will give up his or her job to become an at-home child caregiver or whether they will place the child in the costly care of someone else. In either case, they may have to cut back on their discretionary spending.

Vic and Barb started off differently from the way in which Rachel did. They were single, out of college and each began working and investing through their company 401(k) plans. They met through a mutual friend, dated for two years and then married. Neither had credit-card debt when they married and neither owned a home.

Vic, 27, a lawyer, and Barb, 25, a wellness program manager for a large corporation, came to see me about their financial future. They had been married two years, had purchased a home and furniture, were paying for modest cars, and were saving 10 percent of their income.

When they had married, they agreed that Barb would become an at-home mom when they began their family. Now they were trying to decide if it was the time to begin their family or if they should wait. A larger question loomed.

Barb had always dreamed of being an at-home Mom. She was faced with giving up her dream of that lifestyle or giving up her very valuable stock options and the financial security they would offer in the future.

Exploring the alternatives, Barb asked: "If I give up my job, what will be financially realistic for us to expect? I want our expectations to be within reach. If we could one day afford to buy a Jaguar on just Vic's potential income, let me know. If we'll only be able to afford a more modest sedan, let me know. I can be happy either way. I just want to tailor my expectations to our pocketbook."

Barb wasn't earning much money, but her company was granting stock options as incentive pay. Her options were worth twice her annual salary. If she stopped working to be an at-home-mom, she wouldn't miss the pay as much as she and Vic would miss her stock options. Then the same questions were asked under the "Barb-still-working scenario." She and Vic both knew the valuable stock options would one day give them the chance to buy some "nice-to-have" items or the chance of retiring early.

Analysis and result.   Here is a couple who has it all together. They indeed have a problem of positives. Stock options of significant value at this stage in their lives would give them financial freedom for the rest of their lives if they handled them properly and if the stock does well. But to benefit, Barb will have to work several more years and may not be able to quit even then. She is truly tied to the company with "golden handcuffs." But they are struggling with their desire for their lives to be managed differently from the way the monetary aspects are indicating.

They have asked the right questions. Armed with answers to the questions, they talked and thought for several months. In the end, they chose to postpone having children. They have decided to build their two careers, purchase a larger home in anticipation of having a family, and invest their extra income.

For them, the choice was a logical and wise one. They each had come from very fiscally conservative families. They wanted to secure their financial freedom early and then begin a family. At their young ages, they still have time for a family. I concurred with their decision.

Consider the stresses of a couple who decided to have their children early and live on one income.

Some solutions for couples. It is a good idea for couples to address the important issue of money before marriage. Recognizing the significant stumbling block it can become in a relationship, both partners need to write down their individual money goals and frustrations, and then, as a couple, share their individually generated lists, openly discussing each item on both lists. This helps each person become acquainted with the other's financial perceptions.

This exercise will give each person valuable insight into the other's thoughts and attitudes about money. This open exchange is essential before real communication and eventual compromise solutions can emerge. Both partners should understand and agree to whatever financial goals they mutually set. Both partners also should participate in ongoing financial decisions, and both should evaluate and be clear about what material things they want versus what they need.

If children are part of the long-term plan, young childless couples should factor them into their plans. Many couples are completely surprised to learn of the costs associated with having a child. Planning for a child should take into consideration everything from the cost of diapers to the cost of day care, from furniture for the child's room to formula, as well as the eventual funding of a college education. Couples also should discuss who will take primary responsibility for midnight feedings, doctor visits, and transportation to and from day care (if needed).

Additionally, women and men who assume the role of homemaker and not wage earner should make it their ongoing business to understand the family financial situation, keep at least one credit card in their own name, keep their job skills updated, and maintain their own checking account. Marriage is "'til death do us part," and death, unfortunately, does sometimes come to wage earners. When "marriage" and "death" occur in the same breath, the subject of life insurance is usually not far behind.

Insurance

One cost couples face in building a joint life, especially if they are contemplating children in the near future or if one spouse makes significantly more than the other, is that of insurance.

If you have someone who depends on you for income, you need life insurance. This insurance, which would be payable to your beneficiaries on your death, would be an amount available for investment that could produce income for as long as your beneficiaries wish the income to last. You also may want to provide for the mortgage to be paid off and college funds to be established. If you are single and have no one depending on you for income, you probably don't need life insurance. Also, there is no need for insurance on a child's life.

How much life insurance is enough?   Your first step is to decide how much insurance to buy. Unfortunately, there is no absolute magic number. A few years ago the *Wall Street Journal* asked ten financial advisers and agents to make recommendations for a hypothetical 45-year-old man with a wife and two children. The suggestions ranged from $250,000 of coverage to $1.2 million.

Some advise having about ten times your annual salary. Others say four times your salary plus enough for college funding for each child less your pension and investment accounts is enough. Still others use a worksheet similar to the one provided for you in Appendix B. If both you and your spouse work, you will each need to complete a separate worksheet. Refer to Appendix E for definitions of the various types of insurance.

Do you need disability insurance?   Remember, insurance is there for you if the worst case happens. If your house burns or is damaged in a storm, your insurance pays. If your car is in a wreck, your insurance pays. If you die, your insurance pays. But what happens if you get sick or injured and can't work? Who pays your bills so life can go on? That's why disability insurance is important. Many think buying insurance on the wage-earner, that is, disability insurance, is like insuring the goose that lays the golden egg, while all the other insurances except life insure the eggs. Most 20-year-olds will have the opportunity to buy disability insurance through their company.

If your company does not offer it and you are the sole wage earner with children, you may want to consider purchasing disability insurance. If so, refer to Appendix G for a discussion that will help you turn your disability purchase into a wealth-building strategy even if you are not disabled one single day in your life.

Checklist for couples. Partners in a marriage—regardless of age but especially when getting started—must work to preserve the integrity both of their marriage and their individuality. Often, money issues play a big part in this discovery. A simple structure for discussing money might help:

1. Write down your individual money goals and frustrations.
2. Share and discuss your individual lists.
3. Set mutual financial goals.
4. Make a plan in advance for the time when children will be part of your family.
5. Preserve the financial integrity of each partner and make sure each partner is fully informed about all family finances.

Carol and Bert—Trying to Have It All

Carol and Bert, another couple in their 20s, have decided to do it another way. They chose to start their family early. When they came to me, they wanted to get out of debt and were interested in beginning a college fund for their new baby. Bert knew he should be contributing to his company's 401(k).

Life realities. Bert was a young CPA working long hours and earning $55,000 a year. Carol was not working, but she was busy decorating and furnishing their new $160,000 home. It was costing them $47,924 a year to support their cost of living. As you can see from their "before" cost of living schedule and tax plan, they were spending more than they had available to spend. Before coming to see me, this shortfall had already created a credit-card balance of $8,000—and it was growing. Despite this, both wanted Carol to remain an at-home mom.

Their questions.   Bert and Carol were frustrated. They knew they were falling deeper and deeper into the hole, but they didn't know how to get out. They wanted help with the following questions:

- How can we begin living within our means?
- How can we reduce our credit-card debt?
- How much monthly investment would we need to create a fund to allow our son to attend a state college?
- Should we sacrifice to contribute to Bert's 401(k)?

Analysis.   The first step required them to list and categorize every canceled check and every credit-card purchase for the prior year. This first step revealed a $47,924 cost of living. Notice there is no 401(k) contribution, no college fund investment and only token payments on the credit-card balances.

Together we brainstormed changes in their budget to help answer their questions. With these changes, Bert and Carol will be able to do the following:

- **Begin funding at least 4 percent a year ($2,200) into Bert's 401(k).** This 4 percent contribution would allow Bert to benefit from the firm's match on the first 3 percent he contributes. As Bert's income increases, he and Carol are committed to increasing his contribution rate 1 percent a year until they are at the maximum allowed. Bert will be investing his 401(k) into the indexed stock fund option of the plan. He may choose to be a little more aggressive in the future, but since this is a beginning, he will be a bit more conservative.
- **Put aside $150 per month into a mutual fund for college.** To fund $10,000 a year tuition for four years' college at 6 percent-a-year cost increase for the next 17 years, Bert and Carol would need to invest $150 a month at a projected

rate of return of 10 percent per year. We immediately set up a growth and income mutual fund which would draft $150 a month from their checking account for their one-year-old's college fund.

- **Pay $250 a month toward reducing the principal on their credit cards.** Bert and Carol's primary goal was to reduce credit-card debt. They decided they would make a commitment to pay $250 a month toward principal reduction and not use their cards for new purchases until the balances were paid.

Revised spending is the key to success for this plan. They felt they could cut back their spending for food, since Carol planned to start cooking more and the cost of formula would go away since their son could begin eating food prepared by Carol. They would not have to pay for as much child care since Carol had a friend with whom she could trade off caring for each other's children. Baby clothes had been and would continue to be a big part of their clothing budget, but they planned to limit purchases for their own clothing to absolute necessities. Gifts and vacations were entirely discretionary and they thought they could reasonably afford to hold down those expenditures until the credit-card balances were gone. Furthermore, they planned to visit friends and relatives instead of taking expensive vacations. And of course, they would not charge anything more on the cards than they could pay off at the end of the month.

If they could stick to these changes, they would be able to reduce their debt and begin investing for college and retirement.

Their take-home pay did not change	$42,305
Their cost of living did change to	37,324
The difference to allocate	$ 4,981
Education fund	$ 1,800
Credit-card balance reduction	$ 3,000

This plan would permit them to pay off the credit-card balances in about two and one-half years and at that time increase Bert's 401(k) contribution to about 10 percent (depending on what his salary is at that time).

Their long-range goal would be to reach the maximum contribution of 15 percent allowed by his accounting firm as soon as
possible. This plan would require strict discipline and dedication
to the revised spending plan. They were ready to do it. Details
follow.

Bert and Carol's Cost of Living
Gross Earnings $55,000

	Before	After
Cost of Living	$47,924	$37,324
Home*	15,924	15,924
Utilities	3,000	3,000
Food	4,800	2,800
Diapers and formula	3,000	2,000
Child care and baby-sitters	1,500	500
Meals out	4,000	1,500
Clothes	3,000	1,800
Car payment	4,200	4,200
Car insurance and gas	1,200	1,200
Birthday and holiday expenses	2,700	1,800
Life insurance	600	600
Vacations	4,000	2,000
Total	**$47,924**	**$37,324**

*Mortgage, $11,724; taxes, $3,000; insurance, $600; yard, $600

Tax Planning for Bert and Carol

	Before	After
Salary	$55,000	$55,000
401(k)	0	- 2,200
Personal exemptions	−7,950	−7,950
Itemized deductions	−15,350	−15,350
Taxable Income	**$31,700**	**$29,500**
FICA	−4,200	−4,200
Federal tax estimate	−4,822	−4,495
State taxes (6%)	−2,250	−1,800
Total Taxes	**$11,272**	**$10,495**
After-Tax and 401(k) Income to Spend	**$43,728**	**$42,305**

Result. Five years later, this couple has stayed with their plan. Their credit-card debt is gone and they have $14,000 in their son's college fund. Bert has increased the contribution to his 401(k) to 12 percent, and his balance is $38,000. Carol is pregnant and in a local master's degree program. When she has the baby, she plans to suspend her studies for a year. She eventually wants to be a counselor in the school system.

Gail and Mark—To Rent or to Buy

Whether single or married, many 20-year-olds begin to think about buying a house. This question usually raises both financial and emotional issues. How to make the down payment is the foremost financial issue, and it is always frightening to take the plunge on that first home. For Gail and Mark, both elements were present.

Life realities. Gail and Mark come from families of modest income. Mark is a government employee making $25,000 a year and Gail works as an administrative assistant making $30,000 a year at a large corporation. They came to me with the goal of reducing their $3,000 credit-card debt and accumulating a down payment for a house.

Their $3,000 credit-card balance is a remainder from their wedding costs, which they have been whittling down for the two years they've been married. They are diligently paying $250 per month to reduce the debt. They owe $5,000 on Mark's car and $6,000 on Gail's. They have no other debt.

They have $2,000 in a savings account that Mark has zealously squirreled away because he is extremely anxious to buy a home. They are renting a house for $530 a month. Let's look at their situation in terms of whether they should rent or buy, as well as their cost of living.

A review of Gail's and Mark's budget revealed their monthly living expenses to be about $3,000 against their monthly take-home pay of about $3,100. They are living within their means.

Gail's and Mark's Cost of Living
Gross Earnings, $55,000

	Renting	Buying
Cost of Living	$36,920	$38,100
Apartment/home	8,100	11,640*
Utilities	1,800	2,400
Food and meals out	6,000	6,000
Church	1,200	1,200
Credit cards	3,000	3,000
Savings	2,400	0
Clothes	1,800	1,800
Personal necessities	960	960
Car payments	6,960	6,960
Car insurance and gas	1,200	1,200
Birthday and holiday gifts	1,800	1,800
Life insurance	500	500
Vacations	1,200	1,200
Total	**$36,920**	**$38,660**

*Mortgage, $9,840; taxes, $1,200; insurance, $360; yard, $240

Tax Planning for Gail and Mark

	Renting	Buying
Salary (Gail)	$30,000	$30,000
Salary (Mark)	25,000	25,000
401(k)s	(5,500)	(5,500)
Personal exemptions	(5,300)	(5,300)
Deductions	(6,300)	(17,700)
Taxable Income	**$37,900**	**$26,500**
FICA	$4,200	4,200
Federal taxes	$5,730	$4,020
State taxes (6%)	$2,292	$1,600
Total Taxes	**$12,222**	**$9,820**
After-Tax and 401(k) Income		
to Spend	**$37,270**	**$39,672**

Gail's and Mark's Net Worth Statement

Assets

Savings	$ 2,000	
401(k) (Gail)	10,000	
401(k) (Mark)	8,800	
Invested Assets		**$20,800**
Car (Gail)	8,500	
Car (Mark)	7,000	
Personal property	25,000	
Use Assets		**$40,500**
Total Assets		**$61,300**

Liabilities

Credit cards	$ 3,000	
Car (Gail)	5,500	
Car (Mark)	4,000	
Total Liabilities		**$12,500**
Net Worth		**$48,800**

Analysis. Gail and Mark want to buy a house in the $125,000 range. They think they will need a 10 percent down payment. So far, they have only saved $2,000. But both have been contributing to their 401(k)s for four years.

Gail and Mark need to find the $12,500 for a down payment and have an additional $3,000 to $4,000 available for closing costs. They hope to negotiate to get the seller to pay the closing costs. They plan to use a friend's truck and move themselves for minimal cost.

$125,000	Home cost
−12,500	Down payment
$112,500	mortgage at 8% for 30 years

Monthly Costs:

$820/month	payments
100/month	estimated taxes
30/month	estimated insurance
$950/Month	**Estimated Total**

If they can find the down payment, Gail and Mark will save $2,400 in taxes with the purchase of their home, thus making their real monthly house payment $750 instead of $950. They currently are paying $675 monthly rent. From a cash-flow standpoint, they can afford the house they want.

What are their alternatives for securing the down payment?

- **Borrow from their 401(k) plans.** Both of their 401(k) plans allow them to borrow up to 60 percent of the balance and repay over five years at 12 percent interest. If they borrow the down payment from their tax-deferred plans, their monthly payment will be $220/month. A review of their cost of living after buying shows they can afford $100 a month. For the other $120 a month, they could reduce their contributions to their 401(k)s until they get at least a 2 percent pay raise. When they get their pay raises, they can continue the 10 percent contribution they now make and also repay the 401(k) loan.
- **Seek more income.** Mark can work overtime and earn up to $6,000 each year. They could both seek higher-paying jobs. This option will require them to wait about two years, we estimate, before they will have the money saved for the down payment.
- **Seek help from relatives.** Neither Gail nor Mark wanted to ask their relatives for help. Frankly, they thought no one had the money to help if they wanted to.
- **Save money each month.** Their final option was to save each month from their already tight budget to accumulate the down payment. Since they need about $10,000 more for the down payment, it would take them three years if they invest $250 a month in the stock market at 10 percent per year to accumulate the money they need. If they choose to go this route, they should select a conservative no-load mutual fund. Any time you invest in the stock market, however, you run the risk of your money being lower than you invested if you are unable to leave it invested for a "normal market cycle" of four to seven years. If you need

to fund your objective in less than three years
the money in the stock market: put it in the ba

RULE OF THUMB

If you need your money within three years, don't invest in the stock market.

Result.   Mark applied for another job in the government and got it within three months. His pay increased $5,000 per year. Gail applied for and got a new job with a $3,000 per year pay raise.

Mark discussed his and Gail's desire for a home with his mother who had no way to help them. But when Mark's Aunt Bea heard the story, she offered the $10,000 to Mark that she had earmarked for him in her will. Aunt Bea has no children, so her nieces and nephews are her beneficiaries.

While you can read the account of Mark and Gail in a matter of minutes, this couple agonized over how to own their home for over a year. They wanted to own a home more than anything else. But they jealously guarded their savings in their 401(k)s as well. They wanted to be settled in a home before they even thought about having children.

This couple was truly emotionally committed to owning a home. They were willing to make whatever monetary sacrifices were necessary to make their dreams come true.

This is an example of how emotional commitment can dictate finances in a very positive way.

How Much House Can You Afford?

Here are the rules of thumb most lenders follow:

- Mortgage payments, property tax, and insurance should not exceed 28 percent of your pretax income.
- Payments on all debt including the mortgage, car payments, credit-card payments and any other debt should not total more than 36 percent of your pretax income.

- Suggested expense levels for housing for various income levels are as follows:

Under $50,000	30% of take-home
$50,000–150,000	25% of take-home
Over $150,000	20% of take-home

- Individual circumstances vary and are taken into consideration.

WEALTHBUILDING STRATEGIES FOR THE 20S

These Are Habit-Forming Years

- **Set realistic goals and stick to them.** Set your financial goals and don't let your emotions pull you off course.
- **Choose your friends and companions carefully.** Make sure the ones you choose support your thinking about your financial goals. If others want to ruin their lives, let them; just don't let them ruin yours.
- **Don't spend on too many frills too soon.** These are the years to sacrifice; you have plenty of time to accumulate things.
- **Don't carry credit-card balances.**
- **Accumulate two and a half to three months' cost of living as an emergency cash reserve and leave it in the money market fund or bank savings.** Use that account only if you lose your job, become disabled or need to make major repairs to your house or car. Then rebuild the account.
- **Start investing at least 4 percent of your gross pay.**
- **Invest for growth—at least 80 percent of your invested assets.** Invest the balance for growth and income.
- **Invest regularly and systematically.**
- **Seek higher rates of return and be tolerant of fluctuations.**
- **Know where your money is going.** It is in knowledge that you gain feedback that your plan is working.

The 20-year-old reading this book is probably already on the road to financial success. With good financial habits in place this early in life, most of life's other decisions will become easier.

CHAPTER 4

THE 30S: THE NESTING DECADE

The decade of the 30s brings fresh psychological,
relational, work, and financial challenges.

★ MAJOR FINANCIAL TASK

Facing the Absolute Nature of Money

The decade of the 30s brings fresh psychological, relational, work, and financial challenges into our lives. During this ten-year time span, most of us begin to understand some age-old principles we may have heard all our lives, such as:

"Money doesn't grow on trees."

"You can't have it all."

"This isn't a bottomless pit of money!"

In other words, we come face to face with reality. We begin to realize the finite character of money and we begin to learn that work isn't all fun and games. We have to do things at home and at the workplace that may not be fun. But nevertheless, they have to be done—and we have to do them!

In my CPA's break room, a sign posted over the kitchen sink reads: "Your mother doesn't work here—so clean up after yourself!" Apparently my CPA has encountered some employees who thought their only job at the office was to crunch numbers and turn out tax returns. Part of the responsibilities of maintaining a comfortable and functioning office environment includes the routine cleaning of the kitchen. I never took a college class that specifically told me to clean up after myself, did you? But this is an example of a lesson of life that, if not learned in our 20s, certainly begins to manifest itself in our 30s.

In every area of our lives, personal grooming, home and office routine responsibilities, and managing our money on a day-to-day basis, reality hits us in the face during our 30s. This is especially true for managing investments to lead to retirement. If not, you may face the consequences of retiring with inadequate resources—financial and otherwise. For it is during these years that we practice money and relationship habits that form the basis for a successful future.

LIFE-STAGE RETIREMENT PLANNER FOR THE 30s

Thirty-year-olds of today very likely won't be comfortable in retirement if they don't make retirement planning a priority now. So, while it will be difficult to find the money for it, you should make retirement planning a must. The easiest way, of course, is to have your company take it out of your paycheck first and place your money into a tax-deferred plan. We know these years require heavy cash drains as you buy a larger house, furnish it, buy a larger car, pay for your children's everyday expenses, and begin investing for their college funds. It is for these reasons that we suggest you contribute 10 percent of your income to retirement accounts, not the 12 percent to 15 percent you will want to contribute in future years.

As with the 20-year-olds, you will want to maximize the growth you can get in your account and not worry about volatility. Your time horizon will be to retire at age 65; thus your money will have 25 to 35 years to grow.

Invest according to this formula:

100 – Your age = Percentage of invested assets for growth
in mutual funds with a small amount in
real estate

Your age = Percentage of your invested assets in
growth and income mutual funds

Split your mutual fund investments equally between domestic and global mutual funds.

If you can tolerate great risk in your investments, you could move to 100 percent growth.

Mutual Fund Investments for the 30s

Objective:	Maximize Growth
Time Horizon:	25 to 35 Years
Risk:	Highly Volatile
Investment Vehicle:	Mutual Funds

Investment Type	% Invested
Growth	70% to 100%
U.S. stocks	50%
Global stocks	50%
Growth and Income	30% to 0%
U.S. stocks	15%
Global stocks	15%

When using the diagrams in Figure 4.1 for your own situation, keep in mind your own risk tolerance (the more growth you have the greater risk you will be taking), for all of your invested assets, and your income. Do not include your "use assets" such as your emergency cash, home, car, furniture, boat, or anything else you own that you will not sell to create retirement capital.

FIGURE 4.1   Asset Allocation for the 30s

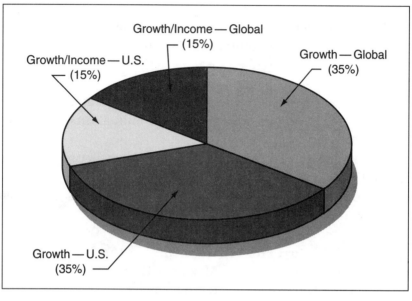

Growth/Income — Global (15%)

Growth/Income — U.S. (15%)

Growth — Global (35%)

Growth — U.S. (35%)

Growth–U.S. = Small and medium-sized companies; REITs; expect fluctuation; minimum holding period: four years.

Growth/Income–U.S. = Fortune 500 companies; dividend-paying stocks and bonds; expect modest fluctuation; minimum holding period: three years.

Growth–Global = U.S. and non-U.S. small and medium-sized companies; best positioned through mutual funds; expect modest fluctuation; minimum holding period: five years.

Growth/Income–Global = U.S. and non-U.S. Fortune 500–sized companies; dividend-paying stocks and bonds; best positioned through mutual funds; expect modest fluctuation; minimum holding period: four years.

The Model Investor Continues in the 30s

The model 30-year-old investor began investing at age 22 when he or she first got a job. As a reminder, the investor earned $1,000 for every year of age and invested 4 percent into retirement accounts from age 22 through age 29. By the end of the 29th year, the investor has accumulated $12,582, and it is invested earning 10 percent per year.

At 30, our model investor is earning $30,000 and will continue to earn $1,000 for every year of age through the 30s. The investor will, however, contribute 10 percent of earnings per year into retirement investment accounts. By the end of the 39th year, the investor will have $91,758 invested for retirement.

So from the beginning of the investor's 30th year to the end of the 39th year, his or her retirement nest egg will look like this:

29th Year	39th Year
$12,582	$91,758

Putting into Place a Lifestyle to Last Many Years

To find the money you will need to properly fund your retirement, you will want to carefully watch every dollar you make to be sure it is allocated in the very best way.

Whether married or single, it is during the 30s that we most often begin to think of "moving up." Our tastes in furniture seem to have crystallized. We begin buying furniture and accessories we plan to keep for a lifetime.

We may move from the small house or condominium we bought in our 20s to a larger one or, if we are married, to one that will accommodate the needs of a child or two. Perhaps this entails a move to the suburbs if we are living in the city. We are, in short, beginning to put into place the lifestyle we will have for a long time.

While in the 20s we were just glad to have a job, in the 30s, we begin to think about moving up the ladder at work. In our 20s, most of us believe we will be successful in our occupations, maybe even world-class successful. In our 30s we begin to see that we must put forth extra effort to make that success possible.

The desire for success in our work is driven not only by ambition, but also by our wish to buy better things. If we have married and children are in the picture, we are keenly aware of the growing amount of money needed to support those family goals. Gradually, in our 30s, our stress levels rise due to the normal maturation process.

Stepping Up to a More Expensive Car

A larger, usually more expensive car is often required for growing families or to meet young career desires. Many times bonuses or an inheritance may have created a small windfall. It is et that money slip through your fingers to become a later

A man in his 50s told me of a time in his life years before, when his wife and daughter had talked him into selling some stock worth about $20,000 to buy a new car. Five years later, his car was worthless and needed to be replaced. The stock would have been worth $50,000 at that time. He carried a grudge for all those years, saying "That was the most expensive car I'll ever buy—and I'll never let that happen again."

The wise 30-year-old will learn from that man's losing experience and adopt our strategy for much shrewder car buying.

Shrewder car buying. Recently Joe, a 30-year-old man, came in to discuss what to do with a $10,000 inheritance he had just received from his grandmother. He, of course, wanted to buy a new car. He wanted to trade in his existing vehicle, add the $10,000 and pay cash for it.

The alternative he was considering was to trade in his existing car, invest the $10,000, and force himself to make payments. "Which would be the smarter move?" he asked.

Let's consider two alternative scenarios to answer his question:

1. $10,000 to buy the new car, and five to seven years from now the new car will be old and will need to be replaced, and the $10,000 will be gone. Joe will have a car payment for the replacement vehicle and the $10,000 investment in the old car will have gotten him nowhere except to have avoided a car payment for the past few years.
2. $10,000 invested at an assumed 10 percent per year annual rate of return (reflecting the unmanaged performance of the S&P 500 since 1926) over 30 years until his age 60 grows to almost $300,000.

Choosing alternative number one means Joe bought a very expensive car. Alternative number two is a better choice. The discipline of making payments won't hurt any 30-year-old. At age 60, those selecting this alternative will be very happy they did!

But what about the old adage of always paying cash for depreciating assets? This makes sense, but only for the wealthy who can afford the luxury of missing the potential return on a healthy pot of money that will be difficult for today's 30-year-olds to replace in 30 years.

In his book, *The Great Boom Ahead,* Harry Dent predicts that the stock markets will be offering returns over the next ten years that only a fool would want to miss. For more information on his predictions, see Chapter 2 of his book, under the section titled, "Projecting the Spending Wave into the Future."

Emotions and Finances

As with every age group, decisions about money are driven by our emotional and family concerns. So once again we face the interlink between financial and emotional concerns.

Pat Malone, M.D., co-author with his father, Tom Malone, M.D., of *The Art of Intimacy,* talks about a central dilemma people in their 30s face in the 1990s. They see costs rising, he says, and incomes not keeping pace. They want to have many of the nicer things they had growing up in their parents' homes. They also want to provide the kind of family life for their children that they had growing up. For many, this means one in which moms did not work outside the home. If moms did work outside the home, their income bought many extras.

In the mid to late 1990s, the two goals seem mutually exclusive. Couples cannot find the money necessary to buy the material things they want unless both work.

"They do not want to be co-opted by the system, but they don't know what else to do," Dr. Malone says. "The question becomes: Do we play the game or sit out?"

Dr. Malone observes three responses by 30-year-olds. They either

1. opt for the larger income and both work,
2. become frequent job-changers in hopes of finding a greener pasture, or
3. decide (in some cases) that money is not the answer and adjust their lifestyle to fit a lower income.

Perhaps it is fair to say that life today is too complex for either spouse to have to shoulder financial or emotional responsibilities alone. If both partners in a marriage work, they certainly are part of the vast majority.

Perhaps, on the other hand, couples who choose to live more modestly can remind themselves that even the lesser amount of goodies they can afford (on one income) represents much more than many of the rest of the world's people enjoy with both spouses working. This financial and emotional decision must rest with the individual couple. In the sections that follow we will look at a single professional woman, a couple who chose downsizing their lifestyle, and a couple where both work.

Last Will and Testament

Everyone should have a will. Your will appoints someone to handle your affairs after you are gone, and in your will, you can make arrangements for your beneficiaries to receive certain assets free and clear immediately or over time. Spreading the transfer over time is especially appropriate for underage children or those you feel are not able to manage the assets themselves.

In structuring the will, be aware that the document itself will be filed with the state as a requirement of a process known as "probate." In writing the will, you should use general language to describe how your assets will be divided and transferred. It is best not to list specific assets in the body of the will. Probated wills become public knowledge and leave beneficiaries prey to many brokers and insurance agents who may be searching the court records for potential clients. Many people who have significant assets like to know that after their death, their financial information will not be available for scrutiny by anyone who is nosy—for whatever reason.

Three functions must be provided for in a will: executor, trustee, and guardian. Those functions are as follows:

Fiduciary functions

Executor

- Offers the will for probate
- Gathers and organizes the assets of the estate
- Pays the valid debts of the decedent

- Pays administration expenses of the estate
- Carries on or liquidates any investments in bus owned by the decedent
- Pays income and estate taxes
- In connection with taxes, makes elections available under the Internal Revenue Code
- Enforces claims on behalf of the decedent or the estate
- Accounts to the beneficiaries
- Distributes the remaining assets according to the terms of the will

Trustee

- Assumes possession of the trust assets
- Pays expenses of the trust
- Invests the trust assets
- Files tax returns and pays taxes of the trust
- Pays income (and if the instrument so provides, the principal) to the beneficiaries on a periodic payment schedule
- Exercises discretion with respect to invading principal or accumulating income, as provided in the trust document
- Distributes the principal at the termination of the trust in accordance with the directions of the settler
- Exercises all other powers and carries out all other duties contained in the trust instrument
- Accounts to the trust beneficiaries

Guardian

Guardian of the person:

- Cares for and takes custody of the minor

Guardian of the property:

- Assumes possession of the minor's property
- Pays expenses of the guardianship
- Invests the minor's funds prudently
- Applies funds of the minor for his maintenance and support under supervision of the court
- Accounts to the court from time to time

- Files tax returns and pays taxes on behalf of the minor
- Distributes the principal and accumulated income of the guardianship to the minor when he or she reaches the age stipulated in the trust document

Establishing a will involves the designation of an executor and a trustee. In addition, a guardian must be named for minor children in case the parents die before the children reach age 18. Also important is the appointment of a guardian if you have handicapped children, regardless of their ages. You will also want to name a trustee to manage the assets your children will inherit and the assets you intend to leave anyone else you think will be unable to properly manage the assets themselves.

Who should you name as executor, trustee, and guardian?

1. **Name as executor** a capable person living in your state of residence who has the time and ability to handle the red tape required in transferring the title of assets as you have outlined in your will. If you name a professional instead of a relative, expect a fee ranging from 1 to 3 percent of the assets they are managing to be charged.
2. **Name as trustee** someone who has sound administrative skills, good investment judgment, and willingness to be responsive to the beneficiaries. Again, a professional or an institution will charge a fee.
3. **Name as guardian** someone who will make a home for your children, love them, and guide them in the way you feel will be most like the way you would if you were alive. You may need to provide some money in your will for them to remodel their home to accommodate your children.

Single and 30

Even if you are single, you need a will. This is especially true if you want to leave your assets to nieces and nephews or other children who are under an age that would make them responsible money managers. After establishing a will, you may want to consider buying a house.

Alice is an attractive lawyer who is in her 30s and single, having recently ended a four-year relationship because it didn't seem to be going anywhere. Alice's mother had once told her, "If you're not married at 35, start thinking about buying a house on your own." She is also buying into a successful law firm after practicing there for eight years. Her goals in coming to see me were to:

- Determine how much house to buy.
- Decide where to place her profit-sharing plan contributions.
- Find out what to do if she wants to retire at 60.

Alice's Net Worth Statement

	Renting	Buying
Assets		
Checking	$ 5,000	$ 5,000
Savings	20,000	6,000
Profit-sharing plan	40,000	40,000
Mutual funds	5,000	5,000
Total Invested Assets	**$70,000**	**$ 56,000**
Home	$ 0	$140,000
Personal property	50,000	50,000
Car	20,000	20,000
Total Use Assets	**$70,000**	**$210,000**
Total Assets	**$140,000**	**$266,000**
Liabilities		
Mortgage	$ 0	$126,000
Credit cards	3,000	3,000
Car loan	10,000	10,000
Total Liabilities	**$ 13,000**	**$139,000**
Net Worth	**$127,000**	**$127,000**

Alice's Cost of Living

	Renting	Buying
Apartment/home	$ 9,600	$ 17,128*
Utilities	2,200	2,400

Alice's Cost of Living (Continued)

	Renting	Buying
Food		
Recreation and entertainment	$ 4,200	
Automobile	2,000	
Medical	6,900	The
Personal necessities	1,500	same
Clothing	800	
Donations/gifts	$ 2,500	
Savings and investments	3,000	
Pet/misc. expenses	15,000	
Total	**$ 48,200**	**$ 55,928**

*Mortgage payments, $12,828; taxes, $2,500; insurance, $600; yard: $200

Tax Planning for Alice

	Renting	Buying
Income	$100,000	$100,000
Interest/dividends	1,500	1,500
Profit sharing	(15,000)	(15,000)
Personal exemption	(2,650)	(2,650)
Itemized deductions	(6,000)	(17,000)
Taxable Income	**$ 77,850**	**$ 66,850**
FICA	$ 5,500	$ 5,500
Federal taxes	19,100	15,700
State taxes	4,300	3,700
Total Taxes	**$ 28,900**	**$ 24,900**
Total income	$100,000	$100,000
Profit-sharing plan	(15,000)	(15,000)
Total taxes	(28,900)	(24,900)
Income to Spend after Taxes and Profit-Sharing Plan	**$ 56,100**	**$ 60,100**
Cost of Living	(48,200)	55,928
Excess	**$ 7,900**	**$ 4,172**

Analysis and result. Alice decided it was important for her to own a town home. She found one for $140,000 and put $14,000 down. Her monthly payments were affordable and gave her a tax deduction for the interest on the mortgage. Buying the town home saved her about $4,000 in taxes. She is now building equity in her own home.

In addition, she wants to continue funding her $15,000 a year into the firm's profit-sharing plan and invest her excess after-tax dollars as well. She wants to retire at 60. Alice is conservative and doesn't like wild volatility. An indexed mutual fund that will mirror the S&P 500 is a good option for her. Performance of such funds since 1926, according to Ibbottson Associates, has been 10 percent a year. If that performance holds for the future, here's how her retirement projections would look:

Alice's Retirement Projections

Profit sharing	$40,000/yr × 10%/yr × 25 yrs =	$433,000
Contributions to profit sharing	$15,000/yr × 10%/yr × 25 yrs =	$1,623,000
Excess to invest	$4,000/yr × 10%/yr × 25 yrs =	$432,000
Mutual fund	$3,000 × 10%/yr × 25 yrs =	$33,000
Total		**$2,521,000**
	Income withdrawal percentage	× 7%
Potential investment income available to spend		$ 176,470

By withdrawing only 7 percent per year to spend, the balance of the return will remain in the account for growth.

If Alice retires early in 25 years, she will want to spend the same amount she is spending now—in inflated dollars. She currently spends $85,000 before taxes. Inflating her current before-tax income (excluding the profit-sharing contribution) by 3 percent a year, she will need $177,000 per year to maintain her same standard of living. According to our projections, she will have about $176,400. Her plan of investing will work according to her time requirements.

Alice won't be waiting around for a "white knight"! She will be financially independent on her own.

Married and Thirtysomething

When Sybil, 35, and Scott, 37, came to see me, they lived in Atlanta with their children, George, 5, and Heather, 2; the family dog, Kramer; and Lily the cat. Their goals, they said, were to be good parents and to be financially independent by the time they were 55.

Sybil, a homemaker, and Scott, a self-employed marketing consultant with prestigious accounts, are from moderately high-income families. They were attempting to maintain an expensive lifestyle reminiscent of their own childhoods. In fact, Sybil and Scott were living above their means, playing the credit-card float with $23,000 total balances.

Sybil and Scott had bought a $400,000 house in a fashionable country-club community where taxes were very high. Monthly payments on the $267,000 mortgage were $2,710, including taxes. They owned two cars valued at $30,000 on which they made monthly payments of $950. (The loans against the cars were $25,000.) They were paying $1,200 a month to send their children to a private school. They paid $600 a month for membership in the country club.

When Sybil and Scott took on those bills, Scott's expectations for his income (based on a future that looked unlimited) were high. But in the early 1990s, he saw many of his accounts cut their budgets or drag their feet on decisions to begin projects he had counted on. Accordingly, the increased income he had planned for had not materialized.

On the plus side, Scott had managed to set aside $77,000 in individual retirement account (IRA)–type investments and $50,000 in non-IRA-type plans. They had a fantastic start. Nevertheless, they were worried.

Scott's stress level was high. Contrary to his usual easygoing manner, a manner necessary to maintaining his creativity, he found himself snapping at Sybil and the children. This was easy to do, since his office was in the basement of their home. But, he rationalized, his office location kept his business expenses low.

Even though they had agreed years before that Sybil would be an at-home mom, the stress drove him to begin pressuring Sybil to find a good-paying job.

One day, Sybil and Scott, at wit's end, began to ask the questions that had loomed in their minds for some time: "Is all this stress worth it?" They were losing their joy of life—their contentment with their marriage. How, they wondered, could they regain their happiness and peace of mind? They also asked each other, "What is the real cause of the stress?" and they came up with an answer: money.

Drastic action would be needed. Long before their peers began downsizing in their 40s or 50s, Sybil and Scott faced their reality. They concluded their only solution was to move to a place where their cost of living would be lower. They chose to move to a small town in north Georgia where their children could still attend a more reasonably priced private school, Scott could rent a small office outside the home and they could afford a very nice house for less money. They made some big changes.

A comparison of the cost of living in north Georgia with the one in Atlanta shows the following:

Sybil's and Scott's Cost of Living

	Atlanta	N. Georgia
Cost of Living	$ 98,376	$ 57,444
Home	$ 32,976*	$ 13,644[†]
Utilities	3,600	2,400
Food and meals out	7,400	6,000
Church	6,000	6,000
Credit cards	3,000	0
Savings	0	3,600
Clothes	3,600	3,600
Personal necessities	800	800
Car payments	11,400	6,600[‡]
Car insurance and gas	1,800	1,200
Private school	13,400	3,800
Country club	6,000	2,400
Birthdays and holiday gifts	3,000	2,000

Sybil's and Scott's Cost of Living (Continued)

	Atlanta	N. Georgia
Life insurance	1,200	1,200
Medical	2,400	2,400
Vacations	1,800	1,800
Total	**$ 98,376**	**$ 57,444**

*Mortgage payments, $24,480; taxes, $6,596; insurance, $700; yard, $1,200
†Mortgage payments, $11,364; taxes, $1,440; insurance, $360; yard, $480
‡Sold the sports car, saved payment of $400

Tax Planning for Sybil and Scott

	Atlanta	N. Georgia
Income	$125,000	$125,000
Business expenses	(5,000)	(15,000)
IRA–SEP	(15,000)	(14,000)
Half self-employment taxes	(2,730)	(2,658)
Personal exemptions	(10,600)	(10,600)
Deductions	(37,600)	(21,260)
Taxable Income	**$ 54,070**	**$ 61,482**
Self-employment taxes	$ 5,460	$ 5,316
Federal taxes	10,070	12,145
State taxes (6%)	3,200	3,700
Total Taxes	**$ 18,730**	**$ 21,161**
Total Income	$125,000	$125,000
IRA–SEP	(15,000)	(14,000)
Taxes	(18,730)	(21,161)
Business Expenses	(5,000)	(15,000)
After-Tax and IRA-SEP		
Income to Spend	**$ 86,270**	**$ 74,839**
Cost of living needed	(98,376)	(57,444)
Excess (Shortfall)	**($ 12,106)**	**$ 17,395**

From a cash-flow perspective, it is easy to see that Sybil and Scott are better off in north Georgia. Let's look at how the changes they made affected their net worth.

Sybil's and Scott's
Net Worth Statement

	Atlanta	N. Georgia
Assets		
Savings	$ 2,000	$ 2,000
IRA-SEP	77,000	77,000
Mutual funds	50,000	50,000
Total Invested Assets	**$129,000**	**$129,000**
Home	$400,000	$200,000
Car (Sybil)	22,000	22,000
Car (Scott)	18,000	8,000
Personal property	125,000	125,000
Total Use Assets	**$565,000**	**$355,000**
Total Assets	**$694,000**	**$484,000**
Liabilities		
Home mortgage	$267,000	$124,000
Credit cards	23,000	0
Car (Sybil)	15,000	15,000
Car (Scott)	10,000	0
Total Liabilities	**$315,000**	**$139,000**
Net Worth	**$379,000**	**$345,000**

Their net worth decreased by only $34,000. They reasoned it was a small loss to suffer in order to gain the peace of mind that a more relaxed lifestyle and less stressful cash flow afforded.

Analysis and result. This couple made an emotion-driven decision and their money pressures dissolved. In Atlanta, they needed $98,376 after tax to support their lifestyle and they had $86,270. In the less expensive north Georgia community they needed about $57,500 after taxes to support the same quality of life. In north Georgia, they had $74,839 available to spend. This decision involved a big risk. At the time of the decision, they weren't sure how it would work out. They thought the money aspects would work out but they weren't sure they would be happy in the smaller community.

Three years later, money pressures relieved, Scott, Sybil, George, Heather, Kramer, and Lily are all settled and involved in their new community. They are involved in church and Sybil works part-time at the children's school. There are no credit-card balances and both of their cars are now paid in full. Scott's income has actually increased. He is investing toward his goal of early retirement at 55. Best of all, Scott has recaptured his old, happy, easygoing self.

The 30s Require Money Everywhere!

By the mid-30s, life usually begins to stabilize. The home is usually furnished, there is no more than one car payment, and credit-card debt is gone. But as 30-year-olds look to the future, if they are married with children, they want to set up college as well as retirement funds. If the wife is going to stay home with children, it is usually during this decade. While the majority of 30-year-olds manage a dual-income household, more and more couples are attempting to live on a single income. So the dilemma centers on how to provide for the increasing needs for money while at the same time giving up some income. This is a problem especially if the couple doesn't want to move to a less expensive community.

Jill's and Elliott's situation provides some insight.

Jill and Elliott

Elliott, 31, has a two-year-old daughter, Brandy. His wife had recently died from breast cancer. Elliott and Brandy inherited a total of $100,000 from Brandy's mother. Elliott paid off his debts of $30,000, set up a $10,000 emergency fund, and invested the remaining $60,000; $15,000 was placed into a mutual fund with Elliott as custodian for Brandy under the Uniform Gift to Minors Act (UGMA), earmarked for Brandy's college funding. The remaining $45,000 had been in a 401(k) and was rolled into an IRA with no tax consequences for Elliott.

During the next three years, Elliott met Jill and they married. One year later they had another little girl, whom they named

Hannah. They came to see me to make sure Brandy's college fund would be adequate and to set up a new account for Hannah.

Elliott was earning $70,000 a year as an industrial engineer, and Jill was earning $40,000 as a graphic designer. They owned a $160,000 home with a $118,000 mortgage, for which they paid $922 a month. They had no other debt and were living within their means.

When Jill and Elliott came to see me, Brandy's college fund had grown to $24,000 and Elliott's IRA rollover account contained $71,000. They had these goals:

- To fully fund college for both girls
- To fully fund a retirement nest egg targeting age 55 for retirement with Jill working only part-time

First, college funding.   Brandy was six at that time, so there were twelve years left for her college fund to build. There were eighteen years during which Hannah's college fund could grow.

Jill and Elliott agreed that both girls would probably go to state college at which tuition, books, and room and board is about $10,000 per year in today's dollars. According to the American College Board, costs at state colleges are inflating yearly at 6 percent.

Assuming Brandy's account grows at 10 percent a year for the next 12 years and college costs inflate at 6 percent a year, there is no need for additional monthly contributions to meet the need for Brandy. However, since there is no balance with which to begin Hannah's account, the monthly amount needed is about $165. On Jill's and Elliott's incomes, they can afford the $165 a month.

Can Jill cut back to part-time and still retire at age 55? Jill and Elliott both have 401(k) plans at their offices. Jill has $25,000 in her plan and Elliott has $75,000. They are both contributing 15 percent before taxes yearly. Elliott is at the maximum allowed of $9,500. They also have $20,000 saved in mutual funds currently growing at 12 percent a year.

Having resolved the college funding issue, Jill and Elliott wondered if it made financial sense for Jill to work part-time, giving her more time in the afternoons with the girls. They think their basic cost of living can be supported by just Elliott's income. They will need Jill's part-time income to pay for diapers, formula, the education fund for Hannah, and the extras of life.

Jill thinks she can earn $20,000 part-time and work out of her home. Both Jill's and Elliott's parents are agreeable to helping with Hannah, thus cutting the cost of child care. Their hope is that Elliott's income will continue to increase.

But if our financial projections show they cannot retire at 55, Jill wants to continue working full time. They are both 35 now. Let's take a look: Jill's 401(k) contains $25,000. If she leaves her full-time job to start a business at home, she can roll over her 401(k) and still contribute 15 percent to an IRA-SEP for her self-employment income. Elliott's retirement fund contains $75,000, so they have a total of $100,000 in tax-deferred plans.

Jill's and Elliott's
Retirement Projections at Age 55

Asset	Amount	10%/Yr	12%/Yr
Tax-Deferred Plans	$100,000	$ 672,750	$ 965,000
IRA Rollover	71,000	477,652	684,900
Mutual Funds	20,000	135,000	193,000
401(k) Contribution	12,500/yr	787,500	1,009,000
Totals		**$2,072,900**	**$2,852,000**
Recommended income withdrawal percentage		× 7%	× 7%
Income estimates		$ 145,000	$ 199,600

Jill's and Elliott's cost of living (shown later) at retirement, inflated by 3 percent a year for 20 years, will be about $74,000. This assumes their spending will remain the same. In 20 years, the children's expenses will go away but Jill and Elliott hope to travel more and health insurance costs probably will be higher when they retire. Therefore, we do not discount any other expenses.

$74,000 × 3% per year for inflation = $133,600

If they stay on their investing plan outlined above, if the investments earn at least 10 percent a year, and their cost of living inflates only 3 percent a year, they will meet their goals and Jill will not have to work full-time.

Let's take a look at their net worth statement, cost of living, and tax plan.

Jill's and Elliott's
Net Worth Statement

Assets

Checking	$ 1,000	
Savings	5,000	
IRA rollover (Elliott)	71,000	
Mutual funds	20,000	
401(k) (Elliott)	75,000	
401(k) (Jill)	25,000	
Total Invested Assets		**$197,000**
Residence	$140,000	
Personal property	70,000	
Car (Elliott)	20,000	
Car (Jill)	15,000	
Total Use Assets		**$245,000**
Total Assets		**$442,000**

Liabilities

Mortgage	$118,000	
Credit cards	1,000	
Car loan (Jill)	10,000	
Total Liabilities		**$129,000**
Net Worth		**$313,000**

Jill's and Elliott's
Cost of Living

Home	$ 15,200*
Utilities	2,500
Food	5,000
Recreation and entertainment	3,000
Car payment	3,880
Gas and insurance	2,000
Medical	2,500
Personal necessities	2,000

Jill's and Elliott's
Cost of Living (Continued)

Clothing	$ 3,600
Donations	4,000
Gifts	3,600
Savings and investments	2,000†
Life insurance	500
Diapers, formula, pet supplies	4,000
"Off the wall"	1,000
Child care	1,000
Total	**$ 55,780**

*Mortgage payments, $10,800; taxes, $2,000; insurance, $600; yard, $600; maid, $1,200
†Education funding: $166/month for Hannah

Tax Plan for Elliott and Jill

	Jill Full-Time	Jill Part-Time
Salary (Elliott)	$ 70,000	$70,000
Salary (Jill)	40,000	20,000
Interest/dividends	1,500	1,500
401(k) (Elliott)	(9,500)	(9,500)
401(k) (Jill)	(6,000)	(3,000)
Personal exemption	(10,600)	(10,600)
Itemized deductions	(20,000)	(19,000)
Taxable Income	**$ 65,400**	**$49,400**
FICA	$ 7,795	6,500
Federal taxes	12,956	8,476
State taxes	3,554	2,594
Total Taxes	**$ 24,305**	**$17,570**
Total Income	$110,000	$90,000
401(k)s	(15,500)	(12,500)
Total taxes	(24,305)	(17,570)
Income to Spend	**$ 70,195**	**$59,930**
Cost of Living	(55,780)	(55,780)
Excess to Invest	**$ 14,415**	**$ 4,150**

FINANCING COLLEGE EDUCATIONS

One of the major concerns for many in their 30s is finding a way to finance their children's college educations. This financial objective sometimes gets moved to the 40s, since many couples are having children in their late 30s. Of course, the later you start building an education fund, the more will be required. The monthly amounts you will need to invest are provided in the following chart. Whether starting a family in your 20s, 30s, or 40s, costs are calculated based on the child's age at which you start your education fund.

We are assuming a state university at $10,000 a year, four-year education, and you will pay for 100 percent of the costs. We also assume the cost of education will increase 6 percent a year from now until your child completes his or her degree.

	College Funding	
Child's Age	Costs for Four Years	Monthly Amount Needed (*Assumes 10% Rate of Return*)
1	$117,798	$ 162
2	111,131	171
3	104,840	181
4	98,906	192
5	93,307	204
6	88,026	218
7	83,043	233
8	78,343	250
9	73,908	269
10	69,725	291
11	65,778	317
12	62,055	348
13	58,542	386
14	55,229	433
15	52,102	492
16	49,153	571
17	46,371	682
18	43,746	1,054

If you plan to send your child to a school where the cost is higher than $10,000 in today's dollars, simply multiply the monthly amount needed by the percentage of increase the higher college cost represents. For example, if the college you plan to use is $15,000 a year, that represents a cost that is 50 percent higher than the $10,000 amount on which the table is built. So you should multiply the monthly amount needed by 150 percent or 1.5 to determine how much you should invest. Alternatively, if the cost you expect is $5,000 a year, halve the monthly amount.

Robin, Larry, and the Triplets

Here's how one couple did it. Robin and Larry had triplets, Susie, Dana, and Tiffany, six years of age, who would be entering college at the same time. While few of us will face the problem of educating triplets, the example of Robin and Larry will help you examine some alternatives to pursue when costs to live are high, both parents work, and there is a strong desire to start a college fund as soon as possible.

When Robin and Larry came to see me, they were doing well in their careers, with Robin earning $70,000 a year and Larry earning $65,000. They were drowning in the expenses of caring for triplets and becoming more anxious about the cost of college educations with each passing year. Let's take a look at their budget.

Robin's and Larry's Income

Salary (Larry)	$ 65,000
Salary (Robin)	70,000
Total	**$135,000**

Cost of Living

Cost of Living $137,000, including taxes

Home	$ 24,500
Utilities	7,400
Food	12,000
Shopping	10,500
Car	4,200
Recreation and personal	$ 3,000

Cost of Living (Continued)

Clothing	
Gifts	$ 2,800
Vacations	2,000
Insurance	5,100
Child care and tuition	10,200
401(k)	5,200
Medical	8,300
Taxes (Federal, State, FICA)	36,131
Miscellaneous	2,500
Total	**$136,831**

Robin's and Larry's Net Worth

Assets

Savings, checking, EE savings bonds	$ 10,000	
IRAs (his and hers)	8,200	
401(k) (Robin)	42,000	
401(k) (Larry)	36,000	
Total Invested Assets		**$ 96,200**
Home	$250,000	
Personal property	90,000	
Autos	34,000	
Total Use Assets		**$374,000**
Total Assets		**$470,200**

Liabilities

Mortgage	$174,000	
Charge cards	5,000	
Car loans	8,000	
Total Liabilities		**$187,000**
Net Worth		**$283,200**

Analysis. Robin and Larry want to begin a college fund. Our analysis shows they are consuming $2,000 more each year than they are earning. They have no significant investment dollars with which to begin. Their $10,000 in savings, checking, and savings ʌovide a cash reserve they feel they need to keep liquid to feel secure. They wanted help in revamping their budget to free up dollars for their goal.

First, how much will they need?

You can see from our chart that four years of college for one child now six years old will cost in future dollars $88,026, and will require monthly investments of $218.

For three, of course, those numbers will be tripled. They couldn't find $654 per month. What options could be created? We decided to make the assumption that whatever they are paying for child care or private school tuition now, they will have to continue allocating for their children—even through college. So let's begin with the need in future dollars: $22,007.

In today's dollars, they are now paying $3,400 a year per child for tuition and child care. Assuming they do not increase that amount to account for inflation for each child even if they are in college, their need will be reduced to $18,607.

Additionally, Larry and Robin are each funding $100 a month into a variable life insurance policy, which will create not only a death benefit of $60,000 on each of their lives, but will (if projected returns hold true) provide $5,000 a year from each policy ($10,000 per year) for the college years. This will further reduce the need by $3,333 per year per child.

$22,000
– 3,400 Continuation of current costs
– 3,333 Loan against life insurance policies
$15,267 **Need per Year per Child for One Child**

Their reduced need per child is $15,267 per year, requiring a total of $61,096 for the four years per child. They need to invest about $150 a month per child or a total for all three of $450 per month in order to meet their goals.

Live-in grandmother.   Robin's father died and Robin's mom, 64, was lonely. She was willing to move into their large home and help with child care after school now costing about $5,000 a year. In addition, she wanted to pay for her housing and board, so she insisted on giving Robin and Larry $400 a month.

Savings in child care	About $400
Additional income	$400 a mon...
Total to Invest or Pay Credit Cards	**$800 a month**
College funding need	$450 a month
Remainder to Be Used for Credit-Card Reduction	$350 a month

If there's no live-in grandmother. Consider sending the children to a local community college for the first two years. It will cut costs considerably, since they can live at home. Average annual cost for a two-year public college during the 1994–95 school year is as follows:

$1,298	Tuition
566	Books
$1,864	**Total**

Reference: Educational Rankings Annual, 1996 edition, Gale Research, Inc., p. 188.

Consider student loans or scholarships. Encourage your child to study hard and apply for scholarships. Good academic scholarships are available. Check with the financial aid office for information. That same office can give you information about low-cost student loans.

The major key to accomplishing this objective, as with most objectives in life, is determination. Set the goal, develop the plan, then stick with it.

WEALTHBUILDING STRATEGIES FOR THE 30s

The 30s are indeed years of choices, choices that have far-reaching implications.

Single or Married

- **Take the plunge—buy a house and live in your tax shelter.** Your home is the best way to reduce taxes. You can write off the real estate taxes and the interest on your mortgage.

- **If possible, maximize your contribution to the tax-deferred savings vehicle available to you.** If you cannot maximize, at least fund 10 percent of your income into that investment vehicle. This applies whether it is an IRA-SEP if you are self-employed or 401(k) if you work for a company. Invest at least 70 percent for growth and don't worry about the fluctuations. You have time. Let only the company matching funds go into the company stock.
- **Maintain a cash reserve account in a money market or bank savings account.** This reserve should be equal to two-and-a-half or three times your monthly cost of living to cover your costs if you should lose your job, become disabled, or need to cover major repairs to your home or car.
- **Invest any other available dollars for growth.** Use mutual funds. See our section in Chapter 2, entitled "Selecting a Mutual Fund." Don't worry if your mutual funds fluctuate. You have time.
- **Don't allocate more than 5 percent of your total invested assets to your company's stock.** While you certainly want to show company loyalty, don't sacrifice your financial future by placing too much money in one asset. Diversification is always best.
- **As you replace your car bought in your 20s, resist the urge to buy new.** Let someone else take the expensive first-year depreciation as they drive off the lot. Force yourself to make payments. (See the section entitled "Much Shrewder Car Buying" in this chapter.)
- **Make your car last at least seven years.** Never finance for longer than four years. Use the three years during which you don't have a car payment to save for additional down payment dollars when you are ready to purchase every seven years.
- **Don't job-hop too much.** Be willing to pay the price of learning and working your way up if you see potential in the future. A good job consists of more than money: A nice workplace, good coworkers, benefits, and money should all be considered as a part of the package.

- **Begin now to balance career, family, and social demands.** Good habits learned now will serve you well in the future.

Married with Children

- Beginning in the 30s with children under six years of age, college funding becomes manageable—about $100 to $150 a month per child if you start when they are born. To have this money to invest, you may have to deny the urge to buy yet a bigger home or to purchase a new car every three years.
- Make sure you have adequate life and disability insurance.
- Teach your children about money—how to spend wisely, save regularly, and give consistently. See Appendix H entitled "Kiddie Money."

The 20s and 30s set the tone for the rest of your life. Manage these years wisely!

CHAPTER 5

THE 40S: THE MOMENT-OF-TRUTH DECADE

"I grow old . . . I grow old . . .
I shall wear the bottoms of my trousers rolled.
Shall I part my hair behind? Do I dare to eat a peach?"

—T.S. Eliot, "The Love Song of J. Alfred Prufrock"

★ MAJOR FINANCIAL TASKS

Stretching Dollars for Children and Parents and
Preparing for Your Own Financial Future

And so it goes through the years. Forty-year-olds may be simultaneously sending the kids to college, trying to find a retirement home for Mom, trying to choose the right investment for their own retirement, and knocking themselves out keeping up with the Joneses. While the available dollars are being stretched, so too are emotions. Balancing the emotional demands of aging parents with the demands of children given a limited amount of time make all the problems loom so much more ominously. Career-building during these years is also typically demanding, often requiring travel and early and late hours.

During our 40s, we tend to find ourselves in a highly social lifestyle trying to balance the maintenance of old friendships with creating new ones. Not only do these add pressure, but the realities of who we actually married (not who we thought we married) have settled in. During this decade, many divorce because they are unable to deal with these realities. If the couple is committed to making the marriage work, additional emotional energy (maybe even counseling) is needed to keep the relationship healthy. An informal survey I took in 1992 revealed the 40s to be the highest-stress decade through which we move as we age.

But the news is not all bad—there is good news, too. First, the good news: You made it through the 30s, and in doing so, chances are you have put together a personal lifestyle: decided to marry or not to marry; to have children or not. Probably you also have learned a lot about how the world works. Your eyes are open wider than they were in your 20s and 30s.

You know what things cost. For one thing, financial considerations definitely are no longer seen through rose-colored glasses. You are aware of the importance of saving for retirement. By now, it is hoped, you have put into place a good savings program and your savings habits are now routine.

Probably your eyes also have been opened with regard to your own career strengths and weaknesses. Let's hope you have found your particular niche in your working life. Maybe you have turned out to be the creative genius you thought you were. If not, perhaps you have found you are a whiz at organization, or maybe at managing and motivating others. You may be a prime innovator, but if not, perhaps you are a great facilitator. You may have found you have a talent for persuasion or the power to persevere when others drop by the wayside. At this age, you should have made great strides toward understanding yourself. Self-understanding is the beginning of wisdom.

Now, the bad news: In the decade of the 40s, things become extraordinarily complicated on every level—personal, interpersonal, and career. As a result, the stresses of life reach their peak. During this decade we are trying hard to manage our personal and working lives. We find ourselves struggling to move up the career ladder not only because we want to do our best, but also because we need to earn more money to meet our spiraling obligations.

LIFE-STAGE RETIREMENT PLANNER FOR THE 40s

It is at 40, or sometime in the early 40s, that the light comes on and people face their mortality with regard to retirement. Single professional women have come rushing in saying that they don't need any more jewelry, furs, or expensive cars. Married couples come in saying that their children were more expensive than they had thought and now that they are grown and out of the house, they want to focus on retirement planning.

Their priorities have changed. They now want to look at slowing down and they realize they may have to play catch-up. Their focus up till this point has been on spending for today for the most and best. Now their focus is on seeing their retirement funds grow. For these reasons, I suggest you contribute 12 percent of your income as a minimum to your retirement account. If you are playing catch-up, you will need to contribute 15 percent or more. With retirement 25 years away, you still have time if you diligently invest between now and then.

As with the 30-year-olds, you will want to maintain a growth objective for 60 percent of the assets in your account and not be worried about volatility for that portion. For the other 40 percent, seek a growth-and-income objective with less volatility. Your time horizon will be to retire at age 65; thus your money will have 15 to 25 years to grow.

Invest according to this formula:

100 – Your age = Percentage of invested assets for growth in mutual funds and a small amount in real estate (probably REITs)

Your age = Percentage of assets invested in growth and income mutual funds

Split your mutual fund investments equally between domestic and global mutual funds. If you can tolerate great risk in your investments, you could move to 80 percent growth.

Mutual Fund Investments for the 40s

Objective: Maintain Growth
Time Horizon: 15 to 25 Years
Risk: High to Moderate
Investment Vehicle: Mutual Funds

Investment Type	% Invested
Growth	60% to 80%
U.S. stocks	50%
Global stocks	50%
Growth and Income	40% to 20%
U.S. stocks	20%
Global stocks	20%

When using the diagrams in Figure 5.1 for your own situation, keep in mind your own risk tolerance (the more growth you have the greater risk you will be taking), for all of your invested assets, and your income. Do not include your "use assets" such as your emergency cash, home, car, furniture, boat, or anything else you own that you will not sell to create retirement capital.

THE MODEL INVESTOR CONTINUES IN THE 40s

The model 40-year-old investor began investing at age 22 when he or she first got a job. As a reminder, the investor earned $1,000 for every year of age and invested 4 percent into retirement accounts from age 22 through age 29. By the end of the 29th year, the investor had accumulated $12,582 and it was invested earning 10 percent a year.

At 30, our model investor was earning $30,000 and continued to earn $1,000 for every year of age through the 30s. The investor, however, contributed 10 percent of earnings a year into retirement investment accounts. By the end of the 39th year, the investor had $91,758 put away for retirement.

At 40, our model investor is earning $40,000 per year and will continue to earn $1,000 for every year of age through the 40s. The investor, however, will contribute 12 percent of earnings a year into retirement investment accounts. By the end of the 49th year, the investor will have accumulated $329,985 for retirement.

FIGURE 5.1   Asset Allocation for the 40s

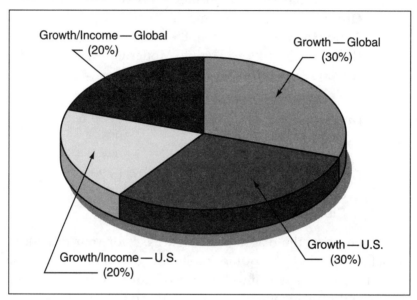

Growth/Income — Global (20%)
Growth — Global (30%)
Growth/Income — U.S. (20%)
Growth — U.S. (30%)

Growth–U.S. = Small and medium-sized companies; REITs; expect fluctuation; minimum holding period: four years.

Growth/Income–U.S. = Fortune 500 companies; dividend-paying stocks and bonds; expect modest fluctuation; minimum holding period: three years.

Growth–Global = U.S. and non-U.S.; small and medium-sized companies; best positioned through mutual funds; expect modest fluctuation; minimum holding period: five years.

Growth/Income–Global = U.S. and non-U.S.; Fortune 500–sized companies; dividend-paying stocks and bonds; best positioned through mutual funds; expect modest fluctuation; minimum holding period: four years

So from the beginning of their 40th year to the end of the 49th year, the retirement nest egg will look like this:

39th Year	49th Year
$91,758	$329,985

Baby Boomers Fear They May Not Be Financially Independent

"It's a scary picture for boomers," said Ken Dychtwald, president and CEO of Age-Wave, Inc., a consulting firm for corporations serving the maturing marketplace. Founder Dychtwald launched FirstWave in the summer of 1997 as a new membership organization to address needs, interests, and quality-of-life concerns of the baby-boomer generation (defined as people born between 1946 and 1964). FirstWave commissioned a study by Roper Starch Worldwide, which surveyed 1,201 baby boomers, ages 32 to 50, across the country to determine their view of the American Dream and its financial implications.

Several issues were identified as being current or potential obstacles to realizing their personal American Dream of financial independence. Following are some of the issues identified by those surveyed, followed by the percentages of those who expressed concern.

Obstacles to Achieving Financial Independence

Issue	Percent Concerned
Caring for aging parents	63%
Financial needs of adult children	54%
Increasingly heavy tax burden	60%
Difficulty making ends meet	37%
Large personal debt	27%
Lack of financial management skills	23%

Source: Seniors Housing News, Winter 1997, p. 21.

There's never enough time! Time becomes a problem. If we are to excel in our work, we often are required to put more time into it. But our lives are also filled with people who need our time: our spouses, our friends, our children, and our parents. We are pulled in many different directions. Somehow, we have to juggle work, at-home responsibilities, and relationships without becoming so completely exhausted that we are unable to do a good job with anything.

We have to do the dreaded—set priorities. Intuitively we know we cannot do it all. For some of us, this is an easier realization than it is for others. But it seems, for all 40-year-olds, giving up something to make time for something else is very difficult. In our 40s, we do have lots of energy. And the thought of not being able to do it all seems almost unacceptable. But sometime along the way, we finally realize the futility of attempting to do it all, and begin to make choices and compromises.

This is where burnout sometimes occurs. We face the realities of life in a more final manner as we begin to see things we thought we would do one day fade away. If we are successful at navigating the burnout waters, we begin to allocate time to handle the top priorities. If it means settling for a job with little or no travel so we can participate in family or social engagements, we do it. It may even mean a pay cut, or no more promotions, but we deal with it.

For single people, this may mean realizing marriage may not be a part of the picture. Therefore, it is at this age that many single people, male and female, start seriously putting together retirement savings plans for themselves and give up on hoping the charming prince or princess will bail them out. This is a smart move earlier in life, but it is essential in the 40s.

There's never enough money!   Managing our time is very difficult during these years. It is equally difficult to manage our income. Two major tendencies peculiar to those of us now in our 40s may complicate our financial decisions. As members of the baby boom generation, many of us expect and even sometimes demand the instant gratification to which we have become accustomed. In addition, we have a related desire to reward ourselves for hard work.

The need for instant gratification, says Philip Wierson, PhD, director of the Counseling Center at Georgia State University, results in an anti-planning bias. "Planning carries with it delayed gratification," he says, "and we're of the now generation. Long-range is next month."

A justification for instant gratification often is the belief that we deserve the best material things: that our children deserve the best school, or that we deserve the most expensive vacation, suit, or dress. This belief may lead us into a pattern of rewarding ourselves with goodies that on the face of it seem innocuous enough—an outfit from Neiman Marcus, a cruise, a trip, the most costly tennis racket, eating out more than once a week. Because we may believe that we deserve expensive things, we may fall into a financial trap that was a danger for us in our 20s: overcharging our credit cards.

Looking wealthy versus being wealthy. independent investor and billionaire businessman Warren Buffett lives in a modest home and drives an older model American-made car. He has said: "Those who are not wealthy often make the total mistake of using their money to buy the things that only make them look financially successful. Those people normally do not ever become wealthy."

It is extremely important to resist the urge to spend more than you are making, especially now. If you have children in college during these years, it is even more important. Even if you didn't have a college fund, some couples make it by the nonworking spouse going back to work. Other couples, where both work already, make it through the college years by making use of financial aid or home equity loans. Interested aunts, uncles, and grandparents who can help are greatly appreciated for doing so. Others borrow against 401(k) plans, though this should be a last resort. The inability to save for retirement during your 40s will mean your retirement date will probably be pushed out to age 70 or beyond.

Topping Out In the 40s

Often as we are busy doing and spending in our 40s, we may run into a topping out of our incomes. If we were accustomed to raises and bonuses through the 30s and maybe even into the early 40s, we may suddenly find ourselves plateauing. Although we are trying to climb, although we want to climb, we discover one day we are sitting on a plateau and are likely to stay there the rest of our working lives. There are fewer jobs at the top and those jobs are filled by 40- to 50-year-olds. Those of us who never get to the top somehow must learn how to be content. We may have to settle for being lower on the totem pole, whether we like it or not. A case in point is Jack, 42 and frustrated by knowing that he has topped out in his company's organization much lower than he would have liked. But he is also convinced he would be unable to replace his employer's compensation package anywhere else, so he has decided to stay. This realization doesn't keep him from being frustrated. He hates being in this stagnating situation. "I'm like a boat without a rudder in this sea of life," he moans.

Jack may need a counselor to help him explore ways to find satisfaction in another aspect of his life, such as by taking leadership roles in church, school, or civic organizations.

In these instances, 40-year-olds have to make conscious decisions to accept the reality of their job future and find contentment somewhere else.

Kicked Out in the 40s

For some, however, having a job—any job—would be a blessing. Those are the people who face the most difficult career scenario. It is the scenario when, in the 40s—in the middle of our career lives—our employer suddenly no longer needs our services at all, forcing us into early retirement or simply eliminating our jobs. This characterizes a situation that has grown more common during the 1990s when so many companies are downsizing.

If that happens, we may find ourselves starting all over. Such a scenario is particularly difficult for 40-year-olds, Georgia State's Weirson says, because, "Until we reach our 50s, we think we're bulletproof."

Gail Sheehy, in *Passages,* puts it another way: We are not "anticipating a major upheaval of the rules and roles that may have comfortably defined us in the first half of life."

The following is an example of just such a situation.

Ellen—Supporting the Family

Seven years ago, John and Ellen Evans had the world by the tail. John, 45, was in middle management earning $70,000 a year, an amount nicely supplemented by Ellen's secretarial salary of $18,000. They bought a nice house in a middle-income Atlanta suburb and furnished it. They bought two previously owned BMWs. Then the large company for which John worked downsized, and his job was abolished. John used his severance pay to buy a small sign-making company but had to dump it after three years before it smothered him financially. He was trying unsuccessfully to create enough revenue to live on and at the same time pay the previous owner their agreed-on purchase terms.

For two years, Ellen's increased $22,000 salary was the chief support of the family. A big evening on the town was two-for-one night at the local fast-food restaurant. After a diligent job search, it became evident John was not going to be able to replace his previous income. He cashed in his retirement savings account from his prior employer to supplement their cost of living.

John settled for a temporary catch-as-catch-can job entering data for the IRS. He would go to bed by 8:30 PM each evening, while his wife waited up. At 10:00 PM she would call the hotline to see if John would be scheduled to work the next day and if so, which shift: 3 AM to 11 AM or 6:30 AM to 3:30 PM. Then she would set the alarm for John and go to bed herself. John earned $6 an hour. For those two years, John and Ellen were on what seemed like a perpetual treadmill: frustrated, tired, struggling to maintain their relationship with their son and each other while maintaining a decent standard of living.

Result. Seven years from the beginning of this nightmare, John turned 52. Here's the picture now. He has managed to move into a full-time middle management government job making $32,000 per year. Ellen changed jobs twice and now earns $35,000 per year. Amazingly, they have no credit-card debt. Ellen insisted on participating in her respective company retirement savings plans. When she left, she rolled them together into an IRA. Her balance is $25,900. John only began contributing to the retirement savings plan two years ago. His balance is $7,200.

John and Ellen have been through some tough times. But their marriage is solid, and their son got an academic scholarship for college. They have no illusions about retirement. They know full retirement for them won't happen until they are in their 70s. And they may have to work part-time even then.

John and Ellen aren't bitter. No one said it would be easy. They're just thankful every day for each other, their son, and their health. They're happy.

Analysis. At 42, Jack hasn't been able to differentiate and come to terms with what is reality for him versus fantasy. John and Ellen have. Jack is not happy. John and Ellen are. The main difference between these two family situations is that the Evanses realize that life consists of more than a job.

Jack will be happier if he somehow finds satisfaction and fulfillment outside his job. Easy to say, hard to do. He will have to make some major lifestyle changes in order to bring about the satisfaction with life he wants. And change is not easy for anyone, especially someone who doesn't want to let go of the dream yet.

John and Ellen, who were fortunate that they had no debt except a modest house payment, will struggle, but they will survive because they possess a key advantage unrelated to dollars and cents: They enjoy close relationships with friends and family that do not depend on an expensive lifestyle.

Balancing Life in the 40s

Weirson's advice is that all age groups need to spend more time with friends and family. Atlanta psychotherapist Don Cabaniss says, "The enlightened 40-year-old is the one who would rather be content than rich—one who has figured out how to make sense of life."

Everybody "wants to live happily ever after—financially, interpersonally, socially, and psychologically," says Cabaniss. "We've all read those 'once upon a time' stories that turn out with perfect endings."

Perhaps, however, those of us in our 40s need to leaven our dreams with a more realistic approach to life. We must come to grips with not only who we are, but where we will likely be in our careers. Peace and happiness will result when we reconcile our expectations with reality.

PRACTICAL STEPS FOR SPENDING AND INVESTING

Spending in the 40s often involves rewarding ourselves for our hard work. Rewards can be expensive and can blow a hole in our retirement planning, but rewards are not the problem.

The problem is the belief that the best rewards cost the most money. Perhaps we can give ourselves less expensive rewards, or rewards that carry no price tag, says Georgia Certified Financial Planner Norm Shirley. You can feel just as rewarded by vacationing in the north Georgia mountains as in New York or Hawaii. You can reward yourself by taking a day off to clean your closets, read a good book, work in your garden, or build something in your basement workshop. The key in this step is to measure your fulfillment by the joy you experience in doing the activity, not by the cost of the activity.

At this age, if you don't already have one, you need a financial plan. Begin by determining what you are spending now to maintain your standard of living. Use the "Monthly Household and Family Expense Worksheet" in Appendix A to find out where your money went last year. From your current numbers, you will be better able to gauge how much you will need in retirement.

Also realistically peg your income potential between now and your target retirement date. Evaluate how much money you will need in the near future to meet your obligations to yourself, your spouse, your children, and your parents. Evaluate how much time you will need to meet all your obligations.

Set priorities. Realize you cannot be all things to all people. Eliminate some things from your time and money budgets. Reduce the time and money spent on other things. Finally, realize you have to "make do" with the time and money you have.

After you have gone through your canceled checks and credit-card statements, placing them in the right categories on your Monthly Household and Family Expense Worksheet, summarize the data on the Summary Sheet in Appendix A. You will need a total annual cost of living in today's dollars to project into the future what it will cost you when you retire. Using the other worksheets in the appendixes, you will be able to produce your own financial plan. The exercise will tell you the retirement capital you will need in order to be financially independent at your appointed date. See the "Retirement Income Calculator" in Appendix C. Go through each step and you will find out if you are currently investing enough for retirement or if you need to add more. In some cases it may be necessary to move your retirement date out a few more years.

The Compromises of Life

It has been said that life is a series of compromises. We learn that fact directly in our 40s.

Muriel, a single mother in her 40s, shows unusual financial acumen, which she attributes to the teaching of her clergyman father and passes on to her 17-year-old daughter.

"Pay attention to money," she tells her daughter, "how it's made and where it's going. Many people have seen too many movies that contribute to the fantasy that money will always be there (or it always won't), and when problems come along they can't see their way out because it wasn't in the movie."

Compromises of life sometimes involve money and other times, time. Sometimes you cut back on the time you spend with various people; other times, you cut back on how much money you spend. Still other times you adjust the quality of what you buy to fit the available cash. And you create quality time with your family and friends. You can't do it all—we have to keep reminding ourselves of this.

Managing Assets from Multiple Marriages

It seems a disproportionate number of divorces and remarriages occur in the 40s. Managing the assets from more than one marriage is sometimes a problem. This is especially true for estate planning. With multiple marriages, it is important to place assets in trust for the current spouse to receive income for his or her lifetime, with the principal going to the children or to other bloodline family members.

Sadly, the failure to draw up a will sometimes creates problems for the family members of the decedent. Consider the case of Nancy, whose family lost her assets to her new husband.

At the time breast cancer took Nancy's life prematurely, she and Dave had been married only four years. Nancy had a nine-year-old son who lived with them and Dave had two grown children from a previous marriage. When Nancy and Dave married, she had sold her home and placed all her equity in their jointly owned home, titled joint tenants with right of survivorship. Dave had contributed no equity to the home purchase.

After Nancy's death, Dave received the home, including all the equity Nancy had hoped would one day go to her son. After they married, Nancy had made Dave the beneficiary on her company 401(k) plan, which had about $200,000 in it. Her son was the beneficiary of a small insurance policy and went to live with his natural father.

What Nancy could have done.   Nancy could have set up a retirement trust to be the beneficiary of her 401(k) plan stipulating that all her 401(k) assets be placed in trust, with Dave receiving the income for life. The trust could have provided for her son's education to be paid, and then upon Dave's death, her son would have received the principal. If the home had been titled only to Nancy, her will could have indicated that Dave could live in the home until sold or until he remarried, then the sale proceeds would go to her son. Saddest of all, with no will upon Nancy's death, Dave's new wife (or Dave's children) will receive Nancy's assets—not Nancy's son, as she would certainly have preferred.

Retirement Planning if Kicked Out in the 40s: Abbey and Mac

When Abbey, now 42, graduated from high school, she went right to work for a large Atlanta company. After 23 years with the company, she had worked her way up to a salary of $45,000 per year. Abbey's salary combined with the $24,000 salary her husband, Mac, made as a mechanic, allowed them to live well—perhaps too well. Never even giving one thought to the fact that their $69,000-a-year income might not be there one day, they spent without restraint on items for their home, their children, and themselves. Gradually their credit-card debt climbed to more than $25,000. Then the unthinkable happened—Abbey's company downsized and she was forced to take early retirement.

Abbey was confident she could find another job to replace her $45,000 salary. She got a severance package of about $30,000 after taxes. She and her husband were thrilled. But they didn't pay off the credit-card debt as I suggested. Instead, with their heads in the clouds, and against my recommendations, they bought a new computer ($3,000) and added a screened porch ($7,500) to their house 30 days before her job ended. In one short month, $10,000 of her severance pay was gone. Abbey soon found that finding a job with a salary comparable to what she was making was going to be impossible. She, the financial leader of the family, was forced to rethink the family finances. Let's look at their situation.

Abbey's and Mac's Net Worth

Assets

Severance receivable	$ 30,000	
Company stock	3,600	
Pension lump sum	45,000	
401(k)	5,000	
Total Invested Assets		**$ 83,600**
Home	120,000	
Personal property	65,000	
Automobiles	23,000	
Time share	8,400	
Total Use Assets		**$216,400**
Total Assets		**$300,000**

Liabilities

Mortgage	$ 99,000	
Screened porch loan	7,500	
Van loan	5,400	
Time share	1,200	
Owed to dentist	900	
Charge cards	25,642	
Computer loan	3,000	
Total Liabilities		**$142,642**
Net Worth (Assets minus Liabilities)		**$157,358**

Results. When Abbey first came to see me, she didn't want to discuss how she was going to create income for her cost of living—she wanted advice on where to invest her pension lump sum and 401(k). So we focused attention there. She said she wanted to invest her rollover for growth and not touch it until she was ready to retire "for good" at age 70.

We discussed her risk tolerance. She said she had been conservative, but realized she must take some risk of principal fluctuation if she wanted her money to grow enough for retirement. We asked her what she would consider a "good" rate of return. She didn't know, but she was sure if her money decreased more than 10 percent in one year, she would lose sleep. So we set a target rate of return of 10 percent per year.

Using our model for how a 40-year-old should invest for retirement at age 65 or beyond, we placed 60 percent of Abbey's money in growth mutual funds and 40 percent into growth and income. We made sure she had at least half of her invested dollars invested domestically and half in foreign funds.

The job search and reality. Her retirement money safely invested, she began to search for a new job. After three months, when she realized she would not be able to replace her salary, she became frightened. It was only then that she was willing to seriously discuss debt reduction. Their monthly cash flow was going to be a problem. So we wanted to explore ways to reduce their monthly payments. Prior to leaving her job, we had encouraged her to refinance her home mortgage—an act that reduced her monthly payments from $1,250 to $950, gaining $300 a month in cash flow. Here's what we did with the severance pay:

Allocation of $30,000 Severance Pay

Debt Reduction	Amount	Payment Saved
Screened porch	$ 7,500	$ 158/month
Computer	3,000	250/month
Van	5,400	470/month
Time share	1,200	220/month
Severance pay used to pay off debt	**$17,100**	
Monthly payment relief		**$1,098/month**
Balance of severance to be used as cost of living until Abbey finds a job		**$12,900**

Monthly cash flow and income needed.   Their after-tax cost of living (after the savings realized by the debt reductions) was reduced to $3,400 a month. Here's how they will share the income responsibilities for the household:

Mac's take-home pay is $1,500 × 12 months = $18,000

Abbey will have to bring home $1,900 × 12 months = $22,800

Abbey will have to earn $29,000 before taxes in order to net the $22,800 needed for her share of the household expenses.

Until Abbey finds a job, she can use the remainder of the severance package to pay the $1,900 a month shortfall. We decided that $12,900 should be placed into a money market account at the bank where they have their checking account. Each pay period (the 15th and the 30th of every month), she will move $950 from savings to checking. This will give her the feeling of "being paid" and she won't run the risk of inadvertently spending their reserve account except as planned. The $12,900 reserve account will last about six-and-one-half months.

Abbey is determined to find a job within that time frame. This time, with more realistic expectations, she will probably be successful.

Analysis.   Until Abbey and Mac came to grips with reality and faced the fact that she could not replace her salary, they had no hope of gaining control over their financial lives. For years they had lived in a fantasy world, spending with no restraint. They have a long way to go yet.

Abbey needs to find a job with more income than is necessary to meet day-to-day expenses so she will have some money to pay down the credit-card balances. They have already destroyed all but one card and it has a low limit. Their commitment is to pay any new balance every month.

In addition, they will pay a set amount against the highest interest-rate cards first while maintaining the minimum balances on the others. They plan to manage their credit-card interest by moving the balance from one card to another every six months to take advantage of lower rates available. We believe they can lower their average interest from about 15 percent to about 9 percent. Under these assumptions, if they pay about $525/month, it will take them about five years to completely pay it off.

By the time Abbey and Mac retire, their children will no longer be the $600-a-month expense they are now. In addition, they should have no credit-card debt by then if, as planned, they never use them again, except for emergencies. Eliminating payments on the credit cards ($525 a month) and the expense now incurred by their children ($600 a month), their present monthly cost of living of $3,400 should be reduced to about $2,300 a month, or $27,600 per year in today's dollars.

If inflation continues to rise 3 percent per year, they will need $63,000 per year in future dollars at their age 70 just to stay even with what $27,600 will buy them today. Before tax, they will need about $80,000 per year to stay even with their current cost of living.

Where will Abbey's and Mac's retirement money come from? At age 70, Abbey should be eligible for about $12,000 per year in Social Security benefits. Mac will be eligible for about $6,000 per year. They will have the nest egg created by her lump-sum pension and 401(k) rollover at age 42, which was invested for growth. They will reposition their invested capital to balanced funds and withdraw 7 percent income annually, paid out monthly. If the past track record repeats itself and the 10 percent return has been realized, the nest egg and available income will have grown as shown below:

Nest egg of $721,000 × 7 percent =	$50,000/year
Abbey's Social Security	12,000/year
Mac's Social Security	6,000/year
Total available income	**$68,000/year**
Total need	$80,000/year
Shortfall	($12,000/year)

There are three ways to meet the shortfall:

1. Cut discretionary expenses. This is the best alternative.
2. Work part-time for two more years (when she is 72) until the house is paid off. Then the absence of a $950-a-month house note will translate into savings of $11,400/year. At that time, their shortfall will only be $600, and with only a little belt-tightening, they should be in good shape. Since it is highly likely that Abbey and Mac will live into their 80s, working past 70 won't be so bad, especially since part-time employment will be all that's needed.
3. Save only $100 a month and invest it at 10 percent per year, creating about $185,000 in additional invested nest-egg capital by age 70. This is the second best alternative.

The message to learn from Abbey and Mac is that if you get into the credit hole by living above your means, it will impact you for the rest of your life. You are better off establishing the habit early in life of living *below* your means.

You simply cannot have it all. If you spend it all today, you will not be able to spend an adequate amount in the future. If you do not spend it all today, you will have some to spend in the future.

RULE OF THUMB

You can't build wealth by spending every dime you make.

AM I MY FATHER'S KEEPER?
MONEY AND YOUR AGING PARENTS

"Do not cast me off in the time of old age;
forsake me not when my strength is spent."
   Psalms 72:9

Although some people are fortunate enough to find that their aging parents are financially independent, others find they must sacrifice to support the father and mother who sacrificed for them. Consider the example of Peter and Dianne, a couple in their 40s.

When Peter and Dianne came to see me, they were sandwiched between the demands of two generations. Money was a problem, but so were the emotional demands they felt. They were trying to meet the financial and emotional demands of their own young children. Simultaneously they were struggling to support Peter's widowed mother, whose assets were almost gone, and help Dianne's widowed aunt, who reared Dianne when her mother died, make ends meet. Their joint income of just above $150,000 was stretched to cover their car payments and the mortgage and home equity loan on their own $300,000 home. In addition, they struggled to make the payments on the $70,000 home in which Dianne's aunt lived as well as the cost of the nursing home where Peter's mother lived.

In my talks with Peter and Dianne, they agonized as they listed their priorities. They wanted to spend quality time with their children and each other. Also they wanted to provide for Peter's mother and Diane's aunt emotionally and financially. At the same time, they wanted to go on with both their careers, which demanded much of them. They basically wanted to do it all. They had some tough decisions to make.

They decided that Dianne would continue to work. They needed her income. Peter would continue to go to work early, before 6 A.M., in order to free the evening hours so he could be at home with Dianne and the children. They decided to continue to spend Sunday mornings at church with their children and to visit Peter's mother only on Sunday afternoons instead of two or three days a week, even though Peter's mom wanted to see them every day. Something had to give.

Meanwhile, we brainstormed ideas to reduce some of the financial stress. Peter and Dianne agreed to give up the season tickets they had been purchasing and the weekend trips they had been taking, sacrificing the private time they had together. They decided they could live without being the proud owners of the Yard of the Month. Believe it or not, this couple took their yard work seriously and felt self-imposed pressure to be the best! As for spending time together, they decided that, for now, they could have tuna sandwiches for lunch together at Peter's office once a week. To cut down costs of family meals out, they could try McDonald's or a cafeteria, instead of paying big bucks for a restaurant meal.

As for the children, Peter and Dianne reduced the amount of money they were putting into retirement savings and redirected it toward private school for their five-year-old. Finally, they needed a way to relieve the emotional pressure. They agreed that it was okay to complain. "We've found it necessary to be able to complain and gripe to each other when the tension gets high," Peter said. "It helps."

This mutual agreement gave each person a way to vent without the other thinking it was a cop-out on the program. The main thing, they agreed, was that they survive the balancing act they felt was necessary for now.

Demanding circumstances, such as those in which Peter and Dianne found themselves, demand a reality test. More and more, today's baby boomers are juggling aging-parent demands with the rearing of their own young children. The pressures of dual demands are exhausting. The relief comes in realizing that no one can be all things to all people all the time. There is only so much time and so much money. Under these pressures, every minute and every penny has to be carefully planned. Needless to say, sacrifices are involved. Like Peter and Dianne, there must be a way to blow off a little steam now and then. Last, do what can be done, and then relax. Nothing stays the same—and this, too, shall pass.

Ten Common Fiscal Faults of Baby Boomers

1. **Mismanaging time as it relates to your private time, time with your family, and demands of your career is a big mistake commonly seen among 40-year-olds.** If you are to excel emotionally as well as financially, you must set priorities. That means there are some things you won't be able to do. It means there are other things about which you will have to compromise your standards of excellence.

2. **For singles, it is a mistake to wait around for that charming prince or princess to come along before you get serious about managing your money wisely.** If you want to be attractive to someone else, get your own financial house in order. It demonstrates your ability to take responsibility for setting a plan in place and sticking to it.

3. **It is a mistake to spend more than you are making at any age; but in your 40s, your retirement savings program should be in full swing.** If you are spending more than you are making, you are probably behind on retirement savings already and you'll be lucky to see retirement in the 70s. Be careful to balance your need for instant gratification with the available cash you have.

4. **It is a mistake to tie your personal reward system to money.** By your 40s, you should be able to distinguish between what carries real meaning in your life and what carries no real meaning. Many times the rewards that carry real meaning don't cost very much. Place more focus on those.

5. **Failing to have a financial plan in your 40s is a mistake.** The plan can be simple:
    - Max out your contributions to your 401(k) or other tax-deferred plan. Your goal should be to invest 15 percent of your gross income. If you've been investing on schedule through your 20s and 30s, the minimum needed now for retirement savings is 12 percent per year.
    - Save to fund at least one-half of your children's college educations. (They can work for the other half—or earn a scholarship. Working for one's own education gives a sense of achievement.)
    - Carry no credit-card balances.
    - Eliminate all other debt except a home mortgage.
    - Have no more than one car note at a time and finance over no more than four years.
    - Carry only the amount of life insurance you need to replace income if the insured dies.

- Live within your income.
- Contribute 10 percent to charity. It's good money management to "give back" a portion of your income to those less fortunate. But choose a church or charity where administrative costs don't erode the charitable contribution and intent.
- Invest at least 60 percent of your investable assets into growth mutual funds. Be sure to diversify among funds which include US and foreign companies.
- Place no more than 5 percent of your total invested assets into your own company's stock. That goal will probably be met by the matching funds your company contributes for you.

6. **Choosing the safe course for 401(k) money can be a mistake.** A study conducted by Oppenheimer Management shows that more than 50 percent of those who participate in 401(k) plans choose guaranteed interest options. A person investing $5,000 per year at a guaranteed 7 percent for 25 years (from ages 40 to 65) would have about $337,780 at age 65. In contrast, a person investing $5,000 per year in an unmanaged S&P 500 index option and receiving an average of 10 percent per year would have about $553,000 at 65. And finally, a person employing a mutual fund management system to manage their money could expect about 12 percent per year and would realize about $783,479 at age 65.

7. **Relying on the company pension is a mistake.** Don't confuse a company pension with a 401(k) or 403(b) plan. A 401(k) is a tax-deferred plan for employees in "for profit" companies; a 403(b) or tax sheltered annuity (TSA) is a tax-deferred plan for employees in "not-for-profit" companies. Such plans allow you to invest for your retirement tax-deferred. A company pension is completely funded by your company and they are quickly becoming extinct.

   Between 1984 and 1994, about 60,000 pension plans were terminated by the respective companies to help cut costs. These actions are leaving many baby boomers unprepared for retirement. Further complicating this problem are the tax changes approved by Congress in 1993, which place a ceiling on the contributions allowed. Fewer pension plans and smaller contributions mean you must take a more active role in managing the money you save in your tax-deferred accounts and in finding other ways outside the tax-deferred plans to save for retirement.

8. **Not funding your IRA is a terrible mistake.** More than 8 million Americans have at least one IRA, but when the tax code changes disallowed the deduction, many people stopped contributing. Should you still contribute even though the tax write-off is gone? The answer (for many) is yes. Consider investing $2,000 per year for 40 years (ages 25 to 65). If you did so, you would have invested $80,000. If you invested in the S&P 500 Index through a mutual fund and earned about 12 percent per year, you would have about $2 million at 65. The conclusion is that, although the $80,000 was not tax-deductible, the growth (i.e. the $2 million minus $80,000 = $1,920,000) on the account was tax-deferred. That means you don't have to pay taxes on it until you withdraw and spend it.

9. **Thinking the equity in your home will bail you out in retirement is a mistake.** Many often plan to downsize their home when they retire. They also think they will be able to purchase a smaller home for cash and have a nest egg left over. With the population declining in the age group behind the baby boomers, that may not be possible. You may be surprised to find your home will sell for less than you paid for it. Real estate prices are determined by supply and demand. The more demand, the higher price you can expect. Fewer people looking to buy higher priced houses will make the price of your house go down, not up.

10. **Don't think you can do it all.** Get help. You wouldn't try to perform surgery on yourself; you'd find a surgeon. Find people to help you carry out your hectic life responsibilities, from housecleaning to taxes to investments. Don't try to do it all—you'll burn out.

WEALTHBUILDING STRATEGIES FOR THE 40s

The 40s are the high-pressure years requiring decisions of priorities about time and money:

- Live within your means. Unless absolutely necessary, try to remain in the house to which you upgraded in your 30s.
- For retirement investing, try to maximize your contribution. If that is not possible, you must invest at least 12 percent per year to stay on target for retirement at age 65.
- Invest 60 percent of your retirement dollars for growth (of which about 5 percent is allocated to real estate) and the other 40 percent for growth and income. Be sure you are balanced 50-50 between U.S. and non–U.S. companies through mutual funds.
- Maintain no balances on your credit cards.
- Make your car last seven years and finance over four years. This strategy will give you three years to place the payment amount to which you are accustomed into savings for an additional down payment when you are ready to trade.
- Balance your time demands in order to maintain your sanity. This will require openness and discussion with family members to bring about relief.

CHAPTER 6

THE 50S: THE HOME RUN DECADE

"It is best to prepare for the days of necessity."

—Aesop's Fables

★ MAJOR FINANCIAL TASK

Preparing for Retirement

For many of us, life settles into itself in the 50s, both emotionally and financially. We are way beyond the uncertainties of the our 20s and the frantic nest-building of our 30s. We have survived the draining demands of the 40s. Chances are, if we've had children, our child-rearing days are over. If we and our children are lucky, they have completed their educations and have launched fulfilling, independent lives.

We may find that we are surprisingly content to be where we are. Although we may have worried about job promotions and reaching the impossible dream in our 20s, 30s, and 40s, in our 50s we may find we no longer do so. Maybe we already have been named CEO. Maybe we already have formed our own company, won the Nobel prize, written a novel, or been named teacher of the year. Some who have gotten there have found the proverbial emptiness at the top, so they begin to adjust their day-to-day priorities to achieve the peace and contentment they found missing as they moved through the late 40s and early 50s.

But if we haven't gotten to the top, chances are good that we are satisfied we gave it a good try or that it simply was never in the cards for us, and we are at peace with it. Even if the dream still is a possibility, chances also are good that we no longer obsess about it; we no longer race through each day driven by an internal hunger to be somewhere we aren't.

Most 50-year-olds have come to grips with their mortality. For many, it is during this decade that they lose their own parents. They begin to ask the right questions about the meaning of life. The 50s decade takes on a different shift from that of the 40s.

Instead of thinking that bigger is better, they begin to think smaller is smarter. Around 55 (maybe somewhat inspired by the tax break available for sale of primary residences) many begin thinking about downsizing their homes. They may think about their "final home." If there is an interest in a vacation or second home, this is the decade to take action.

Their real friends take on more importance in their lives and the cocktail-party circuit is of less interest. Grandchildren begin to be born and the 50-year-olds shift attention more toward family. This is the time of life that investment temperament takes on a slightly more conservative bent. But most 50-year-olds expect to live to 100, so they start thinking about the effect of inflation on their retirement funds.

LIFE-STAGE RETIREMENT PLANNER FOR THE 50s

In the 50s, many of us begin to think seriously about when we will retire, how we will position our investment portfolios to provide income throughout our retirement, and how we will occupy our time in retirement. If we are wise, we have been investing for retirement for many years so that in our 50s, we can just check in on our plan and make sure everything is on target. If we have not stayed with our plan through our previous decades, we will have to play catch-up during this decade. In either case, it is in our 50s that we begin thinking about all the aspects of retirement.

In Metropolitan Life Insurance's statistical bulletin, "The Changing Picture in Retiree Economics," Mark H. Weinstein writes that we are now seeing the "golden age of the golden years," and that baby-boom retirees will be less well off than today's retirees. Pensions and retirement benefits of the elderly may be less in the future and more of the burden for economic security may fall on the individual. This is a result of companies replacing pensions with contributory tax-deferred plans for employees. Further, politicians are constantly warning us of the coming changes in Social Security that will affect those who will receive benefits in the future—not those receiving benefits now. Consequently, baby boomers may well be the generation where all these reductions come together and have an impact.

For these reasons, I suggest you contribute 15 percent of your income as a minimum to your retirement accounts. If you are playing catch-up, you will need to contribute 20 percent or more. With retirement 15 years away, you still have time if you diligently invest between now and then.

Some who are playing catch-up are investing as much as 50 percent of their income for retirement. That sounds like a lot until you realize they are no longer buying furniture for their homes, no longer paying for college expenses (even the incidentals of college), and no longer paying to feed and clothe their children. If working spouses are not caught up in a downsizing, they are probably making more income than they have ever made in their entire lifetimes. With more income and lower expenses, the family experiences a big raise in available cash.

The question is always: Where should we place this money for the best possible return safely? In the 50s, we begin to realize that we don't have time to recreate our nest egg. So we become more safety-conscious. At the same time, we don't have time to lose either, so we want the best possible return without jeopardizing our principal. We therefore move toward more conservative investment positioning.

As with the 40-year-olds, you will want to maintain growth in your account. At 50, that translates to about 50 percent of your invested assets, and you should not be overly worried about volatility for that portion. Without volatility, you get no growth. Therefore, you'll need to accept some volatility to obtain the growth you will need for your nest egg to grow and support you to age 100. For the other 50 percent, seek a growth and income objective that will provide less volatility. Your time horizon will be to retire at age 65; thus your money will have 10 to 15 years to grow before you start tapping it for income.

Invest according to this formula:

100 – your age = Percentage of invested assets for growth in mutual funds and perhaps a small amount in real estate

Your age = Percentage of invested assets in growth and income mutual funds

Split your mutual fund investments equally between domestic and global mutual funds.

If you can tolerate great risk in your investments, you could move to as much as 75 to 80 percent growth.

Mutual Fund Investments for the 50s

Objective:	Maintain Growth and Income
Time Horizon:	5 to 15 Years
Risk:	Moderate
Investment Vehicle:	Mutual Funds

Investment Type	% Invested
Growth	50% to 75%
U.S. stocks	50%
Global stocks	50%
Growth and Income	25% to 50%
U.S. stocks	50%
Global stocks	50%

When using the diagram in Figure 6.1 for your own situation, keep in mind your own risk tolerance (the more growth you have, the more risk you will be taking) for all of your invested assets. Do not include "use assets" such as your home, car, furniture, boat, or anything else you own that you will not sell to create retirement capital.

FIGURE 6.1 Asset Allocation for the 50s

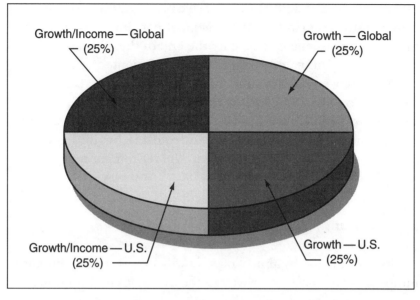

> *Growth–U.S.* = Small and medium-sized companies; REITs good for small percentage; expect fluctuation; minimum holding period: four years.
>
> *Growth/Income–U.S.* = Fortune 500 companies; dividend-paying stocks and bonds; expect modest fluctuation; minimum holding period: three years.
>
> *Growth–Global* = U.S. and non-U.S.; small and medium-sized companies; best positioned through mutual funds; expect modest fluctuation; minimum holding period: five years.
>
> *Growth/Income–Global* = U.S. and non-U.S.; Fortune 500–sized companies; dividend-paying stocks and bonds; best positioned through mutual funds; expect modest fluctuation; minimum holding period: four years.

The Model Investor Continues in the 50s

The model 50-year-old investor began investing at age 22 when he or she first got a job. As a reminder, the investor earned $1,000 for every year of their age and invested 4 percent into retirement accounts from age 22 through age 29. By the end of the 29th year, the investor had accumulated $12,582 and it was invested earning 10 percent a year.

At 30, our model investor was earning $30,000 and continued to earn $1,000 for every year of age through the 30s. The investor, however, contributed 10 percent of earnings a year into retirement investment accounts. By the end of the 39th year, the investor had $91,758 invested for retirement.

At 40, our model investor was earning $40,000 a year and continued to earn $1,000 for every year of age through the 40s. The investor contributed 12 percent of earnings a year into retirement investment accounts. By the end of the 49th year, the investor had accumulated $329,985 for retirement.

At 50, our model investor was earning $50,000 a year and will continue to earn $1,000 for every year of age through the 50s. The investor will contribute 15 percent of earnings per year into retirement investment accounts. So from the beginning of the 50th year to the end of the 59th year, the retirement nest egg will look like this:

49th Year	59th Year
$392,985	$997,176

As you can see, by almost 60, you will almost be a millionaire. I hope that you have seen through the examples in this book that it is not difficult to achieve this goal.

IF YOU HAVE TO RETIRE EARLY

Unfortunately, when we will retire is sometimes not our decision to make. Increasingly, companies are forcing employees in their 50s to take retirement. Most of those people had planned to work until age 65 and aren't really ready to quit work. Those who have invested through the years usually are surprised to learn how well-off they are. Those who were planning to play catch-up are greatly disappointed.

The forced early-retirement scenario is the result of downsizing brought on by three major factors:

1. Information technology
2. The use by companies of outside contractors
3. The elimination of workers, the value of whose functions no longer makes feasible the salaries they receive

Much has been written and spoken about information technology, through which work once performed by several skilled employees over long periods can be set in motion and completed

with lightning speed usually by a single younger, low
ployee. Similarly, the effects of the outsourcing of w
pendent contractors is now well documented. Th
outsourcing, employers eliminate compensation packages that
include large salaries plus benefits.

Not so well documented, however, is the phenomenon in
which, over time, workers simply become redundant. Often this
phenomenon has arisen when companies hired many workers at
low levels. Those workers moved up to middle management
through the years, received automatic pay raises, and finally
reached levels where they could not perform work commensurate
with their salaries. Now, some executives find that Parkinson's
Law—work expands to fill the time available for its completion—
has become all too pervasive in their organizations and downsizings begin.

People in their 50s faced with early retirement fall into two
broad categories:

1. Those who have lived within their means and saved
2. Those who have consistently spent all or more than they
    made

These categories are not new. Aesop wrote about them in his
fable "The Ant and the Grasshopper":

The grasshopper, spending his summer singing and hopping
around, saw an ant struggling by with an ear of corn and asked
him to stop his work and play. The ant replied that he was laying
in food for the winter and advised the grasshopper to do the
same. The carefree grasshopper refused, but when winter came
and he had no food, he asked the ant to help him. The frugal,
industrious ant would not do so. Then, the grasshopper knew, in
Aesop's words: "It is best to prepare for the days of necessity."

You may want to retire early. But even if you don't, you may
be forced to do so. The wise way to prepare for either scenario is
to lay the groundwork early. Here are two guidelines:

1. If you are fortunate enough to still be working in your
    50s, you should be saving from 20 percent to 50 percent
    of your income until you retire.

2. Resist the urge to increase your cost of living with every pay increase. In other words, when you get a promotion or a raise, don't rush out to buy a new car or house. After you establish a comfortable lifestyle, save and invest the raise instead.

Financial Marriages—Disaster or Gold Mine?

When two people marry, they bring with them behaviors primarily learned from their parents. Of course, sometimes one child within a family is financially conservative and another child is not. One often wonders why the two develop such different ways of managing their lives. But that is the subject of much marriage and family counseling, not to be dealt with here. We are interested in observing the marriage of two approaches to money management and how they affect financial independence as we age. A healthy balance between spending today and saving for tomorrow is a good goal. However, often such a balance is not seen.

If it feels good—do it! For example, sometimes two people marry who are interested only in spending for today. This couple enjoys traveling, buying things, and creating memories of today. They don't worry about tomorrow. If neither spouse is financially disciplined enough (that is, strong enough to say no) to control spending and institute a savings program, full and successful retirement will never happen.

But the sky might fall! But suppose two people marry who are more interested in saving for retirement. All their efforts are directed toward the future, often to the sacrifice of today. They usually don't want to spend money to travel, eat out, or have nice things. This approach to money management is too radical, most will agree, but one thing's for sure—this couple will be able to retire early and well.

Stressful but successful. Now consider the couple where one person is financially disciplined and the other is a spendthrift. One will insist on funding a savings program while the other will be pleading to spend for today. If they can strike a balance, this couple will retire successfully—maybe not early—but successfully at age 65. They will also have enjoyed some of the finer things in life along the way. This is the ideal financial marriage; however, they may not have the most relaxed lifestyle. They will have to endure the tension of discussions (read *arguments*) over how to spend money on a day-to-day basis. The resulting compromises will create a financial balance that will work both for today and tomorrow.

Michael and Elle are the first kind of couple. They very likely will never be able to retire completely without drastically cutting their cost of living.

The Grasshopper Model

Michael came to me for financial advice because he was being forced into early retirement. He was 55 years old, had been with the same major company for 25 years, and was receiving a salary of $79,000 a year. I then asked him how much he had in the company's excellent tax-deferred savings plan. His answer was shocking. "I don't have a dime," he said. "It was procrastination," he continued, stretching out a little more on the sofa in my office. "I had the form to sign up on my desk every day, and I kept thinking, 'I'll do this tomorrow.'"

His next bombshell was this: He had only $38,000 as severance pay. His pension, discounted for his age, would be $23,000 a year. He and his wife were accustomed to spending $79,000 a year!

The future was bleak for Michael. Throughout his career he and his wife had spent the money he made as fast as he made it. Time had passed so fast. What could they do now that retirement was upon them? Whatever solution they came up with would have to be a long-term one: Actuaries tell us that a woman who reaches 50 in good health can expect to live to the age of 92 and a man who is still healthy at 50 can expect to live to age 81. Yet, although we can expect to live much longer than our ancestors, many of us, like Michael, are not planning for the later years.

The Bureau of Census also tells us that five out of six people who turn age 65 today have no hope of financial independence.

Those people piece together a retirement life that consists of income from a job, plus their small pension and Social Security. In addition, they move to a smaller house or sometimes to an apartment to reduce their cost of living. For those people, retirement is not the ideal picture of the "golden years."

Analysis.   After much discussion, Michael and I agreed that the following were the reasons for his situation:

1. The expensive family lifestyle his company implicitly expected employees to maintain
2. The personal lifestyle he and his wife enjoyed

Michael had worked all those years for a company that was highly image-conscious. The expectation, although expressed in subtle ways, was that employees would wear expensive clothes, have expensive club memberships, maintain expensive hobbies, and take expensive vacations. They also were expected to live in upscale (read "expensive") neighborhoods and drive late-model, above-average cars. As a result, employees constantly competed with their peers in shows of affluence. If they did not deliberately buck the company "status quo," employees had very little disposable income to save.

Little was said to employees about preparing for retirement. Tax-deferred saving was not aggressively encouraged. Informative meetings about retirement seldom were held and when they were, they often were held after working hours and were sparsely attended. Moreover, the high-profile success of this paternalistic company bred in workers a false sense of security. "When you signed on," Michael said, "you signed on for life. You were led to believe that your company pension was all you needed." As Michael found out, sadly, he had been led down the primrose path.

But the company he worked for was not Michael's real problem. Michael didn't take the responsibility himself to participate in the plans available, nor did he and his wife of 26 years control their spending. This changed, for Michael at least, when he was forced into retirement.

Not so for his wife. Elle had never worked seriously outside the home, but Michael's family still had the best of everything. When Michael was forced into retirement, she still wanted the best of everything. She was angry he had been forced out.

Michael was tired from working under the stress of trying to figure out a way to make ends meet without his high-paying job, but Elle refused to economize. She wanted to remain in the same expensive house, keep their late-model cars and car payments, and continue to take expensive vacations. She also insisted on contributing nothing to the family budget—although she did work part-time and made about $10,000 a year. She refused to spend even a penny of it on family necessities. Instead, she spent it on "nice-to-haves" for herself and their daughter.

Faced with the impending loss of Michael's job, they need a financial austerity program. In order to be able to retire at age 70, they need to do the following:

1. Sell their large home and buy a smaller one.
2. Stop taking expensive vacations.
3. Bring in two full-time incomes.
4. Save and invest for growth at least 25 percent of their income for the next 15 years.

Result. Elle was having none of it.

Today, Michael is struggling. He is self-employed, doing contract work as a trainer. His long-term marriage to Elle is now troubled, to say the least, but he feels trapped. He is afraid that if Elle doesn't get her way, she will divorce him and become an even greater financial drain.

Stories like Michael's are sad. All too often they are the result of the following:

1. Overindulgence of parents way back when or perhaps having had nothing as a child and an overemphasis on the "my family will have everything I didn't have growing up" syndrome
2. A general personal refusal to face reality and take responsibility
3. An unwillingness to stop overspending early in a marriage

Now let's turn to Buddy and Susan, a couple whose financial situation is as different from Michael's as can be imagined.

The Ant Model

Buddy and Susan worked for the same company during their entire careers. Both were forced into early retirement at the same time, Buddy at age 51 and Susan at age 50. But, unlike Michael, they already had built a strong financial foundation for themselves.

Budget while working. Before retirement, their combined income was $88,000, with Buddy making $43,000 and Susan making $45,000. Annual taxes on their combined income were $25,000. Of the remaining yearly income, they were saving $18,000, or about 20 percent, and spending $45,000. Their home mortgage was their only debt. In other words, they were consistently living below their means—and had been for quite some time. As a result, at ages 50 and 51, their cars were paid for, the mortgage on their $94,000 home was down to $40,000, and they had a whopping $640,000 coming to them in a combined lump-sum pension buyout and 401(k) funds.

Of the financial marriages discussed earlier, Buddy and Susan had achieved the balance of the "stressful but successful."

Throughout their marriage, Buddy and Susan, who had no children, were both intent on enjoying life day to day. They traveled, but they didn't take lots of expensive trips. They took short, inexpensive trips. They always looked for travel bargains.

Susan liked to decorate their home and spent money as needed. Buddy wasn't too thrilled over Susan's decorating budget. But Buddy liked expensive equipment for his woodworking hobby, which didn't thrill Susan. But they tolerated each other's preferences.

They both agreed that contributing the maximum to the company 401(k) was important to them. They had both started working straight out of high school and never left their respective companies. So over the years, their savings programs plus the good fortune of being with a company that funded pensions for employees ensured their successful retirement.

Retirement budget. Buddy and Susan completed a Monthly Household and Family Expense Worksheet (see Appendix A) to estimate what they would need as yearly after-tax income to maintain their cost of living after retirement. Some expenses would go away, such as expensive suits for work, car expenses for the long commute they each had endured, and parking expense in the downtown garages. The exercise showed them they would need not $45,000 to support their lifestyle, but only $38,000 after taxes.

Their 401(k) and pension lump-sum funds were rolled over into IRAs and invested in mutual funds balanced between stocks and bonds. They began to receive $45,000 annually from the portfolio on a monthly systematic withdrawal. After taxes they had $38,000 to spend—exactly the same take-home income they had enjoyed while they both worked.

Result. Buddy and Susan are withdrawing only 7 percent per year from the total return of 10 percent they are earning on their IRA rollover nest egg. This will assure them of growth on their principal and growth of their income as they age.

Now Buddy does cabinet-making part-time, and Susan makes and sells crafts. Both are busy, contented, and financially secure—and working a little just because they want to!

Withdrawing Income from IRAs—Without Penalty

One additional point must be made here. Because Susan and Buddy were under age 59½, they were in danger of being subject to a 10 percent penalty for withdrawals from IRAs. However, under Internal Revenue Code section 72(t), they are not penalized at all. They are taking a flat amount from their accounts until age 59½. With the help of their CPA, they made sure they were complying with the rules by taking substantially equal withdrawals over their lifetimes at a reasonable interest rate. Thus, they paid no 10 percent penalty. For specific information on this section, see Figure 6.2.

Internal Revenue Code
Section 72(t)(2)(A)(iv)

IRC section 72(t)(1) imposes an additional 10 percent tax on amounts withdrawn from retirement plans (including IRAs) prior to age 59½. However, IRC section 72(t)(2)(A)(iv) provides that this tax does *not* apply to distributions which are part of a series of substantially equal periodic payments (not less frequently than annually) made over the life expectancy of the planholder or the joint life expectancies of the planholder and the planholder's beneficiary. Some specific provisions of this section are as follows:

- Once a series of payments is begun, it cannot be modified before either:
  1. age 59½, or
  2. five years from the date the payments began, whichever happens *last.*
- Payments are considered to be substantially equal periodic payments if the amount to be distributed is computed using one of the following three methods:
  3. The account balance is divided by the planholder's life expectancy or joint life expectancy from IRS tables.
  4. The account balance is amortized at a reasonable interest rate over the planholder's life expectancy or joint expectancy from IRS tables.
  5. The account balance is amortized at a reasonable interest rate over the planholder's life expectancy from an insurance mortality table. In this method there is no provision for using joint life expectancy.
- If it is determined by the IRS that these provisions have not been satisfied the planholder will have to pay a tax and penalty which would have been imposed under section 72(t)(1), plus interest, for the amounts withdrawn which did not qualify under section 72(t)(2)(A)(iv).

Source: 1997 U.S. Master Tax Guide

The Henny-Penny Model

For the sake of driving the point home, let's look at one more couple who have led fiscally conservative lives. The highest combined salary Aaron and Joan, ages 59 and 57 respectively, received during their working years was $60,000. Yet they were saving $1,400 a month, or about 24 percent of their income. As a result, their retirement nest egg was $347,000. That money was invested for growth and income. When Aaron reached age 59½, they planned to begin spending 7 percent of its total 10 percent per year earnings. This plan would leave 3 percent to 4 percent in the portfolio for continued growth and therefore take care of future inflation.

Aaron and Joan had chosen to stay in the first house they had bought as a young couple. They purchased that house for $30,000 in 1961. Today, it is paid for and worth $100,000. Instead of moving into larger and larger houses, Aaron and Joan chose to buy beach property.

At retirement, Aaron and Joan were continuing to pay for a beach home for themselves and rental property in Florida. They continued their frugal ways. They planned to spend, for example, $50 a month on recreation (which covered the trips they wanted to take to Florida with their son and his family) and $50 a month on auto expenses. Their personal expenses, such as haircuts, laundry, cosmetics, and prescriptions added up to $80 a month. They would continue to tithe, contributing $200 a month total to their church. They also would continue contributions to charities. But the joy of their lives was to be able to give to their only son and his family "care" packages of household items and the "nice-to-haves" they found on sale, which they knew a young couple with two babies would not be able to comfortably afford.

There's more! Shortly after Aaron had to retire, he was hired back on a contract basis, making $60,000 a year, with the company from which he had retired. At this point, Aaron and Joan decided to let their retirement money grow. This couple has done it right through all the years, but not without sacrifice. They never allowed Aaron's pay raises to be consumed in increased day-to-day expenses. They have always been cautious about their spending.

he financial marriages discussed in this section, this cou-
ild be under the "Henny Penny—the sky is falling" model.
This couple focused on preparing for the future no matter what.
It happened that because they kept their spending under control
for many years, money was available for what many see as extras—
the beach house and rental property.

Aaron and Joan embody Aesop's platitude "It is best to prepare for the days of necessity." They also serve as fine examples
of another Aesop saying: "The gods help them that help themselves."

LONG-TERM CARE INSURANCE

Probably because the 40s and 50s are the years in which many
of us help our parents think through long-term care options, we
often wonder about purchasing that type of insurance for ourselves.

The 40s are probably too early for most to think about long-
term care insurance; however, it may be worth it to examine the
feasibility of this type of insurance early, especially if there are
health problems such as stroke, diabetes, and Alzheimer's dis-
ease in your family.

Costs of Long-Term Care Insurance

Costs vary from company to company. The younger you are,
the lower the costs. Once you have the rate quoted and you have
purchased your policy, the premium cannot increase as you age.
Sample premiums quoted here show a range from low to high depending on the company offering the insurance.

Sample annual premiums are based on:

- A 90-day waiting period
- $100/day benefit
- 50 percent home health-care included
- Waiver of premium included

The annual costs for a 55-year-old are about half those for the same coverage for a 65-year-old. As you review the following chart, you can see that the annual cost for this coverage is reasonable regardless of age:

	Age 55	**Age 65**
Single	$450 to $750	$1,050 to $1,500
Couple	$675 to $1,200	$1,600 to $2,850

Think about the cost of one month in an assisted living community or nursing home. If the cost is $100 per day for 30 days, just one month will cost you $3,000. If you went into the nursing home at age 85 and had to stay there for ten years, your total cost for care would be $360,000. Suppose you, as a single person, purchased a long-term care policy at age 55. Your premium would be $450 per year. If you did not go into the nursing home until age 85, you would have paid your $450 a year premium for 30 years. Thirty years times $450 a year would mean your total cost of insurance would have been $13,500.

This book is about building wealth. As you approach and enter retirement, you will need to focus on preserving wealth. The long-term care insurance helps you do that.

Costs of Long-Term Care Insurance Compared with Those of a Nursing Home

Nursing home care from ages 85 to 95	$36,000/year × 10 years =	$360,000
Total premiums paid ages 55 to 85	$450/year × 30 years =	$ 13,500
	Wealth Preserved $346,500	

If you wait until age 65 to buy the insurance the premium cost versus the benefit is:

Nursing home care from age 85 to age 95	$36,000/year × 10 years =	$360,000
Total premiums paid from age 65 to age 85	$1,050/year × 20 years =	$ 21,000
	Wealth Preserved	$339,000

Today, the average nursing home stay nationwide exceeds $40,000. If a person has to go into a nursing home, the average period of time they stay there is three years. In addition, we are seeing assisted living facilities (ALFs) spring up, offering a living arrangement akin to a home with meals provided and various levels of services (e.g., driving, cleaning, hair care) offered for a fee. Assisted living facilities offer a step between independently living in your own home and being totally dependent in a nursing home; they are not at all institutional. They are designed to closely replicate a home as much as possible.

Three alternatives are available to you to pay for this care:

1. If you have enough assets or income, you can pay for the level of care you choose at the time you need it.
2. If you have few or no assets (at maximum, a home, car, prepaid funeral contract, and a $5,000 certificate of deposit), Medicaid will pay your expenses that are greater than your income.

   If you have assets and want Medicaid to help you in this area, you must spend down your assets to the levels specified in the previous paragraph. A cruel aspect of this qualification system applies to the middle class who have worked diligently to provide a nest egg for retirement. Those who prepared themselves are penalized by the spend-down requirements prior to receiving Medicaid coverage. Those who did not prepare themselves are "rewarded" with instant Medicaid coverage.

   Therefore, for anyone over 55 who has more than $200,000 in assets (yes, an IRA counts), long-term care insurance should be a consideration for protecting those assets. While important for anyone with assets, it is vital for a married couple. You are protecting your wealth, not your health, strange as it may seem. You will receive the care whether you or Medicaid pays for it.
3. Transfer this risk to an insurance company through the use of long-term care insurance. The insurance allows you to protect your assets and let the insurance company pay for your health care. One suggestion for paying insurance premiums would be to set up a mutual fund to provide systematic withdrawals to pay premiums monthly, quarterly, or annually. See Figure 6.3 for a summary of key elements of the policy to consider and sample rates.

FIGURE 6.3   Long-Term Care Insurance Summary

Benefits	**$10 to $200 per day**
Benefit Period (How long the insurance company will pay benefits)	From two years up to lifetime
Waiting Period (How long you have to wait to begin collecting from the insurance company)	From no-wait up to a 180-day wait
Home Health Care	Can be purchased or sometimes included
Qualifying for Benefits	Cannot perform 1 up to 3 "ADLs" (activities of daily living): bathing, continence, eating, toileting, transferring
Waiver of Premium (Not having to pay premiums if you go into a facility.)	Often included at no cost
Cost Of Living Adjustment (COLA) (Allows the benefit amount to increase annually with inflation)	Can be purchased

NOT WITH MY MONEY, YOU DON'T: YOUR MONEY AND YOUR HEIRS

It is in our 50s that we begin to realize we aren't going to live forever. Some people wait until their 60s to think about serious estate planning, but with more people retiring early, estate planning issues are being addressed earlier.

While planning ways to best use our money while we are alive is important, it is equally important to provide for its disposition when we are gone. But creating a will is difficult. So it is not unusual for someone to come to me with no will. However, with no will to direct the distribution of the assets after death, many time-consuming problems can occur for those who are living. In Georgia, for example, if there is no will, a surviving spouse receives only a child's portion: That is, all the assets are divided equally among the surviving spouse and the children.

The matter of asset management after death is particularly complex in the case of multiple marriages—yours or those of your children. Partners may worry, for example, that the surviving spouse will end up in a second marriage with some gigolo or red-hot mama who will inherit the assets of the original marriage, after the first partner is dead. That could happen. Is it possible to protect your principal for your children and still give your spouse some income? This section will help you address this question.

As we age we begin to think about transferring assets to children. What if your married child inherits money from you and then gets a divorce? Would it bother you if your child's former spouse got half of the money you intended for your child? There are ways to prevent this from happening.

Your House after You're Gone

Among the problems of remarriages is one related to the primary residence and its disposition upon the death of one spouse. Joe and Sharon, married two years, had been married before. They came to see me for early retirement planning. Joe's company was downsizing and he was being forced out early. He had two children in their 20s—they weren't too fond of Sharon. Sharon had a son who was ten years old and lived with them. Joe and Sharon did not have wills but insisted they would work on that as soon as Joe retired. They had just moved to Georgia one year earlier from a neighboring state. Tragically, the day Joe submitted his early retirement paperwork to personnel, he was taken to the hospital with a heart attack. He never regained consciousness.

The situation was complicated. Sharon had sold her home in the other state and had placed the equity from that sale into the down payment for their new home. Joe had not contributed to the down payment at all. It was jointly titled. Joe had intended that Sharon have full and clear title to the new home if something happened to him. With no will, that wish was not made legally binding. As a result, by the laws of the state of Georgia,

Sharon owned her half of the house outright, but Joe's half was split among Sharon and Joe's two adult children, one-third each. The obvious problem: How could Sharon own it outright? Since Joe's children were not willing to disclaim their ownership of the home, Sharon was forced to pay them for the portion of the house they each owned, even though her down payment had made the purchase of the home possible.

If she and Joe had adequately planned for the transfer of the ownership of the home, they could have avoided this expensive and painful outcome. By titling the home "Joe and Sharon Last-name, Joint Tenants with Right of Survivorship (JTWROS)" the survivor would have received the entire asset upon the death of the first to die.

Your Money after You're Gone

For your surviving spouse. Doug and Jackie, married for 30 years and in their early 50s, with combined assets of about $1 million owned 50-50, wanted to make sure their children got the assets they had accumulated together. If they died simultaneously, no problem. They made sure the children were named in their wills. However, knowing that it is possible for one of them to outlive the other by many years—maybe even 20 years—they became concerned about a second marriage after the death of the first spouse. So we brainstormed and made the following decisions.

They have identical wills. Each provides that all assets be placed in trust for their children, with the surviving spouse receiving an income for life. This plan ensures that the surviving spouse will have the income needed for as many years as needed. Then only at the death of the surviving spouse will the principal of the trust be distributed to the children. This is one way to be sure your spouse has income and your children get the assets. Many are concerned that the surviving spouse not have his or her hands tied in the event he or she needs the principal. Before unilaterally discarding the idea of a trust as a vehicle to help you, be assured that the language can be such that the spouse (often named as trustee) can dip into the principal if needed for specified expenses (such as medical or education) or there can be liberal powers to spend principal (such as for general well-being). These concerns should be discussed in detail with your financial planner and the lawyer preparing the documents.

For your children. Suppose your grown child inherits your assets, holds them jointly with his or her spouse, and then divorces. After a marriage is over, it's over. And most don't want the "ex" to benefit any more than necessary. So it would be particularly distressing to know that family money had gone to someone outside the family if it could have been prevented.

Louise and Byron had been married 33 years; had three grown children, two of whom were married. Louise inherited over $1 million from her parents. The daughter, Susan, received $50,000 when her grandparents died. The money was used to purchase a home for her and her new husband. Three years later they divorced. You guessed it: He got one-half of the equity because all assets were divided equally. Louise was angry and heartbroken. Louise wanted to make sure that upon her death any money passing to her children would somehow be protected and kept in the primary family.

There are several complex solutions that involve family limited partnerships or family corporations. These solutions must be thoroughly investigated with competent legal help. Simpler solutions involve stipulating that your assets be disbursed to the grown child at even more mature ages, thereby increasing the likelihood that the money will stay in your linear family.

In still another solution, an irrevocable trust can be established, giving the income to the surviving spouse, but requiring the disbursement of principal to the children only when they reach mature ages; say, one third at age 35, one third at age 45, and the final third at age 55. While difficult to enforce, unless you name a corporate trustee, which is normally not a good idea, the trust can stipulate that your assets remain in your linear family. If you don't name a corporate trustee, be sure to name a very responsible child or name two to be cotrustees.

The bottom line is: After you are gone, the trustee can do anything he or she wishes. If you name your child as trustee and beneficiary, there is a greater possibility of your wishes being ignored. As always, there are disadvantages to naming lated party to serve as trustee. Generally, trustees are the costs can range from 1 percent to 4 percent per year of the assets in the trust.

Tough as it is, talk about it. No one wants children to lose sibling relationships fighting over assets. So, however you decide to structure the disbursement of your assets, make it a priority to discuss it with your children. Most problems occur when parents fail to clarify their motivations behind their decisions. Money is a highly charged symbol in the parent-child relationship, representing reward, affection, approval, and love, and because this is true, children need to know their parents' intentions and the reasoning behind them. Problems arise when children's expectations about their inheritances do not match reality. Families are sometimes torn apart by resentment, anger, disappointment, and confusion over perceived inequities in the distribution of their parents' money.

Parents are leaving their offspring not just a financial legacy in their wills, but also "an emotional one," Loren H. Plotkin, a partner in a Manhattan law firm, told the *New York Times.* "Your will is your last word to your family. You can't apologize afterward. You can't take it back."

WEALTHBUILDING STRATEGIES FOR THE 50s

If You Are Fortunate Enough to Still Be Working

- **Doggedly invest at least 15 percent of your income into your 401(k) plan.** If you are playing catch-up, invest 20 percent to 50 percent of your income. The exact amount will have to be determined by analyzing how much you already have invested and how much you still need to accumulate to retire by your target date. The Retirement Income Calculator in Appendix C will take you through the steps to tell you the exact amount you need to invest between now and your target retirement date, taking into account what you already have set aside.

- **Position at least 50 percent of your investments in growth and 50 percent into growth-and-income mutual funds.** If you are comfortable with fluctuation in your portfolio, you can invest up to 75 percent in either the growth or growth and income category. (See "Evaluating Risk Tolerance" in Chapter 2.)

    Since we are experiencing positive stock market performance that is unprecedented in our country's history, and since we all know there will be a time when the performance will be negative, it is important to know the mutual fund family you select can weather the storm. So look for performances that date back to the 1973–74 bear markets. Look for funds that are managed through a team approach or through a strictly enforced system of decision-making whose performance dates back to these years. Satisfy yourself that if the worst years should recur in the future, you are comfortable enough with your selected management system to be able to ride out the storm.

If You Are No Longer Working— and Now Withdrawing from Your Nest Egg

- **Position your investments for balance.** Allocate your assets 50 percent to 60 percent into dividend-paying stock mutual funds, and the balance into bond mutual funds. Often you can find funds whose managers manage the balance between stocks and bonds for you. If you decide to use that approach, select no fewer than two and no more than three balanced mutual funds to provide the income and growth. Use the same criteria as discussed in the item immediately preceding for selecting balanced or growth and income funds.
- **Drop the expensive term insurance you possibly carried while you were living off your earned income and needed to be sure your dependents could survive without you.** As you saw through the years, term insurance was an inexpensive way to cover your insurance needs. (Remember, it carried no cash value. See Appendix E for a discussion of

types of life insurance.) But as you have bee
cost of your term insurance has been rising.
toward 60, the costs will become highe

As you get closer and closer to retiren...., ,
need less insurance to provide income for those who depend on you. Think of it this way: If during retirement
your sources of income can support you and your spouse,
certainly the income will support your spouse only. There
is one caveat: If you will be on a pension and opt for the
survivor annuity payout, your spouse may only receive one-
half of your pension. If one-half won't be enough, you will
have to retain some of your life insurance to replace the
lost income.

- **Drop disability insurance.** Disability insurance provides
  income in the event you become unable to create monthly
  income through working. If your income is coming from
  investments as a retired person, you would not have a loss
  of income if you became disabled. Therefore, you no
  longer need this insurance.

Whether You Are Working or Not

- **Don't take chances with your money.** Don't loan money to
  friends or relatives unless you are prepared to kiss it good-
  bye.
- **Concentrate on being debt-free—except for a small mortgage, only if absolutely necessary.**
- **Tightly control spending.** There is never a good time to
  overspend without thought—certainly not now.
- **Reevaluate your need for life insurance.** As you near
  retirement, your need for life insurance will change. Life
  insurance is intended to provide a nest egg that will create
  income for your dependents. If you have a nest egg that is
  providing income for both you and your spouse, certainly
  one of you alone can live on that same income.

  If you have selected a pension that provides a survivor
  annuity for your spouse, the survivor annuity will usually
  be one-half of the amount you are receiving. You may want
  life insurance to cover the lost half of the annuity.

If you selected a pension that provides no annuity for your spouse, life insurance is a good way to make sure your spouse will be able to continue his or her lifestyle if he or she loses your pension. The money from the insurance can be invested and produce an income stream to make up for no pension income.

Life insurance is also needed to cover estate taxes when you and your spouse both die. Proper estate planning can protect up to $600,000 of assets each under current tax laws. But if your estate is more than $1.2 million, there may be a need for some life insurance on the last to die to cover estate taxes. This type of insurance is not terribly expensive and can be purchased as permanent insurance under the whole life, universal life, or variable universal life contract. See Appendix E for definitions of the types of insurance.

- **Many large corporations are now giving employees the opportunity to take a lump-sum buyout instead of a monthly pension.** If you have the choice, take the pension lump-sum buyout. The common misconception is that the company pension is safer. However, if you follow the simple rules discussed in Chapter 2 of this book entitled "Criteria for Selecting a Mutual Fund," or if you simply select indexed funds, you will probably have more income to spend than you would have had with the company pension. However, you must be able to take some risk. (See "Evaluating Risk Tolerance" in Chapter 2.) Remember, company pensions do not usually increase over time to keep up with inflation.

For the person who never touches the principal in the lump-sum rollover IRA and leaves the growth alone, money will likely be left over for heirs.

Furthermore, if your lump sum is rolled over to an IRA, you will only pay taxes on the income you withdraw. You pay no taxes as the money is rolled over. *The only danger is for the person who cannot keep his or her hands off the principal. That person would be better off with the pension.*

- **In your late 50s, begin considering long-term care insurance.** With longer life expectancies, it is essential to protect investment capital. To be covered by Medicaid for long-term care costs, all assets must be spent down except your home, a car, a prepaid funeral contract, and a $5,000 CD. Long-term insurance is especially helpful for a couple whose income is perfectly suited to support them living together, but would be strained if one of them had to go into an assisted living community or nursing home.

CHAPTER 7

RETIREMENT AND THE 60S: THE GOLDEN MILE

The majority of us are going to live a long, long time after we retire. In fact, we may live as retirees as many or more years than we lived as workers.

 **MAJOR FINANCIAL TASK**

To Live Long and Prosper

While you are young, you are creating. When you begin to age, you must focus on preserving.

A fact of life in today's world is that the majority of us are going to live a long, long time after we retire. In fact, we may live as retirees as many or more years than we lived as workers.

More and more people are living to be 100 these days, and more will live to that age and beyond as time goes on. According to an article entitled "Who Is Old?" in the January 21, 1996, issue of *Parade* magazine:

> There are more than 52,000 [people who are 100 or older] in America today, almost three times the number in 1980. They have become the fastest-growing age group not only in this country but also throughout the industrialized world. New studies show that Americans live longer after the age of 80 than other national groups. In fact, after the age of 85, the odds that you will die in the next year or two actually level off . . .

Ask Willard Scott, the NBC-TV weatherman, who started celebrating 100-year birthdays on the air in 1981. "I've got a problem," he says. Instead of the trickle of centenarian letters he received at first, he now gets 400 a week.

What has that got to do with money? Quite a lot. Suppose we begin work at age 20, continue working until age 60, retire, and live to be a century old. We will have worked 40 years, and we will live 40 years after we retire. If we live this long after our working years are over, we are going to need enough money to spend even as the cost of living goes up at the rate of inflation. Furthermore, most of us don't ever want to spend our principal; we want to have some left over for our heirs or charitable interests.

As with every decade so far, emotions are intertwined with our financial decisions. In the 60s decade, our emotional concerns are largely focused on being vibrant mentally. And we need challenges to keep our long lives vital to the end. Finally, we are going to need to be as healthy as possible so that the retirement years we have earned can be good ones. Life in our times places a different burden on us from that our parents and grandparents experienced.

In the 60s decade, those who are healthy can begin doing the things during retirement we have always dreamed of doing. Health and money become the two top priorities. Without either, life loses its fervor. We look at health on two fronts—physical and emotional. In many communities, life enrichment centers offer programs to address both aspects. And good financial planners I know are busier than ever educating retirees on ways to manage their money conservatively while still providing growth for the years beyond. If not purchased during the 50s, the 60s decade usually sees a concern for purchasing long-term care insurance. The successful 60-year-old is financially independent and wants to stay that way.

LIFE-STAGE RETIREMENT PLANNER FOR THE 60s

In the 60s, we are on the home stretch to retirement. It is time to begin thinking about positioning our investments to maintain enough growth so our investment capital will keep up with inflation while at the same time providing us with income. It is now more important than ever to plan how we will spend our time in retirement. If we are wise, we have been investing for retirement for many years and in our 60s, we will be wealthy—we can just check in on our plan and make sure everything is on target. If we have not stayed with our plan through our previous decades, we will have to seriously revise our retirement timetables. In either case, it is in our 60s, as in our 50s, that we look at all the aspects of retirement.

Until you actually retire, you should continue to contribute 15 percent of your income as a minimum to your retirement accounts. If you are playing catch-up, you will need to contribute 20 percent or more. With retirement only five to ten years away, you are finally running out of time to accumulate the wealth you will need. But since you are reading this book, you probably have your finances well managed and under control, and you will be fine.

As with those in their 50s, some in their 60s are playing catch-up. If they are, they are probably investing 50 percent of their income for retirement.

The question is always: Where should we place this money for the best possible return, safely? This question is especially important in your 60s, when you are well aware that you don't have time to lose your money and recreate your nest egg. Therefore, in your 60s, you might move more toward a conservative investment position.

But as with the 50-year-olds, you will want to maintain growth in your account. For growth, allocate 30 percent to 40 percent of your invested assets and do not be overly worried about volatility for that portion. You will want 60 percent to 70 percent of your capital invested for growth and income. The amount you place into each asset category will be determined by two things:

1. **How much income you need and the investment capital required to produce your income by withdrawing only 7 percent per year.** This portion of your capital should be placed into growth and income or balanced mutual funds that provide current income and protection from inflation.

2. **For the balance of the investment capital, you can seek growth.** Choose the relative risk for the growth portion of your portfolio based on how much you could afford to see your principal go down each year and still sleep. See "Evaluating Risk Tolerance" in Chapter 2 of this book to help you determine how much risk you can take. Then for the growth portion, put your money there and leave it alone. Remember, without volatility, you get no growth—and you'll need at least 3 percent per year growth over and above the income percentage you will be withdrawing for your nest egg to keep up with inflation and support you to age 100.

Invest according to this formula:

100 – your age = Percentage of invested assets for growth in mutual funds with a very small amount in real estate

Your age = Percentage of invested assets in growth and income mutual funds

Balance your mutual funds between domestic and global mutual funds by placing 70 percent into domestic and 30 percent into global mutual funds.

If you have excess investment capital at this stage of your life, you can probably tolerate greater risk in a portion of your investment portfolio. If so, you could move to a higher percentage of your assets placed into growth stock mutual funds. This is the balance you will want to have until you start withdrawing income from your accounts. When you begin withdrawing income, you will want to move 100 percent of your assets to growth and income or balanced.

Mutual Fund Investments for Ages 60 to 65

Objective:	Provide Income and Maintain Growth
Time Horizon:	5 to 15 Years
Risk:	Moderate
Investment Vehicle:	Mutual Funds

Investment Type	% Invested
Growth	40% to 60%
U.S. stocks	70%
Global stocks	30%
Growth and Income	60% to 40%
U.S. stocks	70%
Global stocks	30%

CONGRATULATIONS! YOU'RE A MILLIONAIRE!

The Model Investor Continues in the 60s

The model 60-year-old investor began investing at age 22 when he or she first got a job. As a reminder, the investor earned $1,000 for every year of age and invested 4 percent into retirement accounts from age 22 through age 29. By the end of the 29th year, the investor had accumulated $12,582 and it was invested earning 10 percent per year.

At 30, our model investor was earning $30,000 and continued to earn $1,000 for every year of age through their 30s. The investor, however, contributed 10 percent of earnings per year into retirement investment accounts. By the end of the 39th year, the investor had $91,758 invested for retirement.

At 40, our model investor was earning $40,000 per year and continued to earn $1,000 for every year of age through the 40s. The investor contributed 12 percent of their earnings per year into retirement investment accounts. By the end of the 49th year, the investor had accumulated $329,985 for retirement.

At 50, our model investor was earning $50,000 per year and continued to earn $1,000 for every year of age through the 50s.

FIGURE 7.1   Asset Allocation for the 60s

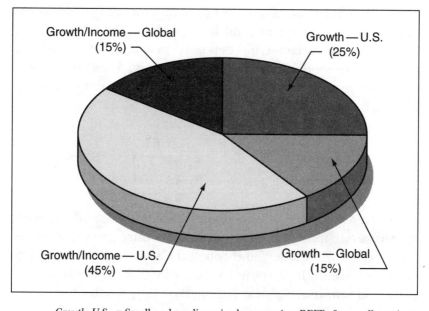

$Growth–U.S.$ = Small and medium-sized companies; REITs for small portions; expect fluctuation; minimum holding period: four years.

$Growth/Income–U.S.$ = Fortune 500 companies; dividend-paying stocks and bonds; expect modest fluctuation; minimum holding period: three years.

$Growth–Global$ = U.S. and non-U.S.; small and medium-sized companies; best positioned through mutual funds; expect modest fluctuation; minimum holding period: five years.

$Growth/Income–Global$ = U.S. and non-U.S.; Fortune 500–sized companies; dividend-paying stocks and bonds; best positioned through mutual funds; expect modest fluctuation; minimum holding period: four years.

The investor continued to contribute 15 percent of earnings per year into retirement investment accounts. By the end of the 59th year, the retirement nest was $997,176.

At 60, our model investor is earning $60,000 per year and will continue to earn $1,000 per year for every year of age through age 65. The investor will continue to contribute 15 percent of earnings per year into retirement investment accounts. From the beginning of the 60th year to the end of their 65th year, the retirement nest egg will look like this:

59th Year	65th Year
$997,176	$1,845,773

At 65, our model investor retired and placed all investment capital into balanced mutual funds. The investor instructed the mutual fund company to send him or her a monthly check for 7 percent of the account and deposit it to a designated checking account. The model investor began receiving $129,204 income and every year his or her income increased 3 percent to keep up with inflation:

	Age 65
Nest Egg	$1,845,773
Income	$ 129,204

Some won't need all the income shown above and will want to leave some money in their account for pure growth. The following chart will guide you through the steps to determine how much to leave in the account earmarked primarily to provide income and how much to leave earmarked for growth only.

How to Divide your Capital between Income and Growth

Determine how much before-tax income you will need in retirement:	$ 100,000
Divide that amount by 7 percent:	÷ .07
This equals the retirement capital you need invested at a total return of 10 percent to produce 7 percent income and still give you modest 3% growth:	$1,428,571

If you are our model investor, you will place $1,428,571 of your nest egg into assets that will produce 7 percent income for you first and still give you 3 percent growth. The balance of your capital, $417,202, will be placed into assets that provide growth. It is from this account that you will secure the money to buy new cars, take vacations, and pay for the extras of life.

So it is highly desirable to have enough capital to split into two accounts: one for growth and income and one for growth only.

TODAY, BEING HEALTHY, WEALTHY, AND WISE TAKES ON ADDED MEANING

The Need to Stay Healthy: or, "You Only Have to Floss the Teeth You Want to Keep."

Several years ago I went to see my dental hygienist, and she asked me a question while she worked: "How often do you floss?"

With my mouth full of various and sundry paraphernalia, plus her hands, I mumbled an answer: "When I get around to it."

She went on: "Well," she said, "you only have to floss the teeth you want to keep."

From her personal soapbox, she went on: "Flossing was not so important for our ancestors, perhaps," she said, "because most people died before they lost their teeth. But times have changed. Today's movement toward preventive dentistry has occurred because we all are living longer. We don't want to have to replace our teeth with false teeth, so we have to impose upon ourselves a discipline our grandparents may never have considered."

My wheels began to turn. There is a sermon in that! What is true for our teeth is true for all aspects of our health. We must keep our bodies fit. We must keep our minds alert. And beyond that, we must be fiscally healthy, as well.

It is true that we must take care of our bodies if we are to live long healthy lives. It is also worth noting that if we are to be healthy, we need money to pay for medical care and to buy the extras in life that contribute to good health. For example, it costs money to buy a water filter or bottled water; an air purifier; organically grown fresh fruits and vegetables; or vitamin supplements. These are the extras in life that in the future may not be extras as much as necessities. And they cost money. Remember the old saying: We are what we eat.

But if you aren't into the bottled water, organically grown foods, or air purifiers, at least be sure you remember the food groups you were taught in high school and eat plenty of fresh fruits, green, leafy vegetables, legumes, and other fiber foods and go easy on refined sugar and meats.

While it takes money to eat the right way, what good is all the money in the world if you aren't here to enjoy it?

Being healthy, wealthy, and wise must all go hand in hand for without one, the others are meaningless.

The Need to Live Wisely: The Importance of Emotional Health

In a similar way, we must be careful to develop a wide range of interests so that the retirement years will be enjoyable ones. This aspect of our lives has to do with emotional health. In a lovely North Carolina mountain community, the Life Enrichment Center conducts courses on a wide variety of topics ranging from flower arranging to "Building Self-Esteem"; from English literature to "Managing Your Money When You Are Alone." In Rock Hill, South Carolina, retired ministers (and my uncle and aunt) Harold and Betty Shirley created and conducted a most successful course entitled "Living Simply, Living Sanely" for retirees who want to learn.

All over the country, churches, colleges, and community groups recognize the need for this growing segment of our population to be stimulated mentally, thereby helping to maintain good emotional health. Here's what can happen if a person loses his or her purpose in life.

Miserable in Retirement: Ed Was Driving Betty Crazy

Ed, 68, and Betty, 64, were miserable—even though their finances were in very good order. Ed felt there was no purpose to his life. Three years before, he had retired from his 40-hour-a-week job.

This man, unable to find meaning in his life, was driving Betty up the wall. In the absence of the work he had always done, he became fixated on his health. Every time he developed the hiccups or a yawn, he went to the doctor, thinking he was sick. Each time he went, the doctor told him he was the "healthiest sick man he had ever seen." (Just as his wife always told him!) He refused to go see a counselor. He dropped deeper into depression, sleeping more and more. His golf game dropped and he became discouraged. He and Betty came to see me for a financial review. They shared their concern about Ed's emotional and mental state. They already had figured it out. Ed was feeling useless. His obsession with his health, I surmised, was his attempt to find a medical prescription to cover his unhappiness. We all agreed it wasn't his physical health. It was his mental health.

Furthermore, we agreed that he needed to find a project to give him a purpose. They talked with their children, who agreed to help. Within a few months, one of the children helped get his dad involved in a community project.

He became a different person. With a reason to get up in the mornings, he became pleasant around the house . . . like his "old self," Betty said. With something to think about besides himself, he no longer worries as much about his illnesses, imagined or real.

Analysis. People—and this is especially true of workaholic types—who pour all their energies into their careers make a fundamental mistake in doing so. We need other interests, interests that will enrich our lives both before and after retirement.

Sadly, Al, a vice president of personnel of a large company, had no interests outside the company. He worked until he was forced out at age 70. During his last seven years, he was a stumbling block to many in the company. He didn't want to retire, but he didn't want to take on any new projects either. Some people can work past 65 and be vital contributors, others can't. For good mental and emotional health, it is wise to develop interests outside work.

Happy in Retirement: Alma and A.D.—Reemployed Retiree

Some people who retire still want to continue to work, but in a different field. It could be a completely new field or one they had given up in their early years. Some set up their own small businesses. Some work part-time for others so they earn a little income and come in contact with people on a regular basis. All of this is tied to emotional health. It is necessary to pursue other interests such as another career, charitable endeavors, volunteering, hobbies, or classes in order to maintain a healthy outlook on life.

My father, A.D. Shirley, retired at age 65 after 40 years as a rural letter carrier and 20 years in the Army Reserves. (My mother never worked outside the home. When they were married, so the story goes, my mother told him: "You make the living; I'll make the living worthwhile!" And so they did!) When he retired, he was a young 65-year-old and wanted to keep doing something.

A friend who owned an engineering and roadway construction firm hired him to do quality control inspections of work they had under contract. At 65, my dad learned the standards that needed to be maintained for construction of airport runways and superhighways. He created systems for the orderly checking of work in progress and fell in love with his second career.

He worked for eight years until he was appointed to the city planning commission which reviewed zoning applications for new project construction in my hometown of Meridian, Mississippi. He served two three-year terms and stepped down at age 79.

In 1997, still vital and active at 81, my dad and my mom, 74, maintain a mailing list of friends and relatives from over the years. They create uplifting messages, have them printed on postcards they embellish with pictures and motivational stickers, and mail to those on their list. They spend hours visiting the sick or their friends who live alone. Regularly, they attend church and military reserve association monthly meetings, and participate in water aerobics and senior citizen activities. They enjoy taking and sharing pictures and get a thrill out of creating "care packages" for the children, grandchildren, and friends. Neither of my parents has aged in mind or spirit. They are the most emotionally healthy people I have ever known. I'm sure there are others out there just like them, but I don't know many. What an inspiration to all of us who are younger!

If you are among those approaching retirement with dread or if you are already unhappy with retirement, think about developing other interests. Work at it as you would a full-time job. Think about others. Help meet their needs and you will be surprised how your needs will be met in the process.

RULE OF THUMB

To remain viable and vibrant members of our world, we need continuing challenges. We must work to create those challenges. In the retirement years, a focus on others will help keep our lives in perspective.

The Importance of Being Wealthy—and Staying Wealthy

If we have been careful spenders and investors throughout our working lives, we are way ahead in retirement; but financial decisions don't simply end when we retire.

Today, the rules are different from those that governed investing strategies of our grandparents or parents. Back then, people worked until 65 and lived to 75 or 80. Today, we are working until 65, but are living to 90 or 100. Look at how your cost of living would go up if you lived 30 years beyond age 65 versus living 15 years beyond age 65.

The Problem: Our Cost of Living Increases

To Maintain This Cost of Living	Increased by 3%/Year Inflation You Will Need	
	In 15 Years:	In 30 Years:
$25,000	$39,000/Year	$ 60,000/Year
$30,000	$47,000/Year	$ 73,000/Year
$40,000	$62,000/Year	$ 97,000/Year
$50,000	$78,000/Year	$121,000/Year

Suppose you insisted on investing only in the safest high-grade bonds where your income would be fixed and your principal supposedly "safe." If your cost of living was $25,000 per year when you retired and you lived 15 years, you actually could afford to spend some of your principal as your income needs went up, and still not run out of money. (For this discussion, we ignore Social Security and assume you have no pension.) We have assumed you are providing your own income stream from your personally invested nest egg of about $350,000. Your nest egg will not increase at all if invested in these bonds.

High-grade bond index performance. For illustration purposes, suppose you could have invested your nest egg of $350,000 in Salomon Brothers High-Grade Bond Index Fund in 1973, the beginning of the two worst consecutive years our markets have known since 1931. You began to withdraw 7 percent ($24,500/year) and you took a cost of living raise each year of 3 percent. Using the actual performance of that index from 1973 forward, by 1988 (15 years from when you began) you would have spent $493,000 and your principal balance remaining would be $190,000.

As your income needs went up with inflation, you naturally would have begun spending your principal. And you could—until 1996. If you had still been living at the end of 1995, you would have spent $790,000, but your principal would be completely gone. In other words, your money would have lasted 23 years. So if you started taking income at age 65 and died at age 88, you would have died when your money ran out. But if you lived beyond 88, you would be out of money.

Where are you going to get the increased income you will need as the cost of living goes up with inflation? At age 88, I doubt you will want to go back to work.

The rules must change from the very beginning. You cannot afford the luxury of a stable portfolio of fixed income, tax-free or not, as your parents and grandparents may have. You will have to take some risk and you will have to configure a portfolio with some sound stocks (preferably inside a conservatively managed mutual fund) to provide growth.

Performance of indexed stock, managed stock, and balanced funds. Take a look at the performance of our $350,000 nest egg invested in an index fund versus a managed mutual fund of some of the same large 500 companies. Contrast those performances with a balanced fund containing large company stocks and high-grade bonds as well.

Comparing Indexed, Managed Stock, and Balanced Funds That All Provide Increasing Income for Retirement

The following assumes $350,000 is invested, and 7 percent is withdrawn systematically each year and increased by 3 percent each year. It also assumes we invested the money in January of 1973. We want to see how long the money would have lasted.

Years	Income Spent	Indexed Stock Total	Managed Stock Total*	Balanced Stock and Bond Total†
10	$280,865	$165,903	$261,222	$410,709
15	$455,673	$ 83,659	$302,607	$541,323
20	$658,324	$ 0	$376,407	$814,843

*The managed stock fund totals are drawn from averaging hypothetical information from three growth and income stock mutual funds: Investment Company of America, AIM Weingarten Fund, and the George Putnam Fund of Boston. All numbers shown are net of all sales loads and annual fees.

†The balanced stock and bond mutual fund totals are drawn from averaging hypothetical information from three funds containing a balance of stocks and bonds: Income Fund of America, AIM Charter Fund, and Putnam Growth and Income Fund. All numbers shown are net of all sales loads and annual fees.

How did the funds perform? Let's recap:

- **Fixed income investments as measured by the highest quality bond index available** would have lasted through bad times and good times—for 22 years through 1995 and be completely gone. This would certainly have been adequate if the person only lived 15 or 20 years. However, with longer life expectancies pushing us out 30 years, this investment choice would not have been adequate.
- **Indexed stock funds** under the same scrutiny would have lasted through bad as well as good times—for 17 years through 1990 and be completely gone.
- **Managed stock mutual funds** (mutual funds whose management system "manages" the stocks within the funds) using the exact same parameters would have lasted through bad times and good times—for 23 years through 1996—and then have almost $400,000 left in the account for your beneficiaries.

- **Balanced stock and bond mutual fund** (whose management system manages a portfolio of roughly half bonds and half stocks) using the same parameters would have lasted through 1996 as well—and have over $800,000 left in the account for beneficiaries.

After learning how the various investment strategies have worked over the years—including the bad years of 1973 and 1974, many people are moving toward a balance between bonds and stocks for producing a growing stream of income with principal growth. This approach will allow your retirement money to grow and to provide increasing income for as long as you live—no matter the number of years.

Joe and Donna Were Having to Cut Back

Joe and Donna, ages 69 and 64, respectively, came to see me about their retirement income. They had been living 15 years off fixed, tax-free income created by trust funds they had inherited, as well as some money of their own. One day they found their bank trust department–managed portfolio had begun to get smaller each year for the past three years. Unknowingly, they had begun to do the unthinkable: spend their principal.

Fifteen years ago, they had put the money in tax-free bonds because they did not want to pay taxes and because that's what their fathers had done when they were alive. At that time, they were receiving $125,000 yearly in income. In 1990, when they came to see me, they were receiving the same amount, but it was not going nearly as far as it had 15 years earlier. That was because inflation had caused their cost of living to go up to about $190,000 per year. But they were cutting back and holding down their costs to about $150,000 year.

"We used to take four golf trips per year," they said. "Now we only can go one time. We used to go to the Virgin Islands twice per year. Now we can go only once."

Yet they were still in good health, and they wanted to continue going and doing. Their parents had lived into their 90s and it was likely they might, too. They had some major changes to make in the way their money was allocated among asset classes.

And they had some major revisions in thinking to do. The
no longer afford the luxury of paying no taxes. They wou
to convert to taxable income and pay taxes—a thought they hated
but finally understood.

Analysis and results. Fifteen years ago, they began with a
nest egg of $3 million. They easily lived on $125,000 per year and
had $25,000 per year to reinvest. Seven years later, they could no
longer reinvest anything and by the time they came to see me,
their principal had dwindled to $2.8 million. They were begin-
ning to get worried. They had two goals:

1. To have enough income to support their lifestyles as the
   costs went up
2. To leave the principal they had inherited intact for their
   children

We reconfigured the portfolio leaving $1.3 million (about 46
percent) in tax-free bonds and placing the other $1.5 million into
mutual funds balanced between about 65 percent in conservatively managed stocks and 35 percent in bonds of large companies. Their tax planning looked like this:

Reconfiguring to Create Growth Means Paying Taxes

Income	Before	After
Tax-free income	$125,000	$ 65,000
Taxable income	10,000	122,000
Social Security	18,000	18,000
Total income	$153,000	$205,000
Income subject to tax	$ 28,000	$140,000
Deductions		
State income taxes	$ 1,080	$ 7,800
Real estate taxes	3,400	3,400
Charitable contributions	10,000	10,000
Total deductions	$ 14,480	$ 21,200
Taxable Income	**$ 13,520**	**$118,800**
Taxes		
State income taxes	$ 1,080	$ 7,800
Federal income taxes	0	28,683
Total Income Taxes	**$ 1,080**	**$ 36,483**

Now let's look at available spendable income before and after these changes were made:

Income	Before	After
Gross income	$153,000	$205,000
Less taxes	(1,080)	(36,482)
Income Left to Spend	**$151,920**	**$168,518**

After reconfiguring their portfolio, Joe and Donna had more income left to spend even though they paid more in taxes, as you can see from the chart. But that's not all they had.

With $1.5 million of their assets positioned to grow at an estimated rate of 2 percent to 4 percent per year net after taxes and net after the income they are spending, they will not be in danger of spending their principal. As a matter of fact, if history is any indication of what they might expect, their principal will probably grow. So I asked them: Would you rather

1. Pay no taxes and spend $150,000 per year, with no pay raise and no growth on your principal;

   or

2. Pay about $37,000 in taxes and have about $165,000 per year to spend—with a 3 percent pay raise every year and growth on your principal but have to endure periods when your principal will be down?

They chose the second alternative. Now what are the disadvantages of this plan?

The disadvantage of using a balanced fund is that in a year during which both stocks and bonds are down, their principal balance would also go down.

If, in 1973, Joe's and Donna's $1.5 million had been invested in the same balanced fund illustrated earlier, their principal would have gone down 30 percent—that is, to $1 million at its lowest—and it would have taken the next eight years to have grown back to the original principal amount.

This investment strategy would only be appropriate for the person who fully understands and can tolerate potential fluctuations in their principal. It requires patience!

By contrast, invested in high-grade bonds, the principal would have slowly decreased each year such that in the eighth year the principal would be down 30 percent, never to go up again.

These illustrations are based only on past performance—not predictions of the future. We all know "past performance is no guarantee of future results." Each investor must decide whether he or she can live with the risk. Furthermore, one must realize that we have illustrated what we think to be the worst time to have invested and begun an income stream.

In 1997, we are becoming spoiled with consistent double-digit returns in the unmanaged stock market indices as well as mutual funds. But it is important to prepare for the worst. Here's one person's opinion of what lies ahead.

THE GREAT BOOM AHEAD (AND THE BUST BEYOND)

In his book, *The Great Boom Ahead,* Harry Dent (New York: Hyperion), says: "There will most emphatically not be a Great Depression of the 1990s. The truth: We are on the verge of the greatest boom in history!"

Dent claims that "nothing matters as much as the Spending Wave" created by the number of people in the 50-year age bracket. The larger the generation between ages 46 to 65, the greater the effect of that spending peak on stock market performance.

He says: "Think about the effect of the baby boom generation. This largest generation of births in our history is far from its peak in earnings and spending. As it approaches this peak, it will have a dramatic impact on the economy, creating the greatest boom in our history." Thus, with baby boomers turning 50 in larger and larger numbers each year beginning in 1996, he predicts a strong stock market response.

Dent says to look for the stock market to continue surging up until around 2008 to 2009, when it will begin a steady decline until around 2015, at which time the baby boomers will be approaching 70.

That time, about ten years from now, will be the most dangerous time to have money invested in the unmanaged index. Think about how old you will be ten years from now. At that time will you want to be worrying about your money daily? If so, stay in index funds and actively move them when the indicators suggest, about ten years out.

The Great Boom Ahead and You

If you don't think you will want to be worrying about your money in ten years, you should seriously consider hiring a mutual fund management system now to make decisions for you. The real value of a management system will be when the overall market goes down—not when everything is trending up. That's what accounts for the excellent manner in which recovery from the bad years of 1973–1974 occurred with the managed strategies when compared with the unmanaged ones.

We are always looking for ways to achieve moderate risk and attempt to make the results come out in our favor. To give yourself the *hope* of future results somewhat like the past, look at our section in Chapter 2, "Criteria to Help You Select a Mutual Fund." Finally, this concern for the future alone should give you reason to find a good, trustworthy financial professional to help you.

Children and Professionals Beware!

Many people in their 60s and beyond have a hard time comprehending how inflation will ultimately affect their cost of living and consequently their income needs. It is often only after their income needs have increased and their incomes have not that they fully comprehend. Therefore, children of parents in their 60s and professionals working with people in this age group need to be aware of this shortfall so they can cooperate to help explain the problem and create workable solutions.

Another blind spot for many in these age groups is that of seeing the "big picture." Periodically, upon receiving his annual investment performance report, Richard, 66 years of age, calls me, for example, and reminds me that he has such-and-such an amount of money—quoting the amount he invested ten years ago. I usually have to remind him that he now has significantly more money due to the growth of his account. He seems to have trouble thinking that the growth in his account belongs to him, too.

Like others his age, he was brought up in the days when retired people followed two simple financial rules: invest the money at a fixed rate and spend the interest only—never touch the principal. There was never any growth of the principal. So the only thought was about the original principal amount. As we have seen through the example outlined above, those rules are inadequate for today and the future.

Now it is no longer enough to avoid spending the principal. Not only must you not spend the principal—you must also not spend the first 3 percent of the earnings. You must leave 3 percent per year inside your account for growth to make sure your principal, and thus your income, will grow to keep up with inflation. Examining the following chart will show you that a flat percentage on a growing principal amount will create an increase in the real dollars available to spend. That's what we want!

Principal Growth Produces Income Growth

Year	Nest Egg	%	Growth $	%	Income $
1	$100,000	3	$3,000	7	$7,000
2	103,000	3	$3,090	7	$7,210
3	106,090	3	$3,182	7	$7,426
4	109,272	3	$3,278	7	$7,649
5	112,550	3	$3,376	7	$7,878

And so on . . .

HANDLING THE UNEXPECTED IN RETIREMENT

Still, no matter how carefully you invest, you cannot cover every contingency, because life is full of surprises. On the one hand, retired people need to live within the means they have accumulated for themselves. On the other hand, emergencies they had not planned for may arise. Let's look at an example.

Bruce and Janie—Pushing the Envelope

Bruce, 66 years of age, came to me wanting to increase his $2,400-a-month income from investments to $3,000 a month. He had retired at 62, at which time he had rolled over a $300,000 IRA that was earning a 12 percent per year total return. He had already had one heart attack and bypass surgery.

His goal was to withdraw 10 percent of the total income and leave the additional 2 percent in the fund to grow and take care of inflation. He especially wanted to protect his principal for his wife, Janie, in the event he died before she did.

Unexpected expenses were making it difficult for Bruce and Janie to live on this income. Once they even had to take $10,000 from the principal. This expenditure of extra money was due not to their fiscal irresponsibility, but to expenses they had not counted on. Janie had been in an automobile accident, which made the purchase of another car a necessity. They also helped pay the hospital costs associated with their daughter's health problems that were not covered by health insurance.

Analysis and results. If he had increased his income by an additional $600 a month, it would have represented a 25 percent increase to $36,000 per year. To create $36,000 per year, we would have to withdraw 12.4 percent, which would leave no growth in the account and over the years, they would have to begin spending principal. There had to be another way. Either they needed to reduce their cost of living or they had to create additional income.

They hadn't planned to take Janie's Social Security income until her age 65, but after our discussion, they decided to begin drawing her Social Security right away. She had just turned 62. Further, he decided to take a part-time job at Wal-Mart to earn the extra money they needed. With her Social Security income of $370 a month and his extra part-time income of $400 a month from Wal-Mart, they found the extra $600 a month. And now their account can continue to grow to take them into the future.

A FOOTNOTE FOR THE WISE: BEWARE OF THE SIREN CALL OF ROMANCE

People in their 60s are not immune to the financial uncertainties of life, nor are they immune to the call of romance. The particular caution for 60-year-and-olders is warranted because, if widowed, the surviving spouse may have more money than a younger person. This is due largely to having had longer for the money to accumulate. Also, the survivor may have been the beneficiary of some life insurance. And the inherited money will be all that person will ever have with little or no time to replace it if it is lost.

All these complications as well as natural loneliness of living alone could put the survivor in a vulnerable position with regard to suitors. This is not to say that as one ages he or she must be so wary that they must live a life alone, but one must be careful that a romantic encounter is based on sincere affection for the person, not for the person's money. Of course, this caution is appropriate for any person, at any age.

Marie and Her Dad's Money

Marie, a widow in her 60s, inherited almost a million dollars from her father. In the eyes of the unscrupulous, Marie might be a very attractive marriage prospect for that reason alone. Marie had been divorced for years when she inherited her father's money. For all those years, she had barely survived on an alimony settlement from a previous marriage and occasional unexpected checks from her father. She had been lonely for many years. In a short time after her father died, she met Sam, fell in love, and married him.

The problem was that Sam had no money of his own and he began to suggest ways for Marie to spend hers. Marie unwittingly let him influence her. Sam and Marie decided they needed a new house.

She had always wanted a new house, closer to where her daughter lived. The house Sam planned and built, however, ended up costing twice as much as Marie and I had planned as a prudent decision. She had to withdraw from the principal of her inheritance to cover the extra cost of the house.

Sam, supposedly feeling bad about causing her to spend her principal, decided to start his own business so he could make some money and pay her for his share of the house and replenish some of her principal.

Of course, he needed money to start the business, and you guessed it—Marie financed it. In one year, Marie built a $300,000 house and set Sam up in business to the tune of $100,000. New furniture, a mobile home for her daughter, a few extras, and another $100,000 was gone.

Analysis and results.   In all, about $500,000 of Marie's principal is gone. Marie is receiving $35,000 per year income from the remaining principal to support their cost of living. If Marie cannot learn to say no to Sam, she will be in serious financial trouble. I'm nervous about the relationship—because Marie is reluctant for me to meet Sam and she seems unable to say no to him. She is treading on the edge now, taking the maximum amount that is prudent from her account. As long as she doesn't spend any more principal, she will be all right. Marie promises me she won't take any more principal. Let's see if she can stick with it. This story is unfinished. We'll pray for a happy ending.

Words about Romance and Money

- **Don't tell a potential suitor anything about your assets or income.** Make sure you each love the other irrespective of money. Remember the marriage vows aren't multiple choice when the preacher asks you to take the other for better or worse. If the person has no money, red flags should go up in your head and heart. Make sure you can handle the worst *before* you marry.

- **Don't hesitate to check out the person.** If your suitor shows signs of having no money (e.g., renting, always asking you to pay for meals out or activities), red flags should shoot up. If, on the other hand, the person is serious and can be trusted, he or she won't mind your checking. Learn about people who have known your suitor for years and inquire as to his or her character and past relationships. If you have access to a credit checking service, don't hesitate to do a credit check for possible bankruptcies or late payments. Permission from the person is always advisable. Then discuss your findings. If your suitor acts defensive, dump him or her.

- **If the relationship looks as though marriage is in the offing, agree ahead of time to a prenuptial agreement.** "But," you ask, "What about sharing and full commitment?" Here's the logic: If you are in your 60s and have accumulated some assets (whether through your own efforts or through an inheritance) there probably have been people along the way who provided you emotional support as you built your net worth. You likely have known those people longer than the person you are considering as a marriage partner. It is not unreasonable to want those who have supported you for years to be the recipients of your assets should something happen to you. You can always set up a provision in your will for your marriage partner after you have been married for a number of years.

  Further, agree to keep separate checking accounts and a strict accounting of what each funds for the other, unless there is a good balance of assets and income between the two of you. If there is a good balance, it still isn't a bad idea, until you live together a while and learn each other's money management habits. The last thing you need at this stage is for someone else's laxness about bill-paying to affect your credit rating or your financial stability.

- **Don't move too quickly.** Yes, you're in your 60s; but you still have time to make sure this won't be a mistake. As with many decisions, there's no substitute for time.

SOME NUTS AND BOLTS ABOUT RETIREMENT INCOME

Your Nest Egg and Inflation

When you retire, you will either have a pension or you will have a nest egg from which you will draw income to support your standard of living. If you have a pension, you will be lucky if your pension income increases with inflation. If that is your only source of income, you must manage your expenses closely in order to live within your income.

If you will have a nest egg due to the rollover of a 40l(k), profit-sharing, pension, IRA, or other tax-qualified plan, you will be able to decide how to invest the money so as to create monthly income withdrawals.

However, if you spend all the income your nest egg earns every year, and if inflation continues to increase as it has every year since 1955, you will not have enough money to do the things you've become accustomed to doing as the years move on and the cost of everything goes up—as it inevitably does.

For example, if in 1974 you had invested $1 in January in a savings account earning 8 percent, you would have earned 8 cents, enough money to buy a postage stamp to send a Christmas card in December. However, your invested dollar in January 1996 would have had to earn 32 percent (32 cents) if you expected to send a Christmas card in December of 1996!

Stamps aren't the only things that go up in price. As prices increase, so does your income need. To stay up with the increasing cost of living over the years, you will need more dollars to spend. To receive more income, you will need more dollars in your nest egg. Those increased nest egg dollars will produce the increased income you will need to pay the increased prices of everything you will want to buy! The percentage withdrawal can remain the same as long as the nest egg grows.

So for lifelong retirement planning that hopefully will be needed for 40 years of successful retirement living, you must make sure your nest egg is invested at least enough to cover inflation (that is, 3 to 4 percent per year) *plus* whatever amount you need to spend.

Suppose you have a $500,000 nest egg and spend $35,000 the first year you are retired. The second year, to keep up with a 3 percent inflation rate, you will need to spend $36,050 to maintain the same standard of living. That means your nest egg will have had to grow to $515,000 to produce $36,050 at a 7 percent spending rate.

Since no one wants to outlive their money, we must be very careful to avoid touching the principal or the first 3 to 4 percent of growth.

Rule of Thumb

There is never a time when you can begin to spend your principal unless you know the exact day you will die.

If Your Income Isn't Enough

Ideally, the decision to retire is yours to make. Since we don't live in an ideal world, the decision to retire is not always yours to make. Sometimes when your company downsizes you, it may be a few years ahead of your schedule.

Regardless of whether the decision is yours or not, you absolutely must know how much money you need to support your standard of living. This is a painful but necessary chore. You must go through your canceled checks and credit card statements and place into categories where you spent your money in the most recent calendar year. Don't guess. Work only from exacts. (To help you do this, I've included a "Monthly Household and Family Expense Worksheet" in Appendix A.)

When you know for sure where your money went last year, you can begin to estimate what expenditures will change during your retirement years. The closer this exercise is to the date of your retirement, the closer your current figures and your retirement figures will be to each other.

Add together your income from all sources and match it with the dollars you need to support your retirement cost of living. For example:

Cost of living needed (before tax)	$35,000 per year
Pension	–12,000
Nest egg income	–14,000
Shortfall	**$ 9,000 per year**

Making Up the Income Shortfall

If you retire before you can begin receiving Social Security income. You will need to work to make up the shortfall. If you are resourceful and have the inclination, perhaps a small business would be appropriate—or a part-time job somewhere. This is the time of your life to work at something you want to do, since your earned income requirements are not very great.

If you retire after you can receive Social Security benefits. Make up the shortfall with Social Security income. If you are still working part-time or if your spouse is working, postpone receiving Social Security benefits until neither of you is working. Otherwise, take your benefits as soon as possible. Remember, if you want to, you can still work and not lose your Social Security benefits if your income is kept below a certain level. Employees who are age 65—but not yet 70—can earn $13,500 in 1997 before their Social Security benefits are reduced $1 for every $3 in earnings over the limit. There is no limit for people over 70 and over.

A new law signed March 29, 1996, gradually raises the limit through 2002 as follows:

1998	$14,500
1999	15,500
2000	17,000
2001	25,000
2002	30,000

After 2002, the annual exempt amount will be indexed to growth in average wages.

Income from investments, interest, pensions, annuities, capital gains, and other government benefits don't apply to the annual earnings limit. (This information is based on prevailing tax laws in 1997.)

Your Taxes after Retirement

Ideally your standard of living will be the same after retirement as it was before retirement, but there is one little-anticipated after-retirement factor that stretches your money. Believe it or not, it comes courtesy of Uncle Sam. It's your reduced tax obligation!

Often people making $50,000 to $80,000 per year before they retire are surprised to learn that they can maintain their cost of living on a much lower income after retirement because their taxes will be much lower. Let's look at the case of Larry and Edna, who in 1995 earned a total of $65,550 and paid $13,228 in taxes (in the 28 percent federal tax bracket). When they retired in 1996, they received an income of $46,550 and paid $4,114 (in the 15 percent federal tax bracket). Even with a decrease of almost $20,000 per year in income, Larry and Edna were surprised to see their standard of living could remain the same.

Tax Planning for before and after Retirement

Preretirement		Postretirement	
Salary (Larry)	$45,000	Pension	$20,000
Salary (Edna)	20,000	Salary (Edna)	0
		Social Security	15,000
		(Only $3,500 taxable)	
15% 401(k)	(9,750)	Nest Egg Income	11,000
Interest/Dividends	550		550
Adjusted gross	55,800		35,050
Exemptions	(5,100)		(5,100)
Item deductions	(10,000)		(8,600)
Taxable Income	**$40,700**		**$21,350**
Federal Tax	6,183		3,203
State Tax	2,072		911
FICA	4,973		0
Total Taxes	**$13,228**		**$ 4,114**

Analysis and result.   Larry and Edna are looking to retire and not change their standard of living. They wanted to know if that is possible. Based on the tax planning above, before retirement, their total income was $65,550. After retirement, their total income will be $46,550. They are currently spending $42,572 to support their cost of living (COL). Take a look:

Cost of Living Comparison

	Preretirement	Postretirement
Total income	$65,550	$46,550
Less 401(k)	(9,750)	0
Less taxes	(13,228)	(4,114)
To Support COL	**$42,572**	**$42,436**

Before retirement, it cost Larry and Edna $42,572 to support themselves. After retirement, when Larry is on a pension, drawing Social Security benefits, Edna is not working, and they are withdrawing $11,000 per year from their nest egg, they will have $42,436 available to spend. Uncle Sam's smaller bite after retirement actually helped them make their retirement decision.

HOME SALE TAX BENEFITS—ONCE IN A LIFETIME

Challenges as well as benefits come with aging. Don't overlook the one-time exclusion from capital gains taxes given for a person selling a home after age 55. Here are the rules under current tax laws: You get to exclude from capital gains taxes $125,000 ($62,500 each for a married couple filing separately) if

1. you sell your home at age 55 or later;
2. you have lived in your home three of the past five years; and
3. you have never invoked the privilege before.

Be careful in your planning if you are considering marriage after age 55.

Suppose a 58-year-old and 59-year-old are considering marriage. Neither has used the $125,000 exclusion in the past. Both own homes and plan to sell them and purchase a jointly owned one. It would be smarter for each to sell their respective homes before marrying, thus sheltering $250,000 from capital gains than for them to marry, then sell the homes and only shelter $125,000.

WEALTH-PRESERVING STRATEGIES FOR THE 60s

The decade of the 60s is the decade to begin fully enjoying the fruits of the investments you have put into place during the decades that went before. It is your time to live life to the very fullest in your most relaxed state. Play golf, work in your garden, travel, enjoy your grandchildren, go dancing, take classes, and spend all the income your investments earn (above the 3 percent you will keep in your accounts for growth). And, ideally, find a way to pass on the wisdom of your years.

Above all, exercise, eat healthy, and keep the cobwebs out of your brain by investing time in others, so you can move into the next decade with vitality and vibrance.

CHAPTER 8

RETIREMENT AND THE 70S: TOO BLESSED TO BE STRESSED OR DEPRESSED

Time waits for no one.

A long life is a mixed blessing.

MAJOR FINANCIAL TASK

Live *Well* and Prosper

The 70s

Many who turn 70 are depressed until they realize that the longer they live, the longer they're likely to live. So, I've noticed in the early to mid-70s, a relaxation with the aging process for the healthy 70-year-old. It is after reaching 70 that the person who was adamant in his or her 60s to have 100 percent of his or her assets in tax-free bonds comes waltzing in asking how to achieve portfolio growth. If they didn't in their 60s, these investors now want long-term care insurance and want to explore the options for independent living without the hassles of home ownership. In the 70s, attention turns to estate planning as never before. Once those pieces are in place, they are ready to go, see, and do until they can't.

The 80s and Beyond

For the healthy and active, these are peaceful and fun-filled years. By this time, you probably have figured out how to manage your money to provide for your needs and have some left over for the finer things in life. These are the years where the most financially successful people can give money to their children and grandchildren so they can see them enjoy it. While they may not be able to move as quickly as before, the most successful people in this age bracket play bridge, golf, do needlework, volunteer, dance, garden, take courses, and enjoy time with friends and family. The successful in this age bracket are fortunate enough to reap the rewards of many years of decisions that turned out right.

The 70s and beyond are called the golden years. Living well during these years isn't just about money. Living well during these years requires meeting life's challenges with grace and humor. As my Aunt Becky, 75, has said many times, paraphrasing—and adding to—Bette Davis's famous words, "Growing old isn't for sissies. I try to stay sassy without being brassy!"

A sense of humor will go a long way to helping you live well through these years. There is plenty of medical evidence that laughter is the best medicine. So even if you don't have anything in particular to laugh about, in the quiet of your own home, work up a good laugh and exercise your lungs and all those stomach muscles. Look at yourself in the mirror and you'll find that a smiling face looking back at you is more uplifting than the alternative.

The 70s and 80s are the years during which we enjoy recalling memories. These are the years during which you will want to put on paper your family heritage for the younger generations. It is also a good time to write down special stories about your experiences or family life. Those are treasures of your mind and soul and will bring inspiration to the generations coming after you. Leave a written memory book as part of your legacy.

"I'll have to forget some things so I'll have room to put more things up there! People who don't have many memories don't have this problem!"
    —Becky Shirley Glasser

LIFE-STAGE RETIREMENT PLANNER FOR THE 70s AND BEYOND

As we progress through the '70s and beyond, we are living examples that, with discipline toward staying with the plan, we will remain millionaires through our golden years and will have assets to leave our loved ones. We will be part of the small number of people who truly are financially independent. This is quite an accomplishment: Only one person in six who turns 65 in our country today achieves financial independence.

It is the time to continue leaving our investments positioned to maintain enough growth so our investment capital will keep up with inflation while at the same time providing us with income. So for your asset allocation, leave 100 percent invested in growth and income or balanced funds.

At this stage, don't worry about moving assets around; you can just check in on your plan periodically and make sure everything is on target. If you have not stayed with your plan through the previous decades, you will have to seriously revise your retirement budget. Perhaps you will have to look for affordable housing for seniors. In this case, you will have to examine your lifestyle and determine how to cut down some expenses.

Margaret, 73, came to see me recently. She wanted to invest some money in a balanced mutual fund. She was tired of getting such low interest in the bank. Her sources of income were a pension from her late husband's company and Social Security, and they were ample.

I told her that we could send her a check from her mutual fund, but she didn't want it. I told her she needed to spend some more money. She told me that she doesn't want to. She said, "Sometimes I go to the mall and look around for something to buy. When I see something, I am reminded that I will either have to dust it or insure it. I don't want to do either. So I go home without it. I'd rather help someone else—bring a smile to someone else's face."

So Margaret volunteers at the VA Hospital and the patients love her!

The Model Investor Continues in the 70s and Beyond

By age 69, our model investor is receiving $141,185 per year in income, and the principal remaining is $2,077,434. We continue this plan through the 70s and at age 79, the investor is receiving $189,741 in income annually and the nest egg is now worth $2,875,055. As you can see, the income continues to grow as the principal grows. This plan will work for the investor's lifetime as long as the overall investment return holds at 10 percent a year.

	Age 69	Age 79
Nest Egg	$2,077,434	$2,875,055
Income	$ 141,185	$ 189,741

YOUR INCOME IN YOUR 70s AND BEYOND

People who retire in their 60s are accustomed to adjusting their lifestyles to fit their incomes. By the time these people are in their 70s, they often are programmed to live as frugally as possible. People often feel better if they continue saving some money. This way of thinking is driven by the way they were reared and by the fear that they may outlive their income.

But with a portfolio balanced between growth and income investments, 70-year-olds can actually spend more and still have a nest egg that will grow (see Figure 8.1). This will perhaps relieve their fear of outliving their income.

Keep Up Your Guard

These are called the golden years. It is well documented that the 60s on are the years during which a person has the most money accumulated. You must be on guard to make sure you don't let anyone unscrupulous get their hands on your gold.

Unfortunately, we live in a financial jungle filled with predators. These crooks prey on older people. Often we read of a con artist who swindled a sweet older lady or man out of large sums of money. When you read about the incident, it may be obvious to you that it was a scam from the beginning. But when it is hap-

FIGURE 8.1   Asset Allocation for the 70s and Beyond

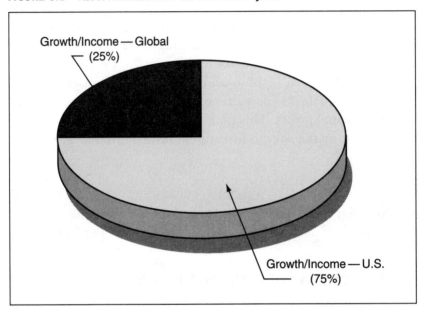

Growth/Income — Global
(25%)

Growth/Income — U.S.
(75%)

Growth/Income–U.S. = Fortune 500 companies; REITs for a small amount; dividend-paying stocks and bonds; expect modest fluctuation; minimum holding period: three years.

Growth/Income–Global = U.S. and non-U.S.; Fortune 500 companies; dividend-paying stocks and bonds; best positioned through mutual funds; expect modest fluctuation; minimum holding period: four years.

pening to you, it is sometimes difficult to detect. These scam artists often call and engage in friendly chatter. They may develop a relationship over several weeks or months before asking for any money. Scamsters love to single out senior citizens who too often are overly polite, too lonely, or too eager for financial help to run the other way. Only trust people you have known a long time or whom your trusted friends recommend to you. Never send money to a stranger for anything no matter how good it sounds.

For a more complete list of suggested ways to protect yourself, refer to our Chapter 2, "Investment Basics—Avoiding Scam Artists."

David and Pauline: Living for Today While Protecting Tomorrow

When David and Pauline came to see me, David was in poor health and knew his days were numbered. He was 73 years old and he was still able to go and do, but he had good days and bad days. His wife was 71. He had been self-employed and they were living on the IRAs he had built through the years through smart investing. However, they were spending only 3 percent of their total return of 5 percent.

They were overly invested in bonds paying 5 percent. David managed their cash flow very strictly. He knew Pauline would outlive him. He wanted to make sure the two of them didn't spend principal and that there was a little growth so that she would be well taken care of for her lifetime. But they wanted to spend some money and enjoy it together, while his health was good enough to travel. They came to see me for help in securing the present income they wanted without doing damage to the portfolio for Pauline.

Analysis and results.   With a rebalancing of their assets, they were able not only to meet his goals, but also to increase their income from 3 percent to 6 percent of their assets and still have growth for Pauline's lifetime. Because of the increase in their income, they were able to take some trips and enjoy his last years by spending a little more income together without jeopardizing their nest egg for Pauline.

Sadly, David died two years later. We rolled over David's IRAs to Pauline's and her income has continued. David's life insurance was owned by an irrevocable life insurance trust, with Pauline designated to receive the income for her lifetime and the children to receive the principal upon Pauline's death. We invested the life insurance proceeds she received in growth and income mutual funds.

Since the IRA income she and David were receiving before his death was enough for the two of them, it certainly is enough for Pauline alone. Because she didn't need it, she decided to give the income from the insurance trust to each of her four children and three grandchildren equally every year.

Since David's death, Pauline has enjoyed taking the trips she loves with her church group and with her children. Last year she took her oldest granddaughter to Europe for two weeks as a graduation present. They took one bag each and Eurailed from one bed-and-breakfast to another all across Europe.

Problems with IRAs and Being Single in the 70s

Many people have IRAs that contain the bulk of their invested assets—especially professional people and entrepreneurs. What these people don't know is that if they die, their children or other nonspouse beneficiaries will be forced to pay income (not estate) taxes on the principal—either all at one time or over a five-year period. If the total assets are greater than $600,000 (under prevailing tax laws in 1997), the children will pay estate taxes also. Now, if your IRA assets are small, don't worry about it. If, however, they are nearing $100,000, you will want to get some help to avoid the problems we are discussing here.

In Pauline's case, the assets are almost $1.8 million, of which $700,000 are in Pauline's IRA. If Pauline died with her IRA still intact, the children would owe the following:

Taxes Owed on IRA Assets

	Total	Per Child
IRA assets	$700,000	$175,000
Taxable income to be spread over five years		35,000/year
Assume 28% federal income tax bracket		(9,800)/year
Assume lowest estate tax rate: 37%		(12,950)/year
Total IRA Assets Left after Income and Estate Taxes		$ 12,250/year
(for five years, this equals $61,250 per child)		

If a child took his or her share in one year:

Total IRA assets per child added to taxable income	$175,000
Assume 36% federal income tax bracket	(63,000)
Assume lowest estate tax bracket: 37%	(64,750)
Total IRA Assets Left After Income and Estate Taxes	$ 47,250

This analysis shows it is much better for a child or other non-spouse beneficiary of an IRA to spread out the inheritance over the five years. But it points out rather dramatically the devastating effect of income and estate taxes on IRA assets.

So what should you do?

1. **Consider using some family limited partnership or irrevocable trust ideas in conjunction with annual gifting to remove non-IRA growth assets from your estate.** As in Pauline's case, consider moving the vacation home to an irrevocable trust. That act alone will remove $200,000 from her estate.

2. **Pay the taxes now.** Pauline is in the 28 percent federal income tax bracket and hates to pay taxes. But her accountant and I agree that she should begin withdrawing principal from the IRA and pay the taxes now. By the time her children inherit it, the asset will be larger and her children may be in an even higher tax bracket. This doesn't mean she has to spend the principal. She can advise the mutual fund company that she wishes to reregister the amount she is removing from the IRA to a non-IRA account. She can keep the same mutual fund and the same income stream she had as an IRA. The only difference is that she will pay taxes on the principal as it moves into a non-IRA account.

3. **Subdivide the single IRA account into four accounts and name each child to one of the accounts as a beneficiary.** Take the income using joint life expectancies. Since the child will be younger, the amounts to be withdrawn will be lower, and on Pauline's death the child will continue to receive the income under the originally established joint life expectancy table, thus spreading the income and principal over more than five years. This is complex, so it is strongly urged that you seek advice from a professional familiar with these types of problems.

4. **Move non-IRA assets into variable annuity contracts so the income and capital gain distributions can be reinvested tax-deferred.** If this is done, growth can occur in

the tax-deferred accounts and the income can come from the currently taxable accounts as they move out of the IRA.

5. **Consider life insurance to cover some of the estate taxes that will need to be paid upon death.** It is not necessary to completely cover the estate tax liability with life insurance—but it is wise to have some ready cash for final expenses and for some of the estate taxes in case the market is temporarily down.

In Pauline's case, we are increasing the income she will take from her IRA nest egg and not taking any income from the non-IRA assets—leaving them to grow. All assets will pass to the children at the appropriate estate tax bracket, but if Pauline lives long enough, the children won't have to pay income taxes as well.

Don't attempt to structure this alone. You should seek advice from your team of financial, tax, and legal consultants. Arrangements should be made during your lifetime.

PREPARING FOR LONG-TERM LIVING ARRANGEMENTS AND MEDICAID

Assisted Living

As reported in "Who Is Old?" in the January 21, 1996, issue of *Parade* magazine, we are seeing more and more people living longer productive lives than ever before, and as a result, in the future we will begin to redefine middle age. According to the *Parade* article, Daniel Perry, director of the Alliance for Aging Research in Washington, D.C., believes we should begin rethinking our ideas about who's old. "The centenarians are helping to stretch our sense of human potential," Perry says. "If people live to 100, how can you think of a person as 'used up' at 65? We're approaching the day when 70 or 80 is going to be middle-aged."

Regardless of how the demographics play out, however, the 70s and 80s represent the years during which most people begin to think about long-term care alternatives, wills, trusts, second-to-die life insurance, and, in general, passing assets to future generations. The reality as we age is that there will come a time when we won't want to cook all our meals or clean our kitchens and bathrooms. As we approach those times, we will begin to think more seriously about help—and many people would rather not be dependent on their children for that help.

Our society is responding to the need for help of our aging population by creating a type of care called "assisted living" for people residing in their own apartments or in a community-style living arrangement. Today, this represents one of the fastest growing segments of the long-term care industry and it goes by many names: preferred care, catered living, residential care homes, personal care homes, adult congregate care facilities, or assisted living facilities.

Whatever the name, assisted living is extending personalized services, providing health care as needed, and giving support where required to enhance the lives of the aging population. These professionally staffed communities consist of bedrooms, efficiencies, suites, or apartments. Personal assistance is available 24 hours a day.

While there is no information on the exact number of assisted living residences in America in 1997, estimates range from 30,000 to 40,000. Approximately one million individuals live in those residences, which may be freestanding or housed with other residential options such as independent living or nursing care facilities, and the number is expected to grow.

The cost of these services ranges from $1,500 to $3,500 per month, with the consumer having the option in many cases of selecting from an à la carte menu (so to speak) and paying for only the services as needed or desired.

For those who worry about having the income necessary to afford the higher end of the spectrum of services, insurance policies are available to help defray the costs. Most of the policies only pay benefits when the person cannot perform two of the activities of daily living (ADLs), but a few policies will pay the benefits if the person cannot perform one of the ADLs. Premiums for the benefits are pegged to the person's age, and the insured can purchase a daily benefit ranging from $20 to over $100 per day. Refer to the discussion of long-term care insurance in Chapter 6 for a definition of ADLs.

Surprisingly, the cost of the insurance is relatively reasonable for a healthy 70-year-old who wants to buy a benefit of $100 a day and is willing to pay for his or her own care for the first 90 days after needing the benefit. See "Costs of Long-Term Care Insurance" at the end of Chapter 6.

Beginning the process—the search for long-term care alternatives. In your 70s and 80s you may begin to think about alternative living arrangements for the future. Maybe you are growing tired of maintaining your home—there always seems to be something going wrong. Maybe you are tired of cooking. You may wonder about where you will live when you don't want to or can't continue to live independently. It is wise to ask your children or friends to help you look into options long before you really need one. Call and obtain brochures. Then visit the options you find most interesting. Find out if you can bring your own furniture, and if you can have a cottage or private room. Of course, find out the cost and all that is included: meals, cleaning, transportation, etc. Meet some people who are now living there. Ask them if they are happy and whether they would make the same decision again. Narrow down your choices and visit several times before making a final decision.

If your income is not sufficient to pay for the assisted living or nursing home care you feel you want, you will need to know the Medicaid rules. Under 1997 laws, Medicaid will cover care in an assisted living facility at the state's option. Only 8 of 50 states now cover assisted living facilities.

In recent years, the law has changed and now states that a person qualifies for Medicaid to pay long-term care costs:

- After all that person's assets are exhausted except a home, a car, a prepaid funeral contract, and a $5,000 CD (viewed as money to defray final expenses), or
- If those assets were transferred to another person five years or longer in advance of the assisted living or nursing home care being required.

Be sure to check with a tax adviser or lawyer specializing in elder care for the rules applicable to your state of residence and the then-applicable federal guidelines, as these rules seem to change often.

Long-term care is not easy to discuss. Long-term care is a tough topic to raise with the people in your life who may need it. Sometimes children will opt to pay the premium for long-term care insurance themselves rather than discuss the transfer-of-assets issue with older loved ones. If you are the person anticipating the need for such care, you may want to raise the issue yourself and make a decision to buy long-term care insurance yourself. Be aware that insurance can only be purchased if you are in relatively good health. Each insurance company has its own guidelines.

Many children have lovingly and sincerely told their parents they will never place them in a nursing home or other facility. However, when and if the time comes, the children may have no choice. The maintenance of many 40- and 50-year-old's households requires that both spouses work and their own children may be of the ages that require a good bit of money. The only practical choice may be an assisted living facility or nursing home, since the cost of in-home care is very high. (As a note, however, many nursing home policies do have riders that pay for in-home care.)

Living Wills and Durable Powers of Attorney for Health Care

It is during the 70s and 80s that most people begin to think about who will make decisions for them in case they are unable to make them on their own. To accomplish this effectively, one needs a legal document called a "durable power of attorney for health care," which appoints someone to work with the elderly person in deciding the best form of care if they should become disabled.

The durable power of attorney for health care also empowers someone to make those decisions if the elderly person is not able to participate. Usually, these documents require the agreement of two or three doctors giving advice to the one or several people to whom the power of attorney has been given. It is usually advisable to appoint one person as the holder of the power of attorney, since it may be difficult for more than one person to reach agreement in a timely fashion.

In the same vein, many people consider making out a living will in which they stipulate up front whether or not they want to be placed on life support systems should they be indicated.

A competent lawyer can be used to properly draw the power of attorney and the living will, but together these documents should cost no more than about $200; in fact, many lawyers will provide these documents at no additional cost if they are also drawing the last will and testament for that person. Also, some hospital foundations help with these documents as a complimentary service, or they can provide a fill-in-the-blank-form that will serve the purpose.

WILLS AND TRUSTS

During the retirement years, you might want to review your will. Think about the people who will be inheriting your wealth. Make sure you set up proper language to prevent your heirs from inadvertently hurting themselves with your money.

Many a person has been ruined for life by inheriting money they were not competent to manage. If they were in their 20s, 30s, or 40s, they may have spent the principal not fully appreciating the tremendous value of the money.

If you want to really help your heirs, set up a trust in your will that specifies they will be able to spend only the income from your assets but not the principal until they are, say, 55, an age at which they will be more likely to fully understand the importance of not blowing through principal for purchases of cars or trips.

This plan has a side benefit of protecting your heirs from inheriting money from you, buying a joint asset with a spouse, getting a divorce, and losing half of their inheritance to the former spouse.

Another stipulation you may wish to consider is stating in the will that assets you bequeath are to stay in the family blood line. Then name executors and trustees you can trust to carry out your wishes. If at all possible, avoid naming an institutional trustee. The fees are very high and the investment expertise available at the institutions is more often than not inadequate. Many people whose fathers or mothers named institutions as trustees have come to see me with extremely disappointing investment results and fees that were eating up their investment returns. You are much better served to name cotrustee children, grandchildren, or other relatives and leave instructions that they seek the services of an investment professional for investment advice.

Testamentary Trusts

Let's revisit the earlier cited case of Nancy, who died after marrying for the second time, only to have her family lose its rights to inherit her estate—instead, her second husband and his family inherited the lion's share of the assets. Especially helpful in Nancy's case would have been a testamentary trust, which is established upon a person's death. Testamentary trusts do not require that you give away anything while you are living, or that you lose control of anything while you are living. They merely spell out your intent for asset transfer after your death. Any of Nancy's assets outside her 401(k) and her home could have been directed through a testamentary trust in the body of the will. A retirement trust with similar provisions would have been needed to handle her 401(k) assets.

Living Trusts

Living trusts do not reduce your estate tax liability at all. They do, however, help your beneficiaries avoid probate; that is, the filing of your will with the state. This is an area where the unscrupulous often approach senior citizens, claiming living trusts will save lots of money, when, in fact, the savings they claim you save is relatively small. For example, in the state of Georgia, probate costs are only about $150. So living trusts actually *cost* you money. For an attorney to create a living trust for you, the cost could be around $2,000.

The unscrupulous often charge about the same amount, to "review your assets and create a living trust" for you. Then after the trust is in place, the scam artists begin to talk you into moving your assets, creating big fees for themselves at your expense.

If you want to protect the privacy of your estate, perhaps a living trust is valuable. But seek the help of a respected attorney whom you have known for years. Don't work with anyone you don't know.

Living trusts simply contain the same language and provide for the same functions to be performed as in wills, as discussed in the earlier section.

Establishing a living trust involves the designation of a trustee or trustees, a surviving trustee, a successor trustee, and an executor. In addition, a guardian or guardians should always be named for minor children in case the parents die before the children reach the age of 18. Also important is the appointment of a guardian if you have handicapped children, regardless of their ages. You will also want to name a trustee to manage the assets your children will inherit and the assets you intend to leave anyone else you think will be unable to properly manage the assets themselves.

Family Limited Partnerships

Many people who are interested in transferring assets without losing control of the assets while they are living establish family limited partnerships (FLPs), which give partnership interests to their children, grandchildren, or other related or unrelated parties. These are very complex entities and require additional tax filings annually. However, if you have assets in excess of $2 million, the desire to learn and a good accountant, lawyer, and financial planner, family partnerships may be useful in transferring some of your assets and thereby reducing estate taxes. In addition to their tax advantages, FLPs usually insulate the transferred assets from the claims of creditors of the limited partners.

CRATS and CRUTS—Charitable Remainder Trusts

For the charitably minded person or perhaps for the single person, a charitable remainder annuity trust (CRAT) or charitable remainder unitrust (CRUT) may be useful.

Simply stated, a CRAT or CRUT provides you with income for your lifetime (and for the lifetimes of any living beneficiaries you wish to name) in exchange for your giving the principal to a charity or charities upon the death of all the income beneficiaries. The neat aspect of this is that you establish this trust while you are living and you receive a charitable deduction on your income tax return while you are living.

Sometimes the charitable deduction is enough to create tax savings large enough to pay for an insurance policy to replace the asset you are giving away if you so desire. That way, if you do have children or other beneficiaries to whom you would like to give assets, you can do so through the life insurance purchased with the tax savings of the asset you gave away. And as a bonus, the life insurance can be *owned* by an irrevocable insurance trust or by the beneficiaries so that your beneficiaries will pay no estate taxes on that amount!

WHAT ABOUT YOUR PERSONAL PROPERTY?

Many people acquire nice assets they use during their lifetimes and then they forget to make arrangements for the transfer of those assets when they will no longer be using them.

Handling Aunt Claudia's Assets

Vickie's widowed Aunt Claudia turned 84 and had no children. On Vickie's recent visit, Aunt Claudia asked Vickie if she would like to have her 24 place settings of sterling silver. Vickie said she would love to have them, but she also reminded Aunt Claudia that a written list of how she wanted her personal items handled would be most helpful.

Vickie is also concerned about Aunt Claudia's accounts and legal records, since Vickie has been asked to handle these things. Yet Vickie does not know the location of records and accounts, and she hesitates to discuss this with her aunt for fear Aunt Claudia will think she is being nosy.

Perhaps Vickie could give Aunt Claudia a to-do list to make life easier for Vickie later. Ideally, the list would include the following:

- On the bottoms of furniture and other valuable items, place stickers bearing the names of the people to whom the items are to go. (This will help avoid the predictable family squabbles over certain things and if one person doesn't want one thing and another person does, they can swap. But at least, a fight is avoided.)
- Create a list of assets and documents and their locations.
- Also list the names and phone numbers of the persons who can most efficiently help Vickie with each account, asset, and document.

TRANSFERRING VACATION HOMES

Many people have acquired vacation homes that all the family members have enjoyed for years. However, after the owner of the home has gone, those left to share the home often find that sharing it is very complex. Most families grow to include children of children, teenagers and their friends, and others. The day-to-day problems of sharing living arrangements (even if they are sequential and not simultaneous) with people who have different standards of neatness and cleanliness and varied decorating ideas creates problems the original owners would never have expected or wanted. Beth and her sisters are a case in point.

Beth and her two sisters now own the farm and 507 acres once owned by their parents. One sister never goes and would prefer to sell the farm. Another sister, Linda, lives close to the farm and her son is a college student who goes to the farm every weekend with a group of his friends—complete with guns for hunting.

Last Christmas, Beth and her daughter and grandchildren reserved the farm for a visit. Beth had looked forward to taking her loved ones to the farm for a week. It turned out not to be pleasant. They found the home dirty and cluttered. Beth almost wore herself out cleaning and restoring the house to order.

Beth was appalled that her sister would allow her son to let the house become so cluttered and dirty. But Beth and her sister don't deal with each other too directly, so Beth doesn't know how to approach the subject. She is afraid she will offend her sister and damage their personal relationship if she brings up the subject.

But Beth is a smart businesswoman and knows if the property is left to deteriorate, it will lose its value. The conflict is that Beth doesn't want to be the one who visits only to restore order to the house. Yet if she doesn't, her part of the asset could go down in value.

Beth's parents had given no thought to how to pass the farm to their children in a manner that would be manageable. Transferring property of this nature is very difficult. It must be done with care and awareness of how each child is different.

Vacation homes or family homes represent valuable assets that must be protected as they move from one generation to the next. People who own such property can avoid these complex family situations by putting creative legal arrangements into place while they are living. They will want to ensure that one person is in charge, that a set of rules is agreed to and followed for use of the house, that certain responsibilities are taken to maintain the property, and that provisions are made for one or more of the children to be bought out if the joint ownership becomes problematic.

But as hard as you may try, transference of a vacation home with all the ensuing management problems sometimes is just not worth it in the long run. Perhaps the most desirable alternative is to sell the home and let the beneficiaries purchase their own vacation homes. Decisions should be addressed early, however, to avoid painful and disruptive relationships in the future.

WEALTH-PRESERVING STRATEGIES FOR THE 70s AND BEYOND

Be Wealthy—Who Would Want to Be Healthy and Have No Money?

- In these years you are probably drawing income from your pension, Social Security, your nest egg, or all three. You can't do anything to alter your pension or Social Security. Your only control is over your nest egg—and it needs to give you increasing income each year.
  1. Protect not only your principal—protect the growth of your principal.
  2. Select mutual funds carefully. Don't just drift into the indexed funds.
  3. Don't be afraid to pay taxes if it means you'll have more money in the long run. But take full advantage of any tax breaks offered for your age group—like the one-time exemption from taxes of capital gain on the sale of your home.
  4. Think about the next generation. Make sure you have a properly drawn will and durable power of attorney for health care. Consider the use of charitable remainder trusts, insurance trusts, and long-term care insurance.

Be Healthy—What Good Is all the Money in the World if You're Not Healthy?

- To live long with a good quality of life, eat plenty of fresh fruits and vegetables. Drink lots of water, preferably filtered or bottled. Take appropriate vitamins and food supplements. Go easy on refined sugar and meats.
- Exercise regularly. Walking is excellent exercise; so are water aerobics. It is never too late to start.

Be Wise—Who Would Want to Be Healthy and Wealthy But Unhappy?

- Make sure you fully develop and use your sense of humor.
- Spend time thinking of and doing for other people.
- Keep your mind active. Find ways to keep learning.
- Keep your guard up. Don't let the crooks of the world get their hands on your hard-earned money.
- Don't think you're too old for romance, but keep up your guard here, too. If you remarry, use trusts, family limited partnerships, and other legal entities to protect your children and other family members. Your new spouse may not have any unworthy intentions, but the language of your will needs to protect your family members after your new spouse is gone.

RULE OF THUMB

A long life is a mixed blessing. Time waits for no one. Enjoy every minute!

CHAPTER 9

PULLING IT ALL TOGETHER: LIVE LONG AND PROFIT!

A big black crow who was about to die of thirst came upon a pitcher. Hoping it contained water he put his beak in, but discovered that while it did contain some water, the water was in the bottom.

He tried and tried to reach the water but it was too far down. Then a wonderful idea occurred to him. He dropped a small stone into the pitcher. Working hard although he was exhausted and weak from thirst, he continued to drop stones one by one until, at last, he saw the water rising near his beak.

He cast in a few more pebbles and was able to quench his thirst and save his own life.

"Little by little does the trick."

—Aesop's Fables

Many of us spend our lives letting our emotions dominate and by doing so often sabotage our financial success.

Some people who grow up without money live in fear that they will not make enough money. They try to hold onto every penny. Other people who grew up with plenty of money or who suddenly receive a large sum of money for which they did not work may not ever develop a sense of urgency about money. These people often do not place a realistic value on the dollar, nor do they appreciate the effort that is required to earn those dollars. These are the people who overspend today at the expense of tomorrow. If you find yourself in one of these groups, it is never too late to make changes in your money management behavior—nor is it too early.

Whether you earn a large salary or small, you can live long and profit as long as you understand what you really want from the symbols of success your money buys. We all know people who make little money, yet have much. We know others who have made a fortune and have little.

It really doesn't matter how much you make as long as you manage the money you do have in ways that do not interfere with your ability to enjoy healthy relationships throughout your life. Key to managing your money wisely is making sure you are not spending more than you are making.

As we have discussed in previous chapters, the emotions that prevent us from making smart money decisions can ruin lives. An obsessive focus on money also can ruin lives. Through each decade of our lives, we must strike a balance between head and heart concerns if we are to achieve the financial wellness necessary for a long, profitable life.

ACHIEVING FINANCIAL FITNESS

Of those turning age 65 in our country today, only one person in six is financially independent (U.S. Bureau of Census, 1995). Financial independence is defined as spending the same thing you are spending today without working. Personal finance is not a favorite dinner-table topic of discussion. This may be why many of us never learned from our parents how to properly spend and manage money.

Nor have the schools done a good job of providing a road-map for financial fitness. I hope the information in this book has been able to fill in some of the gaps in your financial education.

Assess Your Needs Versus Your Wants

Needs are not the same as wants. In *Mind over Money* by Wayne E. Nance and Edward A. Charlesworth, PhD, we learn the difference between the two.

> *Want* means, "I want to feel better about myself, and I want people to look up to me and respect me. I want to be somebody. Therefore, I want to purchase something to make me feel better."
>
> *Need* means, "I have certain survival instincts such as food, shelter, clothing, transportation, retirement, and education for children. Everything else falls into the want category. It is OK to buy sports cars, winter homes, 6,000-

square-foot offices, boats, and home video cameras. But are we using these possessions to buy our happiness at the expense of financial devastation?"

It is particularly important to understand the difference between the two in the 20s, 30s and 40s. It is during those decades that we accumulate most of the symbols of success. To avoid continuing on the treadmill of earning more and more money to feed the addiction of buying more and more things, ask yourself what you really want from your symbols of success.

So you want a sports car. What do you want from the sports car—the feeling of power and freedom, wind blowing through your hair? Or do you want transportation?

What we really want is often expressed as experiences in words such as respect, peace of mind, adventure, success, self-worth, power, and love. To achieve those experiences, we seek symbols of them through our job, clothes, house, car, family, education, travel, and money. There is nothing wrong with trying to reach for the symbols. But it helps to keep us focused if we understand that the symbols are really ways to seek something experiential. Of each thing you buy, ask "What experience am I seeking?"

Then accurately identify the experience you are seeking. Next, make a list of many things that might provide that experience. Knowing the alternatives increases the likelihood of your achieving what you are really seeking.

It also gives you financial freedom. For if you determine you can't afford the sports car, try an affordable alternative you can use to achieve the experience you are seeking. Financial fitness will come when you are not focused on accumulating symbols of success that do not meet your needs.

It's not how much you make, but what you do with it. For each stage of your life, you must live within your means. This suggests you have to know what it costs you to live. If you don't live by a budget, don't feel alone. Very few people do. Our plan, however, is simple. Place into categories (see the monthly Household and Family Worksheet in Appendix A) where your money went last month, and do it every month. Every month you will be reminded of how you spent your money last month.

> ### RULE OF THUMB
>
> **You will be surprised how much just the knowledge of where your money went will influence your behavior in the current month.**

You cannot survive financially if you spend more than you make. And if you are always in the hole, you will be unable to enjoy healthy relationships throughout your entire life.

You can be a millionaire too. One couple who epitomizes the successful application of all the principles we have discussed throughout our pages are Sam and Laura, now in their late 60s.

Sam and Laura live in a lower-income part of town where hard blue-collar work takes place every day. Sam owns a dry cleaning business. Laura watches over the books, family money, and children. They are in control of their finances and always have been.

When their income increased, they didn't let their standard of living consume the increased income. Instead, they remained in their $85,000 home while accumulating money in their mutual funds, IRAs, and annuities. They never allowed credit-card balances to carry over from month to month. Their children went to community colleges for two years and graduated from four-year schools. They each worked and provided about one-third of their college costs. Sam and Laura paid for the other two-thirds from savings and current earnings. They continued to drive an older American-made sedan and pickup truck instead of two newer upscale foreign-made cars as their income went up.

Today, 20 years later, they live in a $175,000 home, drive a sport utility vehicle and an upscale sedan and have over $1 million in net worth. Their children are supporting themselves. They still have no credit-card debt.

By managing their money well, they set up a lifestyle that can be continued on their nest egg. They are a wonderful example of financial fitness. They reached this level of success about two years ago, so it took them almost 20 years to get there.

Remember, Rome was not built in a day. Financial fitness comes one day at a time, slowly and methodically.

Make sure you know what you need and use the information we have provided to help you map a plan for achieving your goals.

Be wary of anyone trying to sell you anything that doesn't sound realistic to you. Educate yourself. Then be content with what you have.

RULE OF THUMB

Some people can live and be very happy on $30,000 a year while others are miserable with $100,000 a year. Which are you?

Taking Financial Responsibility

At every age, to achieve financial fitness, you must pay yourself first. This means you must take a percentage of your income and invest it for your future before you buy anything else.

Pete, a business owner, told me of the conversation he had with three of the 20-year-olds working in his architectural firm. The firm matches dollar for dollar up to 8 percent of every dollar their 30 employees contribute to the 401(k). The three employees are not contributing anything. They told Pete they cannot afford to contribute. Pete told them: "You cannot afford not to!" And Pete is correct.

Young people make a big mistake if they do not take full advantage of every benefit their company offers. In Pete's employees' cases, they are giving up 8 percent of their salary by not participating in the plan. Take responsibility for your own retirement planning. Whatever your income, invest for retirement first. Here's a summary of the minimum amounts you should invest during each decade:

Investments in Retirement Plans

Ages	Percentages
22–29	4%
30–39	10
40–49	12
50–59	15
60–65	15

Set your rate of return goal at a minimum of 10 percent per year.

Take a look at how your money would have grown through your lifetime if you had only earned $1,000 for every year of your age and invested as we have just outlined.

Retirement Investments through the Years

Age	Nest Egg	Income
22	0	0
30	$ 17,140	0
40	106,214	0
50	371,233	0
60	1,106,794	0
65	1,845,773	0
Begin Withdrawing 7% Income		
66	$1,901,147*	$129,204
70	2,139,757	145,420
80	2,875,655	195,433
90	3,864,640	262,645
100	5,193,752	352,973

*Nest egg continues to grow at 3% per year.

As you can see, it's not hard to become a millionaire by age 60. Many reading this book will be earning far more than $1,000 per year of age and if you follow this book's suggestions, you will be a millionaire long before age 60.

Take a look at Figure 9.1 to see how the investment of your assets should change through the years.

IN GIVING, YOU RECEIVE

Sixty-five-year-old Abbott Smith, who owned a New York personnel recruitment and placement service for years and for whom I worked as a young entrepreneur getting started many years ago, told me something I will never forget: "Don't expect to make a dollar from everyone and don't expect to earn a dollar

FIGURE 9.1 Asset Allocation for the Ages

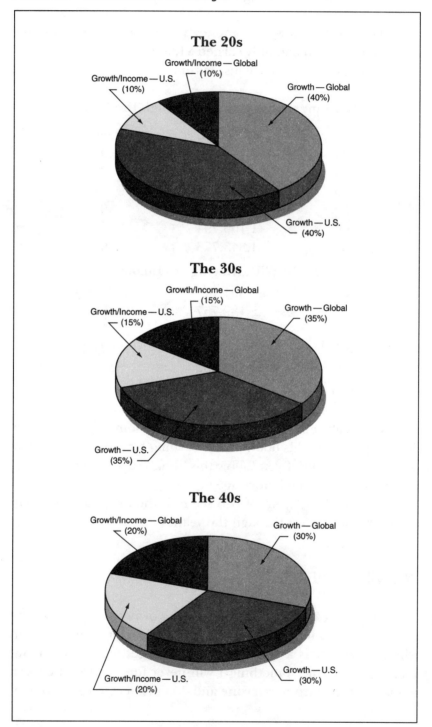

FIGURE 9.1   Asset Allocation for the Ages (Continued)

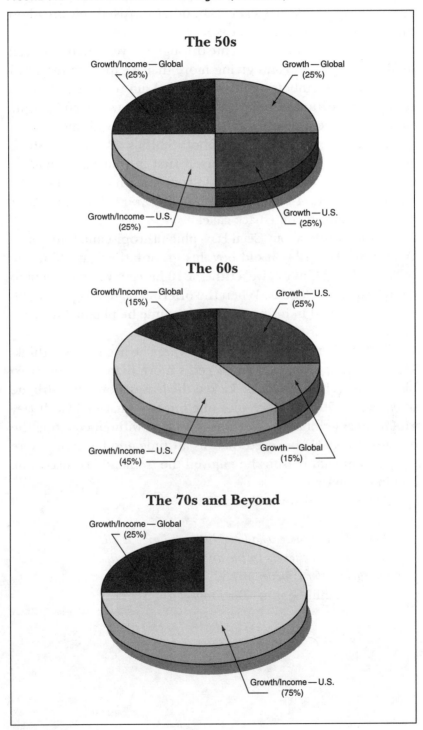

every time you see an existing client. Always give them more service than you think they expect. In other words, throw bread on the water—it will come back cake!"

Those words have guided me through the years to be focused on doing a good job and giving more than I expect to receive. I can testify that Abbott Smith was right. I am truly blessed. As a result, I am fortunate to have a large group of wonderful people who have chosen to plan their financial futures with me.

The financial parallel of Abbott Smith's advice is to share your earnings. After paying yourself first in your retirement investments, give away 10 percent to your church or favorite charity. You will find, I believe, that in giving you will receive. Your bread will indeed come back cake!

A story is told about Cecil Day, philanthropist and founder of Days Inns. As a 12-year-old boy, his grandfather gave him one dollar and told him to give a tithe of 10 percent when he went to church the next Sunday. When the offering plate was passed, little Cecil reached in his pocket for the dime he planned to tithe. He only had four quarters. So he gave one.

Walking home in the small town where he lived, he was thinking about how he had given 15 cents more than the tithe. Two blocks down the street as he kicked the leaves along the curb, he uncovered a 50-cent piece—not one but two quarters! Cecil Day said he decided that day to always give first without counting the exact pennies. He believed that his attitude and his giving were the fundamental reasons he enjoyed the tremendous success he had in his lifetime.

Give first, and you will receive.

"And there are those who have little and give it all.
These are the believers in life and the bounty of life,
and their coffer is never empty."
—Kahlil Gibran, *The Prophet*

ACHIEVING THE FIVE Fs

Motivational speaker Jim Hansberger says the balanced person is one who masters the Five *f*s: faith, family, friends, fitness and finance.

- **Faith.** To be well-rounded and stable, you must have a faith; a faith in something larger than yourself; a faith in God.
- **Family.** To be well-rounded and stable, you must enjoy and spend time with your family.
- **Friends.** To be well-rounded and stable, you must find time to cultivate meaningful friendships.
- **Fitness.** To be well-rounded and stable, you must carve out time to exercise regularly and you must take the time to prepare and eat nutritious food.
- **Finance.** To be well-rounded and stable, you must manage your spending, giving, and investing wisely.

Each of us has a responsibility to have faith in God, ourselves, and each other. With that as backdrop, we must manage our money and our lives well. We must leave a good legacy.

God gives every bird its food.
He does not throw it into the nest.
—Jack Everett, Certified Financial Planner

TIME, ONCE SPENT, IS GONE FOREVER

"Regret for the things we did can be tempered with time,
it is regret for the things we did not do that is inconsolable."
—Sidney J. Harris

Though the whole premise for our book is that we will all live to be 100 years old or older, we may be wrong and die tomorrow. So we should try to spend every minute of every day doing those things that carry meaning and value for us. In order to truly profit in every area of our lives, we must live each day as though it were the last day of our lives and at the same time as if we were going to live to be 100 years old.

I hope that in the pages of this book you have found some ideas that will help you achieve a balance between how you spend your money today and how you squirrel it away for your tomorrows. I hope you found reasons to be patient as you wait for your investments to grow. I hope also that you found reasons to place a sense of urgency on paying off debt and beginning an investment program.

In balancing the dollars you spend, I pray that you will devote thought to balancing the way you spend your minutes. Success in one area will promote success in the other. Ultimately your peace of mind and happiness will depend on how well you achieve success in the spending of both your money and time. For in the end, what matters are the relationships you cultivate and the good you do for others—not just how long you live.

Our focus is on helping you have whatever money you need so you can meet your financial needs and at the same time do good for others for many, many years.

> *If you want to know what has meaning in a person's life,*
> *look in their checkbook, on their refrigerator door,*
> *and in their calendar.*
> —William L. Self, D. Div., Pastor,
> John's Creek Baptist Church, Atlanta

Always Leave Something on the Table

In the cold, hard, hype-driven, competitive world of Wall Street investing where arrogant young hot shots walk around snapping their suspenders as though they have all the answers, the thought of leaving some profit on the table for the next person is almost unheard of.

But if you want to be a successfully balanced person, one whose self-esteem is healthy, fight the urge to be greedy and be content with the profit you have already made. Don't try to grab that last nickel—leave some for the next person.

Who really is the idiot? Wayne moved into a small southern town one summer. One day he went to see the local pharmacist, Lewis, for a prescription. Lewis knew everyone in town. After a warm welcome, he took Wayne over to the window and began pointing out all the locals adding a bit of gossip about each. Presently Phil walked by and Lewis allowed as how Phil is known as the "village idiot."

When Phil came into the drug store, Lewis called him over. He introduced him to Wayne and said, "Phil, let's show Wayne the game we play!" "OK," Phil said. Lewis said: "Here are two coins—a skinny, dull, dingy old dime and a big, fat, shiny nickel. You can have whichever one you want." Phil hesitated a moment, then grabbed the nickel and ran. Lewis broke into uncontrolled laughter.

Wayne was mortified that Lewis would make such a spectacle of Phil's inability to choose the more valuable coin. So he ran after Phil and asked him, "Don't you know the difference between a nickel and a dime?" Phil said, "Mister, all I know is when I take the dime they stop playing the game!"

Set your rate of return expectations at 10 percent to 12 percent and don't be tempted by 18 percent to 20 percent or greater returns sometimes touted.

Leaving a lasting legacy. Look for realistic investment returns, be patient, and when you reach your goals, cash in, leaving profit for the next person. With this strategy, you'll find profits, but more importantly, you'll find peace of mind.

Not only is it important to leave profit on the table for the next person, it is important to leave something lasting for the next generation. Share your values with your children and if you don't have children, with your nieces and nephews—or volunteer with Big Brothers and Big Sisters, Boy Scouts, Girl Scouts, a children's Sunday School class, or other organization where you can fulfill your obligation to leave a lasting legacy.

Our money will not last beyond our lives,
but our ideas and values passed on will.
   —Jim Denison, D.Div.,
   Second Ponce de Leon Baptist Church, Atlanta

DIXES

INSTRUCTIONS FOR COMPLETING FORMS

This is a very important exercise. Your planning will only be as good as the data you put into this document. Be precise and comprehensive.

Monthly Household and Family Expense Worksheet

You will need the data provided by this worksheet (Figure A.1) to determine the amount of life insurance you will need as well as the amount of income you will need when you retire. It is not good enough to include only your fixed expenses such as utilities, rent, house payment, car payment, insurance, etc. You also must include variable expenses such as gifts, clothes, eating out, etc. These last expenses define your "quality of life" and when you retire, you will want to maintain the same or similar "quality of life." So don't leave out a thing. We are not trying to get the amount down as low as possible; we are trying to be *accurate*.

You will need all canceled checks and credit-card statements from the last calendar year to get the most usable data for completing this worksheet. If you use automated teller machines (ATMs), don't forget to include them. Review each check you wrote and each entry on your credit-card statement to determine the most appropriate category for the entry of that amount spent. Place the respective amounts in the appropriate block below.

When you have completed each row, run a total. For each major heading, add the totals you obtained for the rows.

Household and Family Expense Summary

Place the totals you calculated on the worksheet in the appropriate space on the summary sheet shown in Figure A.2. When you have completed each page, you can run a total for the entire worksheet, thus learning what it cost you to live last year.

Determining How Much Life Insurance You Will Need

The column entitled "Survivor Monthly Total" will help you determine how much your dependents will need if the primary wage earner were gone. Estimate those costs and the total will give you the annual amount needed. Use this total in completing Determining How Much Life Insurance You Will Need, in Appendix B.

Retirement Income Calculator

To determine your retirement cost of living, review each line entry and provide your best guess as to how that figure will change when you retire. The total you obtain will be your estimated cost of living at retirement. Use the annual amount you determine in completing the Retirement Income Calculator in Appendix C.

APPENDIX A

Household and Family Expenses

FIGURE A.1   Monthly Household and Family Expense Worksheet

(Year) _____

Expense Categories	Jan.	Feb.	Mar.	April	May	June	July	Aug.	Sept.	Oct.	Nov.	Dec.	Totals
Home													
Mortgage payment													
Insurance													
Taxes													
Improvements													
Yard care													
Inside help													
Other													
Total													
Utilities													
Gas													
Power													
Water													
Phone													
Cable													
Total													
Food													
Groceries													
Meals out													
Other													
Total													

Note: Instructions for completing form are on p. 226.

FIGURE A.1   Monthly Household and Family Expense Worksheet (Continued)

(Year) _____

Expense Categories	Jan.	Feb.	Mar.	April	May	June	July	Aug.	Sept.	Oct.	Nov.	Dec.	Totals
Recreation/Entertainment													
Vacations													
Clubs													
Concerts													
Movies													
Other													
Total													
Automobile													
Payments													
Gas													
Repairs													
Insurance													
Total													
Medical													
Doctor													
Drugs													
Insurance													
Other													
Total													

FIGURE A.1   Monthly Household and Family Expense Worksheet (Continued)

(Year)

Expense Categories	Jan.	Feb.	Mar.	April	May	June	July	Aug.	Sept.	Oct.	Nov.	Dec.	Totals
Personal Necessities													
Hair													
Cosmetics													
Laundry													
Subscriptions													
Other													
Total													
Clothing													
Shoes													
Alterations													
Other													
Total													
Donations/Gifts													
Charities													
Church													
Holidays													
Other (birthdays, etc.)													
Total													

FIGURE A.1   Monthly Household and Family Expense Worksheet (Continued)

(Year) _____

Expense Categories	Jan.	Feb.	Mar.	April	May	June	July	Aug.	Sept.	Oct.	Nov.	Dec.	Totals
Savings/Investments													
Savings													
Reserves													
Investments													
Other													
Total													
Life Insurance													
Personal													
Disability													
Other													
Total													
Depreciating Assets													
Major purchases													
Other													
Total													
"Off the Wall" money													
Personal													
Pets													
Miscellaneous													
Total													

FIGURE A.1   Monthly Household and Family Expense Worksheet (Continued)

(Year)

Expense Categories	Jan.	Feb.	Mar.	April	May	June	July	Aug.	Sept.	Oct.	Nov.	Dec.	Totals
Children's Expenses													
Toys													
Birthday parties													
Camps													
Other													
Total													
Monthly Totals													

FIGURE A.2   Household and Family Expenses Summary

Expense Categories	Current Monthly Total	Percent of Total	Retirement Monthly Total	Survivor Monthly Total	Model Expense Levels: Income:		
					<$50K	$50K–$150K	>$150K
1. *Home* (Mortgage payment, insurance, tax, improvements, yard)	_____	_____	_____	_____	30%	25%	20%
2. *Utilities* (Gas, power, water, cable, phone)	_____	_____	_____	_____	12%	10%	8%
3. *Food* (Groceries, restaurants)	_____	_____	_____	_____	17%	15%	13%
4. *Recreation and Entertainment* (Vacations, clubs, concerts, etc.)	_____	_____	_____	_____	2%	2%	4%
5. *Automobile* (Payments, gas, repairs, etc.)	_____	_____	_____	_____	10%	8%	6%
6. *Medical* (Doctor, drugs, insurance, etc.)	_____	_____	_____	_____	3%	3%	3%
7. *Donations/Gifts* (Charities, church, holidays)	_____	_____	_____	_____	2%	2%	1%

FIGURE A.2 Household and Family Expenses Summary (Continued)

Expense Categories	Current Monthly Total	Percent or Total	Retirement Monthly Total	Survivor Monthly Total	Model Expense Levels: Income:		
					<$50K	$50K–$150K	>$150K
8. *Savings and Investments* (Savings, reserves, investments, education funding)	_____	_____	_____	_____	5%	10%	17%
9. *Life Insurance* (Personal, life, disability)	_____	_____	_____	_____	3%	3%	3%
10. *Personal Necessities* (Hair, cosmetics, laundry, subscriptions)	_____	_____	_____	_____	2%	2%	2%
11. *Clothing* (Shoes, alterations, cleaning, etc.)	_____	_____	_____	_____	5%	6%	8%
12. *Depreciating Assets* (Major Purchases)	_____	_____	_____	_____	5%	10%	10%
13. *"Off the Wall" Money* (Personal, pets, miscellaneous expenses)	_____	_____	_____	_____	4%	4%	5%
14. *Children's Expenses* (Toys, birthday parties, etc.)	_____	_____	_____	_____	–	–	–
Total Monthly Expenses	══════	══════	══════	══════	100%	100%	100%
Total Annual Expenses	══════	══════	══════	══════			

APPENDIX B

Determining Life Insurance Needed

Use this worksheet to help you determine how much life insurance you need, if any. You will need to copy and complete the form for yourself and your working spouse.

FIGURE B.1   Determining Life Insurance Needs—Surviving Spouse

Name of Surviving Spouse _____

	Surviving Spouse*	Example
Annual before tax income needed for the surviving spouse (rule of thumb: 80% of joint cost of living)	_____	$ 75,000
Surviving spouse's current gross pay	_____	– 40,000
Gross Annual Income Replacement Needed	_____	$ 35,000
Divide this figure by 7 percent. (This is the rate of income you could expect to receive from investing the life insurance proceeds in a balanced fund producing about 10 percent a year.)	Divide by .07	Divide by .07
Life insurance capital you will need to provide the needed income stream	_____	$500,000
Optional Additions		
Final expenses	_____	7,500
College fund	_____	75,000
Debts	_____	5,000
Total Insurance Needed	_____	**$587,500**
Less Existing Insurance		
Group policy	_____	$200,000
Policy # 1	_____	$100,000
Policy # 2	_____	75,000
Policy # 3	_____	0
Total Existing Insurance	_____	**$375,000**
Additional Insurance Needed (Subtract total existing insurance from total insurance needed)	_____	**$212,500**

*Surviving spouse could be you or your spouse.

APPENDIX C

Calculating Retirement Income

FIGURE C.1   Retirement Income Calculator

Section 1	You	Example
Line 1: Fill in your current annual before-tax cost of living:	$_____	$ 50,000
Line 2: Multiply your figure from line 1 by 75%: This is your estimated current value of your before-tax annual retirement cost of living.	$_____	$ 37,500
Line 3: Fill in the annual rate of inflation you expect between now and the time you retire (3% to 6%):	_____ %	3%
Line 4: Fill in the number of years you expect to continue working before you retire:	_____ years	15 years
Line 5: Use your figures from lines 3 and 4 to determine in Figure D.1 of Appendix D your appropriate inflation factor:	_____	1.558
Line 6: Multiply your figure from line 2 by the inflation factor from line 5: This is your estimated future value of your before-tax annual retirement cost of living.	_____	$ 58,425
Line 7: Divide line 6 by 7% (.07): This is the total amount of retirement capital in future dollars you will need in order to provide the income in line 6.	$_____	$834,643

FIGURE C.1   Retirement Income Calculator (Continued)

Section 2	You	Example
List assets you currently own that are intended to grow until retirement:		
Asset #1: _____	$_____	$150,000
Asset #2: _____	_____	$ 35,000
Asset #3: _____	_____	0
Line 1: **Total:**	_____	**$185,000**
Line 2: Estimate the annual rate of return you expect to get from your retirement capital between now and the time that you retire:	_____ %	10%
Line 3: Fill in the number of years you expect to continue working before you retire:	____ years	15 years
Line 4: Use your figures from lines 2 and 3 to determine in Figure D.1 your appropriate retirement capital appreciation factor:	_____	4.177
Line 6: Multiply your figure from line 1 by the appreciation factor from line 4: This is the future value of your current retirement capital account.	$_____	$772,745
Line 7: Subtract line 6 of Section 2 from line 7 of Section 1. If the balance is zero or negative, stop here—Congratulations! You have an adequate amount saved for your retirement income needs. If the balance is positive, note the amount:	$_____	$ 61,898

FIGURE C.1   Retirement Income Calculator (Continued)

Section 2 (continued)	You	Example
Line 8: Divide line 7 immediately above by $1,000,000:	_____	.0619
Line 9: Using the figure from lines 2 and 3 in Section 2, determine in Figure D.2 of Appendix D the unadjusted monthly investment amount needed to satisfy your retirement income goal:	$_____/mo	$2,422/mo
Line 10: Multiply line 8 by line 9:	$_____/mo	$150/mo

This is the monthly investment amount needed in order to satisfy your retirement income goal if invested at 10% per year for 15 years.

APPENDIX D

Rates of Return

FIGURE D.1   The Compound Value of One Dollar

Years	3%	4%	5%	6%	7%	8%	10%	12%
1	1.030	1.040	1.050	1.060	1.070	1.080	1.100	1.120
2	1.061	1.082	1.102	1.124	1.145	1.166	1.210	1.254
3	1.093	1.125	1.158	1.191	1.225	1.260	1.331	1.405
4	1.126	1.170	1.216	1.262	1.311	1.360	1.464	1.574
5	1.159	1.217	1.276	1.338	1.403	1.469	1.611	1.762
6	1.194	1.265	1.340	1.419	1.501	1.587	1.772	1.974
7	1.230	1.316	1.407	1.504	1.606	1.714	1.949	2.211
8	1.267	1.369	1.477	1.594	1.718	1.851	2.144	2.476
9	1.305	1.423	1.551	1.689	1.838	1.999	2.358	2.773
10	1.344	1.480	1.629	1.791	1.967	2.159	2.594	3.106
11	1.384	1.539	1.710	1.898	2.105	2.332	2.853	3.479
12	1.426	1.601	1.796	2.012	2.252	2.518	3.138	3.896
13	1.469	1.665	1.886	2.133	2.410	2.720	3.452	4.363
14	1.513	1.732	1.980	2.261	2.579	2.937	3.797	4.887
15	1.558	1.801	2.079	2.397	2.759	3.172	4.177	5.474
16	1.605	1.873	2.183	2.540	2.952	3.426	4.595	6.130
17	1.653	1.948	2.292	2.693	3.159	3.700	5.054	6.866
18	1.702	2.026	2.407	2.854	3.380	3.996	5.560	7.690
19	1.754	2.107	2.527	3.026	3.617	4.316	6.116	8.613
20	1.806	2.191	2.653	3.207	3.870	4.661	6.728	9.646
25	2.094	2.666	3.386	4.292	5.427	6.848	10.835	17.000
30	2.427	3.243	4.322	5.743	7.612	10.063	17.449	29.960

FIGURE D.2   Monthly Investment Needed

Working Years Remaining	Expected Rate of Return	
	6%	10%
5	$14,333.00	$12,927.00
6	$11,573.00	$10,206.00
7	$ 9,609.00	$ 8,281.00
8	$ 8,141.00	$ 6,853.00
9	$ 7,006.00	$ 5,757.00
10	$ 6,102.00	$ 4,893.00
11	$ 5,367.00	$ 4,197.00
12	$ 4,759.00	$ 3,628.00
13	$ 4,247.00	$ 3,155.00
14	$ 3,812.00	$ 2,758.00
15	$ 3,439.00	$ 2,422.00
16	$ 3,114.00	$ 2,134.00
17	$ 2,831.00	$ 1,887.00
18	$ 2,582.00	$ 1,673.00
19	$ 2,361.00	$ 1,486.00
20	$ 2,164.00	$ 1,324.00
25	$ 1,443.00	$ 759.00
30	$ 996.00	$ 446.00

APPENDIX E

Life Insurance Definitions

BUY WHOLE LIFE OR BUY TERM AND INVEST THE DIFFERENCE!

The permanent versus temporary insurance argument has been around for many years. Here's the bottom line.

All Insurance Is Term Insurance

Term insurance is temporary insurance. You are insured for a fixed, pre-specified time. If you don't die, you don't get any money back. The premiums go up every year because you are older—therefore at greater risk of dying. You buy a flat amount of insurance. The premium is quoted for your age and health for that amount of insurance. The younger you are, the lower the premium. This is the lowest-cost insurance available for young people. There is no cash value buildup. When you die, your beneficiaries receive the death benefit—tax-free.

Whole life. This is called permanent insurance, because it is with you for life. You buy it at a flat premium amount greater than the true cost of term insurance at your age. While you are young, you are overpaying for the insurance. As you age, the true cost of insurance catches up to what you are paying each year. The extra money you pay in the early years stays with the insurance company and they invest it with all their assets. Until the true cost of insurance for your age equals what you are paying, the extra cash buildup is called *cash value*. The insurance company pays you interest at a low rate on that cash value. It is your money in a "holding account" until the cost of your insurance goes over what you are paying. The company then dips into the cash value account and pays the difference, thus guaranteeing you a death benefit for your whole life. One final feature: you can borrow your cash value from the policy (usually at very low rates) tax-free. You must never borrow more than about 85 percent to 90 percent of the cash available in your cash value account. Otherwise, everything you had borrowed will be taxable income to you that year and the policy will lapse.

So whole life is a package around term insurance that provides you insurance for your whole life if you pay premiums for your whole life.

Universal life.   This is the contract through which you ask the insurance company to let your premium dollars participate in interest rate fluctuations. In return, the company may ask you to pay premiums for a longer period of time to make up for lower interest rates than originally were expected.

Universal life is insurance that is exactly like whole life *except:*

- Your cash value earns interest rates consistent with money market rates.
- When interest rates go down, you may have to pay more in premiums.
- You can lower the death benefit, thus lowering your premium.
- You could end up with no death benefit if your premiums are inadequate to pay for the term insurance as you age.

Variable universal life.   This is the contract through which you elect to have your premium dollars invested in the stock or bond markets through mutual fund managers' agreements to manage the money for the insurance company. You participate both in the up as well as down markets and your cash value account as well as your premium are adjusted accordingly.

Variable universal life insurance is exactly like universal life
except:

- Your cash value can be directed by you into a variety of different investment options—such as mutual funds.
- Your cash value is held in a separate account within the insurance company for you.
- Because potential stock market returns are somewhat greater than interest rates, you could find enough cash in your policy in your 60s to borrow out as supplemental income for retirement.
- This type of insurance is the hottest product on the market in 1997. Many are using this product to build up cash tax-free for supplemental retirement income.

APPENDIX F

How Fast Does Money Double?

THE RULE OF 72

J. P. Morgan used this presentation when he was asked how to make money or become wealthy.

There are four rules to becoming wealthy:

1. Start early.
2. Save a definite amount.
3. Save regularly and systematically.
4. You must employ your savings productively. (This is the one the savings and loans do not mention.)

To illustrate his point he would show them "the Rule of 72."

$1.00 at 1% simple interest = 100 years to become $2.00
$1.00 at 1% compounded annual interest = 72 years to become $2.00

$$\frac{72}{\text{Rate}} = \text{Number of years to double money}$$

FIGURE F.1   The Rule of 72 Applied to a $10,000 Investment

Interest Rate	Number of Years					
	6	12	18	24	30	36
$\frac{72}{2\%} = 36$						$20,000
$\frac{72}{4\%} = 18$			$20,000			$40,000
$\frac{72}{6\%} = 12$		$20,000		$40,000		$80,000
$\frac{72}{12\%} = 6$	$20,000	$40,000	$80,000	$160,000	$320,000	$640,000

APPENDIX G

Disability Insurance That Pays You Even if You Are Not Disabled

Here are some facts you should know about disability insurance:

- You have to be in good health to purchase it.
- You can only purchase benefits to cover up to 60 percent of your earnings.

Disability insurance is not inexpensive. For a 28-year-old man who purchases $2,500 a month benefit to insure 60 percent of his $50,000-a-year salary, the cost per year is $798. (This example is based on numbers from the Ohio National Life Insurance Company.) This premium is based on the assumption that if he does become disabled,

- He is willing to wait 90 days before his benefits begin,
- He can collect benefits if he is unable to perform the duties of his specific job, and
- His benefits will last until he is age 65.

A few insurance companies allow the insured to purchase a rider to guarantee a return of a certain portion of all premiums paid over a specified number of years if claims made do not exceed that total amount. The cost of this rider almost doubles the total premium, but it allows you to get money back if you do not become disabled.

So in the case above, the annual premium for insurance alone is $798. After ten years, he would have paid in $7,980. If he had not been disabled, he would have lost every dime paid in.

If he buys the return-of-premium rider at an additional annual cost of $636, his total cost per year goes up to $ 1,434 per year. After ten years, he would have paid in $14,340. The return-of-premium rider in this case buys him an 80 percent return of premium (i.e., $11,472 tax-free) after ten years, less any claims he may have made during the ten years. Here's the cost analysis:

Total premiums over ten years	$14,340
Return of premium after ten years	11,472
Net Cost of Insurance over Ten Years	**$ 2,868**

It is smart to purchase the return-of-premium rider if you can afford it. Notice how the premiums increase for a man if he waits till age 35 to purchase disability insurance:

Age	Basic Cost	Return of Premium Cost	Total Cost
28	$ 798	$636	$1,434
35	$1,049	$788	$1,839

Other riders are available for additional fees:

- **Waiver of premium.** With this rider, if you're collecting benefits, you don't have to pay premiums.
- **Cost of living adjustment (COLA).** This rider allows your benefits to increase with inflation.
- **Residual.** If you lose a portion of your income due to disability, this rider allows you to collect a portion of your benefits.

Make sure you purchase benefits if you become disabled to perform duties of your "*own* occupation"—not duties of "*any* occupation." As a general rule, life insurance premiums are slightly lower for females of the same age as the male, while disability premiums are slightly higher.

APPENDIX H

Kiddie Money

*"Train up a child in the way he should go,
and when he is old, he will not depart from it."*

    —Proverbs 22:6

Since most 30-year-olds either have children several years old or have infants, this seems like the appropriate age group to focus on ways to help children learn the smart way to use money. Bad money habits of people I see would be greatly lessened if parents had taught children at earlier ages how to manage money.

The basics are the same for children and adults. Both need to learn how to spend for today appropriately and how to balance savings for the short-term with savings for the long-term goals. Don't forget to teach principles of giving, borrowing, and investing.

Sometimes your efforts at teaching your child to be responsible with money bear fruit when least expected, as in the following example.

One evening my brother Uncle Dunc was visiting D.J. and D.J.'s mom and dad. At dinner, they discussed going out later to the Dairy Queen—a favorite treat for four-year-old D.J. An hour or so later, however, when it was time to go, D.J. said, "I'd rather stay here and play with Uncle Dunc. Besides, we have ice cream in the freezer and it's less expensive." Yes, D.J. was having fun playing, but he probably also was repeating something he had heard from his parents many times before!

LESSONS IN FINANCIAL LIFE

The Piggy Bank

My favorite gift for my clients who have a baby is a piggy bank. When Sarah and Thomas received theirs, we brainstormed ways to fill the bank. They decided, for example, at little Julie's birth to deposit 25 cents each day Monday through Saturday and 50 cents on Sunday in her piggy bank. Thomas said in addition he would empty his pocket change every day into the bank.

They also decided that each time they emptied the piggy bank they would match the funds inside with an equal amount and deposit it into a savings account for her. They decided to continue this schedule of contributions every year. When Julie is old enough to distinguish between coins, at about age four, she will be given an allowance and will be taught to put half of each allowance in the piggy bank. Half of her savings in the piggy bank could be used for purchases over $10 she wants to make, and half would be deposited in the savings account for long-term savings.

When Julie is a freshman in high school, Sarah and Thomas plan to allow her to open a checking account into which half of her allowance and half of her earnings from household chores will be placed (the rest of her earnings will be placed in her savings account). Julie will be responsible for cashing checks as needed and for reconciling bank statements each month. This will be a way Sarah and Thomas can teach Julie the day-to-day money management skills she will need.

Teaching Children about Credit Cards

They also decided that when Julie is about a junior in high school, she will be allowed to have a credit card and will be taught the proper way to use it. This part of a child's financial education is very important, because credit-card companies have begun to focus their advertising efforts on teenagers, trying to hook them early. Unfortunately, many teens and young adults are not aware of how ruinous credit card balances can be, and often quickly find themselves in debt.

Perhaps your children can avoid that pitfall if you take care to help them in the following ways:

- Using your own credit card bills as an example, show them how interest on the amount of money charged begins to accrue as soon as a purchase is made. Point out the high interest rate.

- Teach them to pay off their cards at the end of each month because interest builds quickly. Show them that if they do not, the money they pay in interest is a waste—not reducing the principal at all. Instead, the interest paid becomes profit for the card company.

If you do not want to give your teen a separate credit card, you may want to use one of two alternatives:

1. **Add a second card to your own account.** If you do so, the teen's bills will be sent to you, and you and he or she can set a predetermined payment plan for his or her portion. You may, in addition, want to talk with the credit company about setting a lower spending limit on the second card than on your own primary card.
2. **Allow your teen to use a new debit card,** which deducts money directly from his or her bank account. Under such an arrangement, the teen's credit is gone when his or her money is gone.

Gift Giving

Giving to others can bring us great joy, and holidays can be wonderful times to teach your child about balancing generosity with financial reality. In preparation for holiday shopping, have him or her set aside the amount of money to be used for gifts. You may decide to supplement what the child can afford out of his or her allowance, but once a budget is set, stick to it. Next, make a gift wish list and estimate costs, encouraging the child to buy on sale and to use coupons (The rule is: Never pay full price!). If the budget will not cover estimated costs, the amount to be spent on each gift will have to be revised downward, and maybe the child will consider making some of the gifts. It really is the thought that counts!

Sir John Templeton has been quoted as saying, "Tithing has been the best investment I ever made." Whatever your personal value system dictates about charitable giving should be transferred to your children early. If you are a 10 percent tither, you may want to teach your child to give 10 percent of his or her allowance or earnings. Be reminded that children imitate what they see. If you regularly give, chances are they will, too.

Kiddie Spending

A good occasion when children can be taught to be money-wise consumers is prior to the start of the school year, when you and they can decide together about school clothes and supplies. Here's how:

1. Determine how much money you safely can afford to spend.
2. Help the children make a list of the things they want versus the things they need for school.
3. Estimate the prices of these items and compare the total with your spending limit.
4. If your budget will not cover everything, let the children decide where to cut back. Maybe, for example, they would prefer to cut back on the cost of jeans rather than on the cost of sports shoes.
5. Let your children contribute some of their own money to make up some of the difference if they don't want to sacrifice anywhere.

Children learn the details of money management not by being shielded from financial decisions, but by participating in them from an early age. Make it an ongoing priority. Keep them aware of financial considerations attached to the day-to-day life of the family by involving them in budget decisions that impact them. Let them see you pay the bills every month.

Money Fights

Psychologists tell us there are more marriage disagreements over money than any other aspect of married life. It is a source of tension and disagreement. Often, the problem dates back to childhood where the respective partners learned different ways of dealing with money (or didn't learn a thing!). So whatever your circumstances are relative to money and your spouse, don't pass them on to your children—unless, of course, you've got it all figured out!

On a day-to-day basis, keep your conversations about money low-key and unemotional. If you and your spouse disagree about money, try to keep your disagreements focused on the money itself and out of hearing range of the children. There is the danger that a discussion about money could involve loud voices and accusations, emotionally damaging the other person. This is not good behavior.

Money is, in its literal and simplest sense, "what we use to purchase goods and services for survival," says psychologist Robert Brown of Georgia State University. It should not become a battleground within the family. The more we can keep emotional, crisis-ridden baggage out of money considerations, the better.

RULE OF THUMB

Children learn financial details by doing. They learn core financial values, like many other values in life, by imitating their parents, so make sure you get and keep your own financial house in order both for your sake and theirs.

DO'S AND DON'TS: TEACHING CHILDREN ABOUT MONEY

Do

- Begin when they are young, teaching them to spend, save, and give their own money appropriately.
- Involve them in family budget decisions, and in doing so, make them aware of the bottom-line uses of money: food, clothing, and shelter.
- Involve them in monthly family bill-paying sessions.
- Make them aware of types of money: cash, checks, and credit.
- Make them responsible for some of their own expenses.
- Demonstrate the ability to discuss money unemotionally and resolve differences of opinion amicably.

Don't

- Indulge them by buying everything they ask for. This gives them a warped view of life.
- Pay for good behavior. In real life, people receive money for time and products, not behavior.
- Pay for everything yourself. If you do so, they lose the sense of being part of a family.
- Restrict spending too much. Overrestriction in money matters is as harmful as overindulgence.
- Reward their overspending by always picking up the part of the tab they can't pay.

RESOURCES FOR TEACHING KIDS ABOUT MONEY

For information on Internet sites that can get kids started early and involved in investing, see Appendix I.

APPENDIX I

Web Sites

COLLEGE AID ON THE WEB

The Web offers information on financial aid from a wealth of resources. You can find government assistance, information on individual schools, scholarship-search firms, and searchable on-line databases.

FinAid, the Financial Aid Information Page
http://www.finaid.com

Sponsored by the National Association of Student Financial Aid Administrators, this site offers numerous links for every financial aid category. This site is well organized and easy to navigate.

fastWEB (Financial Aid Search through the Web)
http://www.fastweb.com

This is a searchable database of more than 180,000 private sector scholarships, fellowships, grants, and loans from more than 3,000 sources.

COLLEGE COSTS CALCULATORS

College Board's Online College Savings Adviser
www.collegeboard.org/css/html/save.html

College Savings Bank's "Create Your Own College Plan"
www.collegesavings.com/createl.html

COMPUTERS, USED

If the price of a new computer is making you hesitate, try purchasing a used one. Due to corporate downsizings and overstocked retailers, many late-model, lightly used computers are now available through secondhand retailers. Check your yellow pages for an outlet or try one of these sources:

Rumarson Technologies
www.rticorp.com
908-298-9300

Affordable Business Technologies
www.abcinternet.com
916-635-7727

INVESTING, GENERAL

Dun and Bradstreet Information Services
http://www.zpub.com/sf/arl

In addition to in-depth analysis of companies for a fee, this site also contains useful, free information such as an on-line directory of over 60,000 companies with Web Sites.

Standard and Poor's
http://www.stockinfo.standardpoor.com./

This site offers a wealth of information, including breaking financial news and Standard & Poor's stock reports, which include recommendations, stock outlooks, fair value and risk, Wall Street consensus opinions, industry analysis, and investment-oriented news.

United States Savings Bonds—Savings Bond Wizard
www.publicdebt.treas.gov

With the entry of the savings bond number to this web site, you can learn the current market value of the particular bond.

Interactive Financial Asset Search Technology
www.ifast.com

If you think a dear departed relative failed to mention a certain securities account, you can ask the folks at Interactive Financial run by CapitaLink's online database. You'll need an address and the first four digits of their Social Security number. If there's a match, you'll be given the assetholder's phone number to call to stake your claim before the state seizes the account.

Dictionary of Financial Risk Management
utah.e1.com/amex/findic

This site provides definitions to terms as simple as *risk* and as esoteric as *up-and-in option.*

MEDICARE BENEFICIARIES OPTIONS

Seniors Health Cooperative (USHC) has issued a 12-page report entitled *Medicare, Medigap, and Managed Care: 1997 Consumer Update* to help consumers understand their options in today's changing health insurance market. The report is available for $3.50 from USHC, 1331 H Street NW, Suite 500, Washington, DC 20005–4706.

RESOURCES FOR TEACHING KIDS ABOUT MONEY

Investing for Kids
www.tqd.advanced.org/306

The SIA's Stock Market Game
www.smg2000.org

Young Investor Website
www.younginvestor.com

INDEX

ABOUT THE AUTHOR

Dr. Kay Shirley is president of Financial Development Corporation and a registered principal and branch manager for Titan Value Equities Group, Inc., a nationwide association of independent financial planners. Dr. Shirley is also a licensed life, health, and disability insurance agent. Dr. Shirley earned her B.S. in mathematics from Mississippi State University and a Ph.D. in educational administration and management from Georgia State University. With more than 1,000 clients to her credit, Dr. Shirley recommends only investments in which she, personally, has invested. She prides herself on educating her clients, so that each person is able to make his or her own decisions.

Dr. Shirley hosts financial planning seminars and is a frequent speaker at civic, business, religious, and community meetings. She has been a regular guest on *Good Day Atlanta* and was the creator of the Atlanta-based television show *MONEYTALK*. Dr. Shirley has appeared on the same program as *Wall Street Week* host Louis Ruykeyser and General Norman Schwarzkopf, retired, as well as on a program alongside Dr. Joyce Brothers.

Dr. Shirley is a member of the International Association for Financial Planning, the Women's Commerce Club, and a founding member of the Buckhead Club. She has been honored as one of Atlanta's Top Twenty-Seven Self-Made Women, one of Atlanta's Fourteen Women on Top, as well as being lauded as one of Atlanta's top women executives. Dr. Shirley was honored as one of 24 outstanding Georgia State University alumni and was named to serve on the Board of Georgia State University Alumni.

Dr. Shirley has been featured in *The Atlanta Business Chronicle* and *The Atlanta Journal/Constitution Intown Extra,* and has been published in *Atlanta Magazine* and *Commercial Real Estate & Business.*